10 D0321836

ONE WEEK LOAN

The Business of Water and Sustainable Development

THE BUSINESS OF
WATER
AND
SUSTAINABLE
DEVELOPMENT

EDITED BY
JONATHAN CHENOWETH and JULIET BIRD

Greenleaf
PUBLISHING
2005

© 2005 Greenleaf Publishing Ltd

Published by Greenleaf Publishing Limited
Aizlewood's Mill
Nursery Street
Sheffield S3 8GG
UK
www.greenleaf-publishing.com

Printed on paper made from at least 75% post-consumer waste
using TCF and ECF bleaching.
Printed in Great Britain by William Clowes Ltd, Beccles, Suffolk.
Cover by LaliAbril.com.

British Library Cataloguing in Publication Data:
  A catalogue record for this book is available from the British Library.

ISBN 1 874719 30 6

Contents

Introduction

Jonathan Chenoweth

University of Surrey, UK

Juliet Bird

University of Melbourne, Victoria, Australia

In a document published in 2000 the World Health Organisation (WHO) and the United Nations Children's Fund (UNICEF) reported that 82% of the population of the world, or 4.9 billion people, had access to basic safe-water supplies, while basic sanitation facilities were available to 60%, or 3.7 billion people (WHO/UNICEF 2000: 8). Efforts by local and international authorities during the 1990s, which followed the UN International Drinking Water Supply and Sanitation Decade, 1981–90, enabled the extension of water supply services to an additional 816 million people, with sanitation services for an extra 747 million. However, owing to global population growth, from 5.3 billion to 6.1 billion, over the same period, the proportion of the world's population served increased only slightly, by just 3% and 5% respectively (WHO/UNICEF 2000: 7).

The definition of 'reasonable access' to basic safe-water supplies used in the WHO/UNICEF study was the availability of at least 20 l of clean water per capita from a source located within 1 km of the person's dwelling (WHO/UNICEF 2000: 77). A range of technologies for water supply was accepted as meeting this criterion, including not only centralised piped supply systems but also public standpipes, protected dug wells and rainwater collection. Sources such as unprotected wells, vendor-provided water and water provided via tanker trucks were excluded on the grounds of quality, cost or reliability (WHO/UNICEF 2000: 77). Allowance was also made for the use of local technologies in assessing access to basic sanitation, considered adequate if it included private or shared facilities that separated excreta from human contact, but inadequate where only public facilities were available. Clearly, although considerable progress has been made, many of those deemed to have adequate access to water and sanitation under the standards adopted by the WHO and UNICEF study still have services much below those regarded as satisfactory in most developed nations.

In the Millennium Declaration of the UN General Assembly in 2000 a commitment was made to halve the proportion of people in the world without access to safe drinking water (United Nations 2000). This commitment was confirmed and extended by the international community in the 2002 Johannesburg Declaration on Sustainable Development (UNCSD 2002a). Although many of the statements in the

Declaration were vaguely worded, making it hard to measure progress or success, the Plan of Implementation of the Summit, agreed by the delegates to the conference, clearly stated that 'we agree to halve, by the year 2015, the proportion of people who are unable to reach or to afford safe drinking water . . . and the proportion of people who do not have access to basic sanitation' (UNCSD 2002b: paragraph 7).

Given the predicted growth in global population from 6.1 billion in 2000 to 7.2 billion by 2015, using the medium variant projection of the United Nations (UNPD 2002), this commitment will pose formidable challenges. To meet it, by the end of just a decade and half, approximately 6.6 billion people will need to have access to supplies of safe drinking water. This is more than the current population of the world and involves not only maintaining existing levels of supply but also providing new or upgraded services to 1.7 billion people. The challenge for sanitation is equally daunting: 5.8 billion people will need to be serviced, including new access provision for 2.1 billion.

Put in a different way, over the 14-year period from 2001 to 2015 these targets equate to more than 300,000 extra people every day gaining access to safe drinking water and more than 400,000 people per day gaining sanitation services. It is difficult to imagine, therefore, that these targets are achievable even if they are the result of the best of intentions which themselves are backed up by real and effective action. Even if these ambitious targets are somehow met, which would represent a major achievement for the global community, there would still be approximately 650 million people in the world without access to safe drinking water and 1.4 billion without sanitation.

What is clear from the above overview of the challenge facing the international community in terms of water supply and sanitation is the magnitude of the problem and the fact that there is a political will at least to try to tackle the problem even if success is far from certain. Continuation of the status quo and the type of progress made during the 1990s will not permit the Johannesburg targets to be met. Instead, it will be necessary to promote a combination of many different and innovative approaches, each of which will contribute towards to the overall targets. These approaches must include: technological advances that identify new sources and improve the quality of those already in use; managerial techniques that increase the efficiency and effectiveness of service delivery at both the micro and the macro scale; and fiscal approaches that tap into additional financial resources to make improvements affordable. Economic development in some parts of the world may facilitate achieving the goals but if previous trends are any indication of the future then in some regions economic pressures and the resulting population movements will greatly hamper improved access to water and sanitation.

In the past the provision of water and sanitation was seen primarily as the responsibility of government, which had the task of supporting research into technology, managing supply and disposal systems and providing the funds to pay for those systems. This view has changed: since the 1980s, and increasingly so in the 1990s and 2000s, there has been a growing trend towards privatisation of many aspects of the water sector. Underpinning this has been a shift away from seeing water as a public good that is essential for life, with subsidised supply provided as part of an overall welfare system, to a more market-oriented approach where the state, although still responsible for maintaining universal access to water services, uses market forces to meet this aim. Some form of well-regulated privatisation is now seen by many experts as providing the cheapest means of maintaining and extending water and sanitation systems at the least political cost, thus leading to a rapidly growing global market for the private management of water services (Haugton 2002).

Fully privatised water-supply and waste-disposal systems are still rare, supplying less than 6% of the world's urban dwellers. However, partial privatisation and related operations such as concessionary schemes or build–own–operate–transfer (BOOT) schemes are becoming more common, for a variety of reasons. In many developing countries in particular, governments have found it increasingly difficult to fund expanded water-supply and waste-disposal systems through large-scale borrowings, and they have been under pressure from international agencies to pursue options based on private-sector participation (Marvin and Laurie 1999: 346).

Global institutions such as the World Bank and the International Monetary Fund (IMF) can use their funding programmes in individual countries and regions to promote their agenda of developing an international free market (Marvin and Laurie 1999). The World Bank in particular has been active in facilitating the commercialisation of public water utilities and the development of regulatory frameworks (Pitman 2002). As an example, in the case of the concession for the Buenos Aires water and sanitation system that was put in place in 1993, the World Bank and Inter-American Development Bank (IADB) had both been involved in the sector for several years and assisted with the overall implementation of the process (Loftus and McDonald 2001).

In more developed parts of the world privatisation is often seen as a means of improving the existing services provided by a supposedly inefficient government-owned water and sanitation sector. The expectation is that privatisation will bring improvements, partly through the injection of additional capital and partly by facilitating access to the management skills and expertise of local or international private companies.

There remain some concerns about the effects of privatisation of water systems because the supply of water and disposal of waste are effectively natural monopolies, especially for urban communities where delivery and removal are dependent on pipe networks that cannot economically be duplicated. Thus strong government regulation of price and quality of service is regarded as a necessity, especially given that the cost of water tends to bear disproportionately on poorer citizens, with disastrous consequences for human health if the water becomes unaffordable. There is also a risk that services to rural communities may be less attractive to investors, particularly given that the water industry has come to be dominated by a relatively small number of large international companies.

The role of the private sector in the provision of water and sanitation supply is a significant issue relating to the implementation of the goals set at Johannesburg, but it is only one of a number of problems that must be tackled by water and sanitation practitioners and by the international development community more generally. New technologies are urgently needed, together with measures that ensure that they can be effectively utilised in developed and less-developed countries. There is also a need for a greater understanding of issues reflecting the specific conditions of individual countries and regions.

The contents of this book

This book is divided into five parts in which the authors address the above concerns. It begins with a group of chapters discussing general theory and goes on to look at aspects of water and sanitation privatisation and new technologies. In the final two parts it presents regionally focused papers, looking first at rural areas and then at urban areas.

Part 1: General theory

In Chapter 1 Renzetti examines the issue of demand-side information in water utility operations and planning. In the past it was assumed that consumers' water needs were not sensitive to policy measures open to water utilities; hence, the provision of domestic water focused on the management of supply rather than demand. Renzetti argues that the available empirical evidence indicates that by making more extensive use of demand-side information, such as information on consumers' sensitivity to pricing or willingness to pay for new infrastructure, major benefits both for utilities and their consumers will result.

In Chapter 2 Terrill further explores one of the key themes of Renzetti's chapter: namely, the pricing of water. He argues that provision of a water supply can be expensive because of the significant investment that is generally required and because scarcity limits supply. Particularly when scarcity is a factor, effective use of pricing can reduce wastage and inefficient use. Terrill argues that in order to harness appropriate levels of innovation and research expertise in water we need to accept that water prices must increase under certain circumstances and that they must vary according to supply conditions.

In Chapter 3 Bixio, Thoeye and De Gueldre focus on the provision of reliable treatment in water and sanitation projects from a risk management perspective. Cost implications must be balanced with the benefits of compliance by means of probabilistic risk assessment techniques and the imperfect information that is available to decision-makers. Bixio et al. argue that the ability to identify, manage and share risks effectively can greatly reduce the costs for projects with certain types of risk profiles. The starting point is a clear understanding of the risk assignments, which is achievable only when an explicit link between the risks and uncertainties that generate those risks is developed.

In Chapter 4 Gminder examines how strategic management, daily operational management and sustainability can be balanced within water utilities that are operating in a commercially oriented environment. He explores how corporate sustainability can be incorporated into the concept of the 'balanced scorecard' in the context of a large water utility and finds that it offers a management tool that is flexible enough to deal with environmental and societal issues. A major benefit of the technique is the ability to translate the strategies of corporate sustainability into action and integrate them into general management so that sustainability no longer has to be managed apart from other management tasks and systems.

These first four theoretical chapters collectively point to the need to make maximum use of informational resources in an integrated fashion in the operation of water utilities so that water costs to consumers are kept as low as possible, profit levels are sufficient to ensure that reinvestment in the sector continues and resource sustainability is maintained.

Part 2: Privatisation

Owen begins the part on privatisation by providing in Chapter 5 an overview of the recent global trend towards privatisation and examines the degree to which privatisation now influences the water and sanitation sector globally. He argues that international and locally based private water companies have developed a diverse suite of financial and contractual arrangements that offer flexibility for the future development and management of the sector. Although private-sector participation in developing countries is a relatively recent phenomenon, certain management approaches have benefits that exceed the alternatives. He further emphasises the need for the industrial and academic communities to engage better with each other to promote a more constructive dialogue between the various interest groups involved in the sector.

In Chapter 6 Rothenberger and Truffer examine alternative private-sector participation contracts in the water sector, analysing whether high transaction costs involved in contract setting increase the risk of opportunistic behaviour by the contract parties. They argue that, in order to limit the impact of problems with asymmetric information and of transaction costs, short-term and easy-to-define contracts should be used where possible to improve the performance of inefficient public service providers. Conventional economics, with its focus on production efficiency as indicated by the 'lowest bid for water price' criterion when awarding concession contracts, is too narrow to form a real base for overall welfare improvements.

In Chapter 7 Renzetti and Dupont assess what is known regarding the relationship between the ownership and performance of water utilities. Theoretical arguments predict that privately owned water utilities will outperform public ones, but Renzetti and Dupont show that there is no compelling empirical evidence to support this. However, they argue that the available evidence supports the view that public–private partnerships may facilitate efficient and sustainable operations.

In Chapter 8 Morris and Cabrera examine the effects of private-sector involvement in the water sector by focusing on how water pricing and allocation policy affects specific principles of sustainability, particularly the implications for the urban poor. Although they find that tariff increases following privatisation may result in serious challenges for low-income households, they argue that through more carefully structured water-pricing policies it would be possible to provide water both equitably and in an environmentally sustainable manner.

In Chapter 9 Bremer and Nebiker ask the question of whether joint-use munici-pal–industrial infrastructure projects could help promote service coverage expan-sion while reducing the cost of that expansion. They suggest that corporate invest-ments to meet water and waste-water treatment needs in manufacturing facilities could be structured in a way that also provides water and waste-water services to nearby municipalities.

To those familiar with the field, it is no surprise that the range of perspectives and issues covered in the five chapters in this part on private-sector involvement in the water sector fail to present a clear-cut picture either for or against privatisation. Rather, a very complicated situation is identified with regard to privatisation, the implementation of privatisation and its relative benefits and costs. In part, this may be attributable to the monopoly nature of water and sanitation supply, so that the privatisation of these services is more complicated and problematic than private-sector involvement in other areas that were formerly seen as the responsibility of government. The five chapters presented here suggest, however, that the private sector does have a significant role to play in the water industry in certain situations but that the negative externalities of private-sector involvement must be carefully managed, otherwise any benefits gained may be outweighed by the resulting disad-vantages.

Part 3: Technology

In Chapter 10 Nowak examines the potential use of geothermal energy to power a desalination plant on Milos, a small Greek Island where demand for fresh water greatly exceeds natural supply. Despite the expected benefits of the project, the project met with a degree of opposition by the local community and certain interest groups, meaning that there was a need to convince the local community of the benefits of the project. The geothermal desalination plant has been a success, as it is economically, environmentally and socially sustainable and is accepted by stakeholders.

In Chapter 11 Simpson-Hebert, Rosemarin and Winblad examine the possibility of using dry sanitation options to make the task of expanding the proportion of the world serviced with adequate sanitation more attainable. The ecological sanitation systems they describe operate on natural processes of desiccation and decomposi-tion, are cost-effective and environmentally sound and do not depend on elaborate technology or the significant quantities of water that are required for flush systems. Particularly in water-stressed regions they make sanitation much more affordable, but even in more humid regions they have a potential role to play preventing the pollution of fresh water resources that results from the inadequate treatment of sewage.

In Chapter 12 Johnson explores the potential for water metering in rural areas to improve water services in those areas. Although metering is generally accepted as necessary in urban settings, in rural areas it is often regarded with hostility by engineers, development workers and project beneficiaries alike, and it may be rejected both on philosophical and on technical grounds. Johnson argues that a pragmatic and appropriate use of meters in rural water supply systems can promote fair and equal distribution in a manner acceptable to the community and can also make the water delivery process more efficient, businesslike and profitable.

In Chapter 13 Mann examines how water can be supplied sustainably to isolated rural populations. Broken hand-pumps can be found across much of southern Africa, their users unable to maintain them once those who designed and built the systems have left. Mann argues that the sustainability of any technology is dependent on the knowledge, capacity and confidence of community members who use the technology to maintain and repair the equipment. Systems need to be put in place at the time a water project is implemented to ensure that the community can maintain the project once the international aid funding has come to an end and external resources cease to be available. As in the chapters by Simpson-Hebert *et al.* (Chapter 11) and by Johnson (Chapter 12), Mann finds that high technology is not required to solve some rural water supply problems but rather that it is the careful use of appropriate low technology that is needed.

These four chapters on the use of technology to support the extension of water and sanitation services show that low-technology solutions are just as important as more high-tech solutions. In either case, though, it is dealing with the associated social issues that is most critical as this is the only way to ensure that the proposed technology is accepted and effectively used to facilitate water and sanitation coverage extension.

Part 4: Regionally focused case studies: rural environments

Social issues are further highlighted by Akiwumi, in Chapter 14, in which she analyses the effects of contrasting concepts of water in Sierra Leone, where the national government and global interests promote water as a marketable good, in contrast to the more holistic view of water in traditional society. Conflict between these two viewpoints arises when community water sources are taken over for commercial use without adequate consultation, Often, the resulting indigenous protests have limited project success and caused loss of capital investment. Akiwumi concludes that water scientists must broaden their knowledge base to encompass a variety of relevant disciplines such as history, sociology and anthropology, enabling them to work with greater sensitivity in indigenous systems.

In Chapter 15 Howlett explores the potential for a professional association to create a water aid charity in conjunction with a non-governmental organisation (NGO), in this case the American Red Cross. The Water Relief Network established in 1996 by the US-based Chlorine Chemistry Council seeks to promote access to clean water and sanitation through a range of sustainable initiatives. Howlett argues that such partnerships between the public and private sector, as demonstrated by the Network's work in Guatemala, allow the leveraging of resources to support improvements in the water sector. It is only through global co-operation and partnerships such as these that sufficient resources will be made available to meet the water and sanitation challenge. Howlett acknowledges that at the same time such partnerships are, in the long term, commercial interests of industry bodies as, in the long run, they will promote the development of new markets.

In Chapter 16 Sarantakos, Kontogianni, Skourtos and Dimitriou examine the distortions arising from the inappropriate water management that can lead to unnecessary inefficiencies. Using as a case study the Axios River Basin in northern Greece, an important agricultural area that faces severe seasonal water scarcity and pollution problems, they show that water pricing policy is strongly linked to agricultural policy and that there is an urgent need for radical reform and immediate action to address water-related problems. They conclude that reform of the agricultural policy at national and EU level needs to include a consideration of the viability of crop species under the specific geographical and environmental (climatic) conditions present and the intoduction of measures that promote the most efficient crop species for each climatic area. Effective use of water pricing can promote reduced usage of water and greater economic returns for the community.

In Chapter 17 Stephen describes the work in South Africa of Umgeni Water as the implementing agent for water projects in rural areas of KwaZulu-Natal. The projects are being developed in the context of rapid reforms in the water sector and a changing role for local government in the region. He highlights the wide range of different factors that must be considered if available funds are to be used effectively and if water and sanitation backlogs are to be reduced.

WHO figures indicate that access to basic water supplies in rural areas is poorer than in urban areas and that the disparity for sanitation services is even greater, so the extension and improvement of rural water and sanitation coverage is critical to global development efforts. These four rurally focused regional chapters (and the chapters in Part 3 of the book) show how difficult it is to generalise about the range of problems or solutions to rural water supply because of the diversity of environments and social systems that are found around the world. One thing that is common to each of these four chapters is the emphasis on the importance of working with local communities and organisations. Done effectively, this will ensure that the use of existing knowledge can be maximised and systems be put in place that are appropriate to the local social environment and that are therefore more likely to be sustainable in the long term.

Part 5: Regionally focused case studies: urban environments

Constraints on urban supply and sanitation systems are often rather different from those in rural areas. In Chapter 18 Venkatachalam examines the extent to which urban water supply schemes in India fail as a result of financial scarcity: a poor quality of service leads to a low willingness to pay on the part of households, therefore resutling in low revenue for the water supply authority, which in turn leads to a poor quality of service. Drawing on a case study in the State of Tamil Nadu, Venkatachalam argues that it is not necessarily a fundamental lack of finance that causes a scheme to fail; rather it is the overall management approach adopted by supply authorities that may be contradictory to the expectations of the actual users.

In Chapter 19 Goh analyses the water supply options open to Singapore. Despite being located in a climatically wet region, the densely populated and highly industrialised island city-state is considered to be a water-stressed nation. At present much of Singapore's water supply is imported from Malaysia, but this dependence on one external source is seen as rendering the country vulnerable to supply issues beyond its control. In trying to overcome this, Singapore has evolved a highly efficient internal water management system that provides a model of how to create an effective water supply for a nation with poor water resources but excellent human and financial capital.

These two urban-focused regional chapters point to the importance of having effective structures for managing the water supply and sanitation systems of urban areas. Indeed, it can be argued that they illustrate that appropriate and effective management is considerably more critical to a good water supply system than plentiful natural water supplies.

Overview

In 2000 there were more than 26 countries with fewer than 1,000 cubic metres per capita of fresh water available as internal renewable water resources, a level described as water-scarce; 16 of these countries had fewer than 500 cubic metres per capita and are thus considered to be facing absolute water scarcity (WRI 2001). As populations grow, and with the that likelihood that water consumption per capita will continue to increase, this situation can only get worse. This collection looks at some of the ways in which those responsible for water management can respond to the problem.

We have sought to illustrate the range of approaches that will be necessary if the percentage of the global population having access to adequate and safe water and sanitation is to be increased in line with the brave assertions from the Johannesburg Summit. The contributors have been selected to illustrate the variety of organisations that must contribute to this task. They include academics, the staff of water-management organisations, industry personnel, consultants and employees of NGOs.

Some of the approaches that are advocated are large-scale 'Western-style' improvements involving the creation of new business models, their effectiveness measured by the traditional approaches of fiscal and social analysis. Such schemes may be instigated and partly funded by governments, but governments are increasingly turning to the private sector for money and expertise. In contrast, in many smaller communities it may be more beneficial to follow a different path to improved water supply and sanitation. Because of their size, location or traditions better results may be obtained through the adoption of local small-scale solutions. NGOs have been very active in this area, but to extend their operations many are seeking to adopt a more business-like model.

All acknowledge that governments and water supply and waste disposal agencies, large or small, need to support and encourage continued research into technological solutions that seek out better, more sustainable, ways to use our increasingly scarce supplies of good-quality fresh water. The research needs to be tempered by a better understanding of the social and cultural environments into which the technology will be introduced, thus ensuring that optimum use is made of new and existing systems.

The challenge of fulfilling the water and sanitation goals set at Johannesburg is formidable. Nonetheless, the chapters presented in this book collectively portray many issues that must be addressed as part of this process. They also point out some of the technological, social and managerial solutions that can be adopted in attempting to fulfil water and sanitation goals.

References

Haugton, G. (2002) 'Market Making: Internationalisation and Global Water Markets', *Environment and Planning A* 34.5: 791-807.

Loftus, A.J., and D.A. McDonald (2001) 'Of Liquid Dreams: A Political Ecology of Water Privatization in Buenos Aires', *Environment and Urbanization* 13.6: 179-99.

Marvin, S., and N. Laurie (1999) 'An Emerging Logic of Urban Water Management, Cochabamba, Bolivia', *Urban Studies* 36.2: 341-57.

Pitman, G.K. (2002) *Bridging Troubled Waters: Assessing the World Bank Water Resources Strategy* (Washington, DC: World Bank Operations Evaluation Department, lnweb18.worldbank.org/OED/OEDDocLib.nsf/DocPgNmViewForJavaSearch/water_resource_strategy/$file/water.pdf).

UNCSD (United Nations Commission on Sustainable Development) (2002a) *The Johannesburg Declaration on Sustainable Development* (Johannesburg: United Nations, www.johannesburgsummit.org/html/documents/summit_docs/0409_l6rev2_pol_decl.pdf).

—— (2002b) *Plan of Implementation of the World Summit on Sustainable Development* (Johannesburg: UNCSD, www.johannesburgsummit.org/html/documents/summit_docs/2309_planfinal.htm).

United Nations (2000) *Millennium Declaration* (New York: United Nations).

UNPD (United Nations Population Division) (2002) *World Population Prospects: The 2000 Revision. III. Analytical Report* (New York: United Nations).

WHO (World Health Organisation) and UNICEF (United Nations Children's Fund) (2000) *Global Water Supply and Sanitation Assessment 2000 Report* (Geneva: WHO/UNICEF).

WRI (World Resources Institute) (2001) Facts and Figures: Environmental Data Tables (www.wri.org).

Part 1
General theory

1

Incorporating demand-side information into water utility operations and planning*

Steven Renzetti

Brock University, Canada

In the past, the efforts of most water utilities to provide potable water flows focused primarily on issues related to the supply of water to meet the needs of water users. The underlying assumption in this approach was that these 'needs' were exogenously determined and not sensitive to policy measures available to water utilities. A number of factors, including declining funding from senior levels of government, rising costs of raw water supplies, expanding knowledge regarding the economic features of water demand and rapidly growing levels of water use, have led researchers and utility managers to promote the principle of incorporating demand-side information into utility operations and planning. Another factor supporting this trend is the growing participation of private firms in water supply and the growing interest on the part of public utilities of adopting 'business models' of operation (Hargreaves 2001).

Operational areas that have been affected include pricing, forecasting and investment planning. The goal of these efforts is to promote efficient and environmentally sustainable utility operations by balancing supply and demand considerations more equally. As Wegelin-Schuringa (2002: 1) argues, 'It has been demonstrated in many countries that saving water rather than the development of new sources is often the best "next" source of water, both from an economic and from an environmental point of view.'

The purpose of this chapter is to examine the application of demand-side information to water utility operations such as pricing, forecasting, drought management and capital investment planning (more detailed discussions are found in Baumann *et al.* 1998; Renzetti 2002a). It should be pointed out that the topic of

* This chapter was written while the author was a visiting scholar at the Centre for Social and Economic Research on the Global Environment at the University of East Anglia, Norwich, UK. The author thanks Diane Dupont, Don Tate and Mike M'Gonigle for helpful comments and discussions.

demand-side management is seen here as only one of several possible ways in which information regarding water demands can be incorporated into water utility planning and operations. In the next section I address conceptual issues relating to the employment of demand-side information; in Section 1.2 I report on several specific operational areas where water utilities may employ demand-side information.

1.1 Principles

In economic theory, an allocation of productive resources (capital, labour, water, etc.) is said to be efficient if the economy's pattern of production and consumption cannot be changed in such a way that improves the welfare of any individual without lowering the welfare of another. It can be shown (Boadway and Bruce 1986) that this rather general-sounding definition has direct implications for the operations of any specific industry—including those that supply water.

The general definition of economic efficiency implies that each industry's output should be produced at a level where the marginal benefit from the last unit of consumption equals the marginal cost. In a competitive market, this is brought about by fluctuating market prices. In the case of local water supply, this must be brought about through administratively set prices. If this is to be the case, then information regarding the costs of supply and the benefits of consumption is needed. As a result, it is difficult to imagine a water utility achieving an efficient level of output without having collected information regarding its costs and the demands for its output and using these to determine the marginal costs and benefits of differing levels of output.

This principle of comparing costs and benefits extends beyond choosing the efficient level of output. As the specific applications in Section 1.2 demonstrate, a number of aspects of utility operations (including investments, forecasting and rationing) need to follow this dictum if they are to be carried out efficiently. Different applications, however, will require different types of information. In principle, there are a variety of features of water demand that water utilities would need to ascertain prior to implementing the types of applications discussed below.

There are two broad sets of information that water utilities need to collect. The first relates to those factors that influence decision-making regarding the quantity of water consumed. In the case of residential water demands, economic theory predicts that water use is a function of such factors as the price of water, the prices of other goods (e.g. the price of electricity), household income, the stock (and age) of household water-using appliances and climate. The sensitivity of household water use to each of these variables is something that can only be assessed empirically by applying econometric estimation techniques on locally collected data (Renzetti 2002a). In the case of commercial and industrial water demand, economic theory predicts that non-residential water use is a function of the price of water, the prices of other inputs, the uses to which water is put (e.g. in cooling, processing and steam production) and the level of production. As in the case of residential water demands, the sensitivity of commercial and industrial water use to each of these factors is something that must be determined empirically (Renzetti 2002b).

The second type of information relates to users' valuation of various features of water supply. Although the average person's valuation of the small amount of water drunk each day is obviously quite high (as evidenced by the recent rapid increase in sales of bottled water—often at 500 times the cost of tap water), much less is known about households' valuation of less important uses of water such as for showering, watering the lawn and garden and for washing clothes. Furthermore, relatively little is known about the role played by socioeconomic factors such as income and family size in determining these values. The same can be said for industrial users of water. In some cases, the use of water (such as in the production of some foodstuffs) is of critical importance and thus highly valued. In other cases, where the use of water is not critical (perhaps because of the presence of substitutes such as alternative means of cooling the intermediate inputs), firms' valuation of water can be expected to be much lower.

1.2 Applications

There are a number of facets of water utility operations for which the efficiency can be improved through the incorporation of demand-side information. As indicated in Section 1.1, in order to achieve an efficient level of water use (and the related efficient level of investment) it is necessary to balance the marginal costs and benefits of consumption, where the benefits can be estimated only by determining households' (and other consumer groups') valuation of water use. In this section I review these areas and, where possible, present empirical evidence of the reform of water utility operations.

1.2.1 Use of efficient pricing

From the point of view of the allocation of scarce water resources, one of the most important facets of water utility operations is pricing. This is because changing prices provide a signal to consumers and suppliers of the changing costs of consumption. Increasing water prices encourage consumers to conserve and search for alternatives; such increases also act as an incentive for utilities to search out previously unattractive supply options. This may be done by reducing system losses, investing in more efficient pumps or water meters or leasing water rights.

Historically, however, the primary goals of price setting were to recover sufficient revenues to cover costs and to assign common capital costs across user groups in an equitable fashion (AWWA 1991). In keeping with the view that water demands are exogenously determined, the potential role of water prices to signal the opportunity cost of consumption and, thus, allocate water to its highest valued uses has not been emphasised in the industry. This perspective has had a number of negative consequences. Most importantly, water prices have failed to reflect the marginal cost of supply and typically have been invariant in relation to distance from source, time of use or season (Renzetti 1999). The implication of these inefficient prices is that consumption has grown past its socially optimal level and all components of water supply and waste-water networks have correspondingly expanded to accommodate this.

There is a growing body of empirical evidence that moving to efficient water pricing will provide a number of benefits to water utilities and often will raise social welfare (Hall 1996; Renzetti 1999; Saleth and Dinar 1997). An important feature of these prices is that they are designed to reflect the marginal cost of water supply and also to ensure that demand equals supply. As such, they depend crucially on the nature of water demand and cannot be calculated without fairly detailed information regarding the water demands of all customer groups. Another characteristic of efficient pricing is that prices can be tailored to reflect local cost and demand conditions. Efficient non-linear pricing (i.e. price schedules where the marginal price rises or falls with the level of consumption) can be designed to take account of observed variations in demand elasticities across user groups, in different time-periods or over different levels of consumption. More sophisticated price schedules, however, require greater information regarding the nature of water demand and the distribution of socioeconomic characteristics across households (Brown and Sibley 1986).

Despite these informational challenges, a number of studies demonstrate the feasibility and benefits of moving to efficient water pricing. In cities as diverse as Vancouver, Los Angeles, Manila and Hyderabad researchers have demonstrated that implementation of efficient pricing increases social welfare while encouraging water conservation (Hall 1996; Munasinghe 1992; Renzetti 1992; Saleth and Dinar 1997). For example, in earlier work (Renzetti 1992) I looked at the welfare gains from reforming water prices for the Greater Vancouver Water District and estimated the potential improvements to be approximately 4% of households' welfare (as measured by aggregate consumer surplus). It is worthwhile pointing out that these welfare gains are net of the costs of introducing universal residential water metering in Vancouver.

1.2.2 Management of demand

One area where water utilities have demonstrated an interest in applying demand-side information is in the management of household and other users' water demands (Opitz and Dziegielewski 1998). Although there remains some debate regarding the definition and assessment of demand-side management (DSM) policies (Dziegielewski 1999) it is clear that many utilities, when faced with rising use of water and/or inadequate levels of service capacity, are examining the efficacy of alternative measures to encourage water conservation (a partial list of potential measures is found in Box 1.1).

Given the variety of price-related and non-price-related measures to encourage water conservation, an important area of research has been to assess the relative efficacy of alternative DSM policies. Renwick and her co-authors have recently examined the experience of Californian water utilities that have employed a variety

Water utilities have employed a variety of policies and measures to encourage water conservation. A partial list of options includes the following:

- Education and advertising campaigns ~non-price
- Revision of plumbing, building and landscaping codes "
- Pricing instruments (and installation of metering, if necessary), such as increasing block-rate structures, seasonal pricing, charges for excess use and zonal pricing
- Other financial incentives, such as rebates, subsidised retrofits and water audits
- Leak detection, the reduction of system pressures and the removal of illegal connections NP
- Rationing, such as limiting the time of use or the quantity used (e.g. through banning the use of water outdoors, such as for watering gardens, or through the imposition of alternate-day rules)
- Moral persuasion (i.e. through calls for voluntary reductions)
- Encouragement and training regarding recycling and/or recirculation of water
- Demand modelling and estimation

BOX 1.1 Alternative demand-side management policies and instruments

Sources: Guy and Marvin 1996; Opitz and Dziegielewski 1998; Wegelin-Schuringa 2002

of methods ranging from requests for voluntary compliance, price increases and penalties for overusing water as methods of coping with the drought that hit that state in the 1990s (Renwick and Archibald 1998; Renwick and Green 2000). Renwick and colleagues' statistical models of water demand and household retrofit decisions demonstrate that price and non-price measures curb demand. Non-price measures vary in their effectiveness, with policies that mandate reduced use of water being more effective than voluntary measures. Renwick and Green (2000: 51) conclude that,

> In general, relatively moderate (5–15%) reductions in aggregate demand can be achieved through modest price increases and 'voluntary' alternative DSM policy instruments such as public information campaigns. However, to achieve larger reductions in demand (greater than 15%), policy-makers will likely need to consider relatively large price increases, more stringent mandatory policy instruments (such as use restrictions), or a package of policy instruments.

In his study of water conservation efforts in low-income countries, Brooks (1997: 4) echoes this conclusion, asserting,

> Although regulations have a bad name, they are often both appropriate and efficient for managing water demand. Exhortation is also more effective than generally believed, particularly in times of drought. The range of options is wide enough to preclude generalisation, but one can say that they should be chosen to support, and if possible reinforce, the effects of market-based measures.

1.2.3 Investment decisions and forecasting

The traditional approach to water utility investment planning has been to schedule major infrastructure extensions and improvements according to expected growth in water use. The most important feature about the growth in water use has been that utilities assumed it to be outside their sphere of influence. As a result, water utilities perceived a need to provide infrastructure to support water use wherever and whenever it occurred. As described in Section 1.2.1, the lack of efficient pricing (such as peak-load or zonal pricing) reinforced this investment strategy by failing to promote water conservation.

An alternative approach to infrastructure planning balances households' valuation of infrastructure with the costs of that infrastructure. Specifically, additions to a water utility's infrastructure are scheduled so as to maximise the present value of the stream of discounted future net benefits deriving from those investments. Net benefits in this context are measured as the difference between benefits (measured by consumers' willingness to pay for increments to capacity, reliability or water quality) and costs. A significant part of the scheduling of infrastructure projects involves forecasting future water demand (and, thus, the benefits from additional capacity). Furthermore, sophisticated forecasts of water demand can incorporate the effects of policies such as pricing, development charges and plumbing standards that are available to municipal governments (Billings and Jones 1996).

The interaction between pricing and investment planning is especially important. In an earlier publication (Renzetti 1992), for example, I demonstrated that one of the most important benefits of introducing prices that are based on estimates of customer demand is the utility's ability to delay costly expansions to its delivery capacity. Another emerging application of information regarding households' valuation of water supply and waste-water treatment infrastructure is found in a number of low-income countries. In areas such as rural Africa and Asia that are often plagued by inadequate infrastructure the ability to demonstrate households' willingness to pay for improved access to potable water supplies plays an important part in signalling the financial viability of infrastructure investments (WBWRT 1993). Asthana (1997), for example, conducted a contingent valuation study of rural Indian households in which the female head must often carry water from distant standpipes and communal wells. Asthana found that these households place a high value on improved provision of water supplies, stating that, 'on the average, the amount that they are willing to pay for saving in time is equal to half the wage for unskilled rural labour' (1997: 147).

1.2.4 Evaluation of performance

In the private sector, a key measure of success is customer satisfaction. The public sector, however, has been much slower to measure customer satisfaction or to incorporate these measures into the evaluation of its performance. An interesting exception to this general rule can be found in the use of consumer satisfaction ratings by England's Office of Water (OFWAT). Since the time that water and sewerage utilities in England and Wales were privatised OFWAT established levels of performances (e.g. regarding system reliability) and has commissioned surveys into consumer satisfaction and willingness to pay for system improvements (Reid *et al.* 2002).

The discussion in Section 1.2.2 indicates that there is a growing body of research and acceptance among water utilities regarding the benefits of incorporating demand-side information into pricing, investment decision-making and performance evaluation. This list, however, does not exhaust the possibilities for incorporating demand-side information. There are at least two other ways in which demand-side information may be utilised. These approaches, however, have only recently been suggested and, thus, a significant amount of research is needed before they can be implemented. They are included, however, to give the reader an idea of the full range of possibilities for employing demand-side information to enhance water utility operations.

Reliability

A crucial feature of the design and operations of any water supplier is its targeted level of reliability. It is well understood that demands (which are in some cases closely dependent on uncertain factors such as climate conditions) can at certain periods threaten to exceed system capacity and that unexpected breakages can inhibit supply reliability. As a result, no system is 100% reliable. In addition, increases to system reliability can often be very expensive. Traditionally, engineers have designed water utilities to meet targets of arbitrarily set reliability (such as meeting peak demands 95% of the time). However, in choosing to meet an arbitrarily defined target, designers rarely attempt to determine whether these targets are the ones desired by consumers and taxpayers. Once again, the absence of demand-side information means that there can be no assurance that the efficient level of reliability (i.e. where the marginal costs and benefits of an incremental change in the level of reliability are equated) is achieved.

An alternative approach to the decision regarding reliability is to balance the costs and benefits of differing levels of reliability. This approach recognises that households and other water users value increased reliability but that the investments needed to achieve this have their own opportunity costs. Those funds can be invested in improved roads, schools and hospitals—all things that households also value. In order to balance these benefits and costs, however, information regarding households' (and other customers') valuation of differing levels of reliability must be ascertained. For example, Howe and Griffin Smith (1993) conducted a contingent valuation survey of households and found that residential users of water in the state of Colorado were willing to pay approximately US$60 annually beyond their current water bills in order to halve the likelihood of a major system failure. Once aggregated, these willingness-to-pay estimates could be compared with the costs of achieving this increase in reliability in order to determine whether the investment was merited.

Rationing

The same type of argument as found in the above section can be made regarding the methods used by water utilities to ration water use in times of drought when water demands threaten to exceed available capacity. Traditionally, water utilities have employed some form of administrative rationing such as allowing even-numbered houses to use water for outdoor purposes only on even-numbered days, or limiting outdoor water use to specific periods of the day. These methods of rationing consumption are relatively straightforward to design, implement and enforce but they do nothing to guarantee that the scarce water resource is allocated to its highest-valued uses. As a result, they will typically result in an inefficient allocation of water.

An alternative approach that employs households' valuation of access to the supply network may be feasible and result in a more efficient allocation of scarce water. Specifically, it may be possible to design a rationing scheme that relies more heavily (but not exclusively) on users' valuation of access to the network. For example, at the beginning of each year, households could signal their valuation of continued access in times of rationing by purchasing differing levels of service reliability. Higher levels of service reliability would cost more. As water supply must be maintained for indoor and fire-protection needs, this scheme would be applicable only to outdoor use of water (and, possibly, some types of industrial use of water). Once households have signalled their respective willingness to pay for reliability, a ranking of differing households could be established. The higher a household has paid for access, the lower the likelihood of it having its access interrupted or curtailed. In times of rationing, such a scheme would ensure that only the households with the highest valuation of water would be using the scarce water resource as households with the lowest valuation would be the first to be excluded from use. Such a price-based rationing scheme is already in place for industrial consumers of electricity where higher levels of reliability entail higher prices (Brown and Sibley 1986).

1.2.5 Summary

This list of applications is suggestive of the range of activities that could be reformed through a greater reliance on demand-side information. It is valuable to note that there are, in all probability, synergies between the applications. For example, if a utility were to collect and analyse data on the factors shaping household and commercial water demands with the aim of reforming its pricing practices, then the utility could also use the same data and estimated demand models for enhanced forecasting and investment planning. Similarly, the estimated consumers' valuation of alternative levels of reliability could be used for enhanced evaluation of performance.

1.3 Conclusions

In this chapter I have considered the application of demand-side information to a number of facets of water utility planning and operations. For many utilities, the idea of gathering and analysing data on features such as consumer sensitivity to price change and consumer willingness to pay for infrastructure improvements is unfamiliar. Nonetheless, many other utilities (including those in Los Angeles, Seattle and Toronto) have experimented with price and non-price measures to conserve water use and have used information regarding water demands to assess the costs and benefits of major infrastructure projects.

What is clear is that economic theory and a growing body of empirical evidence support the redirection of the attention of water utilities towards a more balanced approach that incorporates benefit and cost information in their planning and operations. It should be remembered, of course, that there will be costs associated with moving in the directions indicated here. These include the costs of data collection and analysis, the costs of hiring new staff and of retraining existing staff and the costs of public consultation and education as well as a potential increase in the degree of uncertainty faced by the utility. The main new source of uncertainty may stem from the linking of prices to demand conditions, thereby making revenue more uncertain. Nonetheless, the available empirical evidence indicates that, even accounting for these costs, the reorientation of the focus of water utility operations in the direction of a greater reliance on demand-side information will bring benefits to the utility and to its customers.

References

Asthana, A. (1997) 'Where the Water is Free but the Buckets are Empty: Demand Analysis of Drinking Water in Rural India', *Open Economies Review* 8.2: 137-49.

AWWA (American Water Works Association) (1991) *Water Rates Manual* (Denver, CO: AWWA, 4th edn).

Baumann, D., J. Boland and W.M. Hanemann (eds.) (1998) *Urban Water Demand Management and Planning* (New York: McGraw-Hill).

Billings, R.B., and C.V. Jones (1996) *Forecasting Urban Water Demand* (Denver, CO: American Water Works Association).

Boadway, R., and N. Bruce (1986) *Welfare Economics* (Oxford, UK: Basil Blackwell).

Brooks, D. (1997) 'Water Demand Management: Conceptual Framework and Policy Implementation', in D. Brooks, E. Rached and M. Saade (eds.), (1997) *Management of Water Demand in Africa and the Middle East: Current Practices and Future Needs* (Ottawa, Canada: International Development Research Centre): 1-8.

Brown, S., and D. Sibley (1986) *The Theory of Public Utility Pricing* (Cambridge, UK: Cambridge University Press).

Dziegielewski, B. (ed.) (1999) 'Water Demand Management: Unresolved Issues', *Water Resources Update*, Issue 114, Universities Council on Water Resources, Southern Illionois University at Carbondale, Carbondale, IL.

Guy, S., and S. Marvin (1996) 'Managing Water Stress: The Logic of Demand Side Infrastructure Planning', *Journal of Environmental Planning and Management* 39.1: 123-27.

Hall, D. (ed.) (1996) *Marginal Cost Rate Design and Wholesale Water Markets: Advances in the Economics of Environmental Resources. Volume 1* (Greenwich, CT: JAI Press).

Hargreaves, J. (2001) 'Developing a Sustainable Water Industry in a Competitive Environment', in D. Moody and P. Wouters (eds.), *Globalisation and Water Resources: The Changing Value of Water* (Proceedings of the American Water Resources Association/University of Dundee International Specialty Conference, Dundee, Scotland, 6–8 August 2001).

Howe, C., and M. Griffin Smith (1993) 'Incorporating Public Preferences in Planning Urban Water Supply Reliability', *Water Resources Research* 29.10: 3,363-69.

Munasinghe, M. (1992) *Water Supply and Environmental Management: Developing World Applications* (Studies in Water Policy and Management; Boulder, CO: Westview Press).

Opitz, E., and B. Dziegielewski (1998) 'Demand Management Planning Methods', in D. Baumann, J. Boland and W.M. Hanemann (eds.), *Urban Water Demand Management and Planning* (New York: McGraw-Hill): 237-81.

Reid, M., J. Elgood and C. Gevaux (2002) The 2004 *Periodic Review: Research into Customers' Views* (London: United Kingdom Office of Water).

Renwick, M., and S. Archibald (1998) 'Demand Side Management Policies for Residential Water Use: Who Bears the Conservation Burden?', *Land Economics* 74.3: 343-59.

—— and R. Green (2000) 'Do Residential Water Demand Side Management Policies Measure Up? An Analysis of Eight California Water Agencies', *Journal of Environmental Economics and Management* 40.1: 37-55.

Renzetti, S. (1992) 'Evaluating the Welfare Effects of Reforming Municipal Water Prices', *Journal of Environmental Economics and Management* 22.2: 147-63.

—— (1999) 'Municipal Water Supply and Sewage Treatment: Costs, Prices and Distortions', *Canadian Journal of Economics* 32.2: 688-704.

—— (2002a) *The Economics of Water Demands* (Norwell, MA: Kluwer Academic).

—— (ed.) (2002b) *The Economics of Industrial Water Use* (Cheltenham, UK: Edward Elgar).

Saleth, R.M., and A. Dinar (1997) *Satisfying Urban Thirst: Water Supply Augmentation and Pricing Policy in Hyderabad City, India* (Technical Paper 395; Washington, DC: World Bank).

WBWRT (World Bank Water Research Team) (1993) 'The Demand for Water in Rural Areas: Determinants and Policy Implications', *The World Bank Research Observer* 8.1: 47-70.

Wegelin-Schuringa, M. (2002) 'Water Demand Management and the Urban Poor', IRC International Water and Sanitation Centre; document accessed 4 January 2003 at www.irc.nl/themes/urban/demand.html.

2

The price of water
SEPARATING THE NATURAL FROM THE OPTIMAL IN WATER SUPPLY: ENSURING THE BROADEST COMMUNITY ACCESS TO SAFE WATER

Daniel Terrill

ACIL Tasman, Australia

The tenet that nature provides us water for free and therefore should either be provided free of charge to us or heavily subsidised by government is widespread throughout the developed world. It is a view reinforced by the fact that access to water is considered a basic human right that is a crucial component of human survival. Yet, owing to the many competing demands for water (e.g. for household, agricultural, industrial, environmental flows), the notion of 'free' or almost free water is no longer valid. Undervaluation of water is, in many cases, condemning people to inadequate water supplies, particularly in the developing world.

As the level of competing demand for water increases, the disciplines of economics, law, politics and hydrology are drawn inexorably closer. Drawing on these various disciplines, in this chapter I explain how these competing demands can be minimised through a careful use of key instruments, such as designated rights, capacities to trade and variable pricing that reflects scarcity. Although these approaches do not provide all the answers to the problems of water supply, I believe that these key instruments offer the means to better balance many competing demands.

2.1 Existing water supply and pricing regimes

It is not possible here to provide a detailed overview of the water supply and pricing regimes in place around the world. However, global water supply and pricing regimes tend to exhibit a number of key characteristics. A 1997 report from the World Bank identified a wide range of factors influencing the pricing methods employed by governments in various countries (Dinar and Subramanian 1997), including many seemingly conflicting goals. Key factors included cost recovery, distribution of income, improvement of water allocation and water conservation. The net result of these various pricing regimes is that water utilities recover, on average, only a small proportion of total costs in user charges. In developing countries, for example, Cowen and Cowen (1998) suggest that water utilities recover, on average, only around 30% of total costs from user charges.

The World Bank has also found that water prices vary enormously across countries, with wealth and water availability not an adequate explanation for these differences (Dinar and Subramanian 1997). Further, there is little consistency in the pricing mechanisms in place throughout the world, with various mixes of fixed and variable pricing.

In many countries, especially in the developing world, simplistic pricing methodologies that incorporate average cost pricing are in place. Furthermore, within countries and regions there is frequently little variation in prices, despite often large variations in the cost of supplying water. The World Bank has also found that agricultural irrigation users around the world typically pay between 20% and 75% of the total cost of water supply, with the capital costs of providing water infrastructure rarely recovered. This gap between revenues and costs has usually been funded by general government revenue.

In some countries over recent years there has been movement towards the reform of water pricing (Jones 2003). In the developed world, many countries have replaced flat fees for urban water users with a two-part tariff, incorporating a fixed and variable charge. These pricing mechanisms aim to price water according to the long-term cost of water supply, including the cost of funding future infrastructure requirements. Thus, concepts such as full cost recovery are increasingly being applied to the water sector.

In addition, there have been considerable changes to the method of funding water services, most notably a decline in the reliance on government funding. This movement away from government funding to user charges, although far from complete, has seen water markets begin to emerge on a limited scale throughout the world, with Australia, Israel and the USA being prominent examples (Arlosoroff 2002; Garrido 2002; Landry and Anderson 2003).

2.2 The cost of water supply

The business of water supply is fundamentally different from the supply of most other goods and services. It is different because, unlike the supply of most other goods or services, the supply of water into catchment areas and rivers occurs largely independently of any price signals. When the price of a typical market good or a service rises, more people are attracted to producing that good or service such that, over time, and assuming no major constraint on supply, prices will either stabilise or fall in response to the increased supply. Thus, supply is inextricably linked to price. Yet, for the hydrological systems of the world, there is no equivalent response when the price of water rises. Rainfall does not respond to 'the invisible hand' (Smith 1791).

This physical reality means it is easy to dismiss the role of markets in the supply of water. There is a temptation to assume that, because nature provides water into our catchments and rivers for free, water should also be provided to consumers for free and that the only way to extend the availability of water as widely as possible is to provide it for free.

However, nature providing water into our catchments and rivers for free does not mean that water supply to users is free. Although we can rely on nature for the rain to fall and for the water to end up in rivers or groundwater systems, we cannot rely on nature to deliver it into our homes and to our farms and businesses in sufficient quality and quantity to meet all demand. Demand can be met only by human capital and water infrastructure, which, unlike rainfall, are not provided for free.

Unless one is drawing untreated water directly out of a river, water supply requires investment in assets such as dams, pipes, canals, pumps, treatment plants, rainwater tanks. The planning, building and maintenance of this water infrastructure requires long-term investment, as does research and innovation in areas of the creation of more efficient water infrastructure and alternative water supplies. Most importantly, continued progress in the business of water supply requires continued application of human effort, innovation and ingenuity.

Importantly, the level of such investment is related to the price of water, as it is price that determines whether public and private investors in these areas make an acceptable return on their investments. The definition of an acceptable return relates to the levels of return investors can make in other sectors of the economy, which requires that water prices need to go beyond merely meeting the cost of investment. 'Full cost recovery' sounds like a noble goal for water investment, and it is certainly more than many areas have achieved historically, but who wants to invest in an industry that at best only meets costs? To harness the same level of innovation and research expertise in water that currently characterises industries such as information technology and communications we need to accept that water prices must increase. Returns on investment in the water industry need to promise similar returns as in other areas of the economy.

Where the levels of returns on investments in the water sector are too low, underinvestment is likely. In turn, any underinvestment necessarily undermines water supply. For example, David *et al.* (2000) point out how the undervaluing of urban water in the Philippines has led to a wasteful usage of raw water by water utility firms, the misallocation of raw water, the worsening of water pollution problems and a failure to anticipate the necessary investments for water supply expansion in a timely manner.

2.3 The cost of water use

The discussion in this chapter to date has focused largely on the physical costs associated with water *supply* and the need to distinguish between the component of water supply that is natural and the component that depends on human effort, ingenuity and investment. Such a distinction, between what is natural and what is not, becomes relatively less important in the other key dimension to the cost of water—the cost of water *use*. Indeed, within the context of overall water pricing, the costs of water supply are often less significant than the costs of water use. Even if there were no costs associated with water supply, such as with the earlier example of everyone drawing their water straight out of a river, there would remain sound economic reasons against providing the river water for free.

The reasons for this relate to the potential of the pricing mechanism to act as a demand management tool, ensuring that water is used most efficiently. Fundamental to this is the concept of scarcity and the recognition that that there is a limit to the amount of water that can be extracted from a natural source. When water is used for one purpose it is not available for use for other purposes. This is not a great problem if water is abundant and there is ample water for all potential water users. However, when one use of water occurs at the *expense* of another potential use, as inevitably occurs under conditions of scarcity, then the lost opportunity represents a cost of the chosen water use.

Any failure to use price as a key rationing device in the face of scarcity only makes the scarcity problem worse, with wastage and inefficient use inadvertently encouraged. When scarcity drives up the price of a resource such as water, users of the resource are motivated to find alternatives sources of supply, new technologies or substitute resources (Krause *et al*. 2003).

Note that the issue of scarcity is not just about water quantity; water pollution can also create conditions of scarcity through a lack of water quality. The issue of water quality relates to the issue of externalities—another important component of the economic cost of water supply and use that is rarely reflected in the price (Ahmad 2000). Many externalities of water supply and water use are evident in environmental impacts, particularly the environmental impacts of dams and the regulation of river systems and water uses such as irrigation. For example, many of the irrigated basins in Australia suffer from increasingly extensive salinity problems resulting from the use of irrigation water, which in some cases is undermining the very agricultural production that the irrigation was meant to promote (Smith 1998). The existence of externalities and a perceived inability of the market to accommodate them motivate some to dismiss the role of water markets entirely. They tend to do so under the banner of market failure. Yet water prices that attempt to internalise the cost of externalities, such that they are a factor in decisions over the supply and use of water resources, are possible. In fact, they are a most important component of optimal water prices.

2.4 The role of variable pricing

The cost of water is not static. Being a function of water supply and water demand, both of which tend to be highly variable, the true cost of water can vary enormously over time. Fixed pricing ignores this reality.

The argument for variable water prices, which would tend to rise during times of drought and fall during periods of high rainfall, may be dismissed on the grounds that water is a basic human right that is crucial to survival. This logic proceeds that it would be wrong to subject something so important to the perceived vagaries of prices determined by supply and demand. In particular, it is feared that in times of scarcity, prices determined by supply and demand may place even minimum water requirements out of the reach of low-income earners (Brocklehurst *et al.* 2002). As a result, many jurisdictions either set a water fee regardless of water use, a set flat rate for water use or a flat rate up to a certain point and then variable pricing for any additional use. The unspoken premise of this argument is that if something is crucial to our survival then it must be protected from market forces.

However, this principle is not extended into other goods and services that are also crucial to our survival, and for very good reason. We all know and expect that when there is trouble in the Middle East the oil price will rise and we will have to pay more for petrol at the pump, or that a drought may ultimately mean more expensive vegetables or meat on the supermarket shelves. Such variations in price are necessary signals for consumers to consume less and for producers to produce more. With few exceptions, countries that have experimented with removing market forces from food production have found that the scarcity problem becomes worse in the absence of markets.

There is generally great resistance to paying more for water during a drought. Instead, many areas begrudgingly accept alternatives such as water restrictions, which force people to preserve water, or the even less palatable alternative of no supply when supplies run out. Prices that rise to reflect scarcity achieve the same conservation measures as restrictions except that they act far more efficiently and proactively (Saleth 2001). Conservation promoted by rising prices occurs progressively as the drought progresses and prices gradually rise, not at the point at which some sudden and somewhat arbitrary trigger for water restrictions is reached.

Water conservation gains have been most evident in areas where such price signals have been present in water markets. For example, in Tucson, Arizona, average peak daily water demand was reduced by 20% in the mid-1970s by using a combination of price increases and other forms of rationing (Anderson and Snyder 1997). Beattie and Foster (1980) found that a 10% increase in water prices reduced urban water consumption by between 4% and 13%, and Anderson and Snyder (1997) suggested that water demand in the agricultural sector is also highly sensitive to price because of the possibilities of improved irrigation technology and modified cropping patterns.

The benefits of variable pricing are not just limited to demand management and related issues of conservation and efficient use. Variable pricing can also influence supply. To illustrate this principle, it is useful to draw an analogy with food supply and the role of markets in directing farmers' decision-making. When a drought occurs, we rarely resist higher food prices, on the grounds that food is crucial to our survival and, therefore, must also be a basic human right. We begrudgingly accept the price rises because we know that food is not provided to us as a matter of right. Rather, farmers must first grow the food, and farmers listen to price signals that tell them what to grow and how much (they do not always succeed in growing what the market demands because, just like water supply, food supply is subject to a host of variables, many of which are outside the dimension of human endeavour). As such, rising food prices during a drought attract more farmers to eventually grow more food.

Because variable pricing can influence supply, any preference for water restrictions during a drought rather than relying on a price signal represents a missed chance to provide incentive for increased investment in water supply. Ironically, this missed chance represents lost investment that could otherwise minimise the impacts of future droughts.

The argument here is not against providing assistance to those who could otherwise not afford to meet their basic water needs in a market situation. Rather, it is against helping them by artificially subsidising the water to all. Just as we do not meet the dietary needs of the underprivileged by providing free or subsidised food for all, there are alternative ways to meet the water needs of the poor without inadvertently providing perverse economic incentives for undersupply, wastage and inefficient use. Indeed, expanding the availability of water as widely as possible, including to those who may otherwise be left out, requires that wastage and inefficient uses are minimised.

In fact, it is often the poor who often suffer *the most* under conditions of scarcity. David *et al.* (2000) point out how in the Philippines, where urban water rates are the lowest among the Asian countries, the poor are paying more for their water consumption than those who can afford to pay more. This is because these poor households are located mostly in areas that are not yet connected to the waterworks system. They rely more on water rationing and alternatives sources of supply, which are typically very expensive.

2.5 Property rights and risk management

A message from some of the literature in this field is that increasing the prices alone, without any accompanying institutional change, may fail to promote either increased supply or more efficient use of water. Evidence from China, for example, suggests that increasing the cost of water by using pricing mechanisms alone will not necessarily encourage water conservation unless the increase is accompanied by clearly defined and legally enforceable water rights that are tailored to local conditions (Yang *et al.* 2002). Similarly, from Spain, Berbel and Gómez-Limón (2000) stress that use of water pricing alone to control water use is not a valid means of significantly reducing agricultural consumption of water. Significantly, they found that many farms merely absorbed the higher prices, and that water demand did not decrease significantly unless farm income was decreased by around 40%.

Clearly defined property rights are one such instrument that can further improve the efficiency of water use. Property rights over water consist of the right to consume, earn income from or sell the water. The ability to trade water rights can further enhance the efficiency of water use by allowing the highest-productivity water users to use the water rather than the lower-productivity and inefficient users (Pigram 1999). Until relatively recently, in Australia any legal entitlements to water tended to be tied to a specific parcel of land, meaning that the entitlements could not be traded unless the land itself was traded. Recent moves to disaggregate property rights to water from property rights to land have made trading in water rights more possible. Ahmad (2000) warns that, in the absence of well-defined, transparent and freely traded water rights, markets may actually encourage higher use rather than conservation of water.

Water pricing, especially where it is ordered and where contracts are arranged for its delivery well in advance of its actual delivery, also needs to incorporate risk. Rights to water are often sold and prices agreed on well before the water is ready to be delivered. Indeed, this is a necessary precondition for the planning of efficient use of water, yet there can be no guarantee that water ordered in advance will actually be available for delivery. There is no guarantee how much water will flow down a river in any one year, nor how full a reservoir will become. The economically inefficient solution to this uncertainty is either to sell in advance only what can be guaranteed (in all but the most severe drought situations) or to distribute any water shortfall when it occurs across all water users (e.g. to impose restrictions or to give users only a proportion of what they have ordered). In the absence of any deliberate risk management in water pricing, many jurisdictions inadvertently rely on the latter approach. In doing so, the inherent risk in water supply is distributed equally across all users. Capacity sharing—one of the solutions that has been put forward to allocate water property rights in highly variable climatic regimes such as Australia (Pigram 1999)—involves users being allocated a share of the capacity of water in storage as well as inflows and seepage and evaporation losses rather than a set volume of water. In this way, the inherent uncertainty involved in rainfall, stream flows and storage capacities are managed.

Yet even this approach represents an opportunity lost: the opportunity to allow those most able to accommodate the risk to do so, so that those who are least able to accommodate risk do not have to do so. In practice, some water users are more able to cope with risk than others. For example, a rice farmer can increase or decrease the size of the area planted to accommodate variation in supply. The decision on how much to plant can be made on a year-to-year basis. By contrast, a vigneron is unable to easily change the area planted to vines to accommodate variable water supply, with the area planted generally being the cumulative result of many years of decision-making, not just the one. Therefore, for the vigneron, many years' investment is threatened if the supply of irrigation water fails in any one year. As such, the vigneron will be more willing to pay a premium for the lowest-risk water that is *most* likely to be supplied, while the rice farmer may be more willing to accept the far cheaper but higher-risk water.

Under most water pricing structures this potential is not yet available. This represents a lost opportunity for efficiency gains. Just as a market in water can provide for more efficient use of water, a market in water risk can allow for the more efficient distribution and accommodation of the inherent uncertainty in water supply.

2.6 Conclusions

Efficient use of water demands that the price of water needs to reflect both the cost of water supply and the cost of water use. In costing water supply, explicit recognition is needed of what is naturally provided in water supply and what is optimal. Progress in the business of water supply requires human effort, innovation and ingenuity. To harness appropriate levels of innovation and research expertise in water supply we need to accept that water prices must increase under certain circumstances and that they must be variable according to supply. They must rise during a drought to encourage investment in the industry and to encourage conservation in conditions of scarcity, just as rising food prices on the supermarket shelves during a drought encourage people to waste less and farmers to produce more. Use of the variable pricing mechanism needs to be accompanied by careful use of other economic instruments, such as clearly defined property rights to water and capacities for trade. The temptation to divorce economics from water supply must be resisted. Water may well be a basic human right insofar as it is crucial to our survival, but what use is such a right when the rivers run dry?

References

Ahmad, M. (2000) 'Water Pricing and Markets in the Near East: Policy Issues and Options', *Water Policy* 2.3: 229-42.

Anderson, T.L., and P. Snyder (1997) *Water Markets: Priming the Invisible Pump* (Washington, DC: Cato Institute).

Arlosoroff, S. (2002) 'Integrated Approach for Efficient Water Use. Case Study: Israel', report delivered at the World Food Prize International Symposium, 'From the Middle East to the Middle West: Managing Freshwater Shortages and Regional Water Security', Des Moines, IA, 24–25 October 2002.

Beattie, B.R., and H.R. Foster Jr (1980) 'Can Prices Tame the Inflationary Tiger?', *Journal of the American Water Works Association* 72 (August 1980): 444-45.

Berbel, J., and J.A. Gómez-Limón (2000) 'The Impact of Water-pricing Policy in Spain: An Analysis of Three Irrigated Areas', *Agricultural Water Management* 43.2: 219-38.

Brocklehurst, C., J.G. Janssens and P. Kolsky (2002) 'Designing Water-pricing Policy, Tariffs and Subsidies to Help the Poor', *Waterlines* 21.2: 4-10.

Cowen, P.B., and T. Cowen (1998) 'Deregulated Water Supply: A Policy Option for Developing Countries', *Cato Journal* 18.1: 21-41.

David, C., and A. Inocencio, R. Clemente, R. Abracosa, F. Largo, G. Tabios and E. Walag (2000) *Water Pricing: Metro Manila and Metro Cebu* (Policy Note 2000-9; Makati City, Philippines: Philippine Institute for Development Studies, July 2000).

Dinar, A., and A. Subramanian (1997) 'Water Pricing Experiences: An International Perspective', in A. Dinar and A. Subramanian (eds.), *Water Pricing Experiences: An International Perspective* (Washington, DC: World Bank): 1-12.

Garrido, A. (2002) *Transition to Full-Cost Pricing of Irrigation Water for Agriculture in OECD Countries* (Paris: OECD).

Jones, T. (2003) 'Pricing Water: Water Pricing is Becoming More Widespread, with the Dual Aim of Expanding Supply and Encouraging More Responsible Use', *OECD Observer* 236.

Krause, K., J. Chermak and D. Brookshire (2003) 'The Demand for Water: Consumer Response to Scarcity', *Journal of Regulatory Economics* 23.2: 167-91.

Landry, C., and T. Anderson (2003) 'The Rising Tide of Water Markets', in *ITT Industries Guidebook to Global Water Issues*, itt.com/waterbook/toc.asp, accessed March 2003.

Pigram, J.J. (1999) *Tradeable Water Rights: The Australian Experience* (Taipei, Taiwan: Taiwan Institute for Economic Research, Taipei, 21 June 1999).

Saleth, R.M. (2001) *Water Pricing: Potential and Problems* (2020 Focus 9: Overcoming Water Scarcity and Quality Constraints; Brief 10 of 14; Washington, DC: International Food Policy Research Institute, October 2001).

Smith, A. (1791) *An Inquiry into the Nature and Causes of the Wealth of Nations* (ed. R.H. Campbell and A.A. Skinner; Indianapolis, IN: Liberty Fund).

Smith, D. (1998) *Water in Australia* (Melbourne, Australia: Oxford University Press).

Stein, R. (2002) 'Water Sector Reform in Southern Africa: Some Case Studies', in A.R. Turton and R. Henwood (eds), *Hydropolitics in the Developing World: A Southern African Perspective* (Pretoria, South Africa: African Water Issues Research Unit [AWIRU]).

Yang, H., X. Zhang and A.J.B. Zehnder (2002) 'Water Scarcity, Pricing Mechanism and Institutional Reform in Northern China Irrigated Agriculture', *Agricultural Water Management* 1,801: 1-19.

3

Balancing the cost implications and benefits of compliance with advanced risk analysis

Davide Bixio, Chris Thoeye and Greet De Gueldre

Aquafin NV, Belgium

In recent years, among the several sources available for water supply, the use of non-conventional water resources such as recycled municipal waste-water has received increasing attention, particularly in the arid and semi-arid regions (Anderson and Iyadurai 2003).

One of the primary reasons for using recycled water is its availability at a relatively low incremental cost, even in drought years. However, possible constraints that may limit expanded use are (a) the concerns over the possible presence of chemical and microbiological agents that could be hazardous to human health and to the environment and (b) public acceptance.

On the one hand, current technical feasibility can provide water quality that can meet any prescribed standard. On the other hand, aiming for complete safety may impose a heavy compliance cost (Shuval *et al.* 1997). Ensuring that the use of treated waste-water does not result in adverse health and ecological effects or in heavy compliance costs requires the development of a systematic and transparent risk-based approach.

The aim of this chapter is to contribute to the setting of best practice for business and public administrations to reduce the risks to acceptable social, economic and environmental levels. It is worth noting that acceptable risk is generally very location-specific and therefore does not fit within international guidelines (Anderson *et al.* 2001). Thus there is a need to reach international agreement on standard practices on the assessment of risks rather than on the definition of acceptable risks.

3.1 Traditional quantitative risk assessment of water re-use projects

A generally accepted practice for quantitative risk assessment (QRA) comprises four main steps, which are given in Box 3.1 (adapted from NRC 1998). In the case of the re-use of waste-water of domestic origin, a large number of priority pollutants can potentially be hazardous (US EPA 1998; WHO 1989, 1996). The decision whether or not to include a pollutant in the list of hazardous substances is based on a number of criteria, which can be categorised in two main branches, the health effects and the expected environmental levels. The health effects concern the nature and severity of the effects and the predicted no-effect concentrations for the target eco-system (the predicted no-effect concentrations [PNECs]). They can be established based on the available epidemiological and toxicological data in the scientific literature. The expected environmental levels concern the amount and duration of the exposure and can be quantified by the modelling of pollutant emissions, their removal in downstream pollutant barriers and their dilution in the receiving water body.

The steps are as follows:

- Hazard identification, involving definition of the human health and/or ecological effects associated with any particular hazard
- Assessment of the strength of evidence in support of an association between the environmental indicator under consideration and illness, involving characterisation of the dose without adverse effects on human health
- The quantification of the exposure of the community, involving determination of the size and nature of the population exposed and the route, amount and duration of the exposure
- Risk characterisation or integration of the three steps in order to estimate the magnitude of the public health problem and the impact of any proposed pollution barrier option

---

BOX 3.1 Different steps in quantitative risk assessment

Source: adapted from NRC 1998

A generally accepted practice for estimating the risk of exposure to the identified hazardous compounds is to compare the predicted environmental concentration (PEC) with the PNEC. Risk-management actions are then envisaged if the ratio PEC–PNEC is found to be inadequate.

The difference of the predicted ratio from unity represents the margin of safety. The adequacy of the margin of safety to the likelihood of the occurrence of a threat or hazard depends on a number of factors. Critical points are the potential seriousness of the impact on community health and the uncertainties of the predictions. Unfortunately, many of the processes and models that experts rely on to make their predictions contain significant uncertainty, either in the quantification of the exposure or in morbidity. QRA approaches account for these uncertainties by deliberately choosing precautionary values that lead to a 'somewhat conservative' estimate of PEC and PNEC:

- Model uncertainty: based on the precautionary principle—that is, the most conservative conceptual model is applied. For instance, in the case of the prediction of the removal of pathogenic viruses, the modelling of bacteriophages MS2 or PRDI is generally performed (Schijven and Hassani-zadeh 2000), as those viruses generally show the worst attachment, detachment and inactivation values.

- Input and variable uncertainty: the traditional approach to input and variable uncertainty is to use conservative values of input parameters and variables (i.e. by making a a worst-case scenario analysis). The total uncertainty factor is accounted for as the product of the uncertainties for each element. The larger the number of multiplied variables for which conservative values are selected, the higher the resulting margin of safety. The larger the number of multiplied variables for which conservative values are selected, the higher the likelihood of deviating from the actual worst-case situation.

As the calculations on which the simulations are based may require worst-case estimates of a large set of parameters (e.g. combination of highest emission levels, low kinetics in treatment removal, low-dilution levels and so on), traditional QRA approaches may impose, at best, dissatisfactory allocation of resources (Shuval *et al.* 1997) or, at worst, may cancel or delay projects that are potentially beneficial to society and the environment.

The major problem of traditional approaches does not lie in conservatism per se but rather in the absence of any ideas about the limits of error or uncertainty associated with the 'somewhat conservative' assumptions. We need to know *what* causes *what* to determine risk, degree of protection and costs—both their magnitude and their likelihood of occurrence. However, these approaches fail explicitly to link risk, natural variations and uncertainty.

3.2 Proposed quality risk assessment approach

Planning and design decisions can be improved by augmenting judgement, experience and safety factor methods with an explicit link between risk and the uncertainties that generate such risk. In this section we will attempt to set out an alternative approach that provides a way of explicitly taking into account the amount, duration and frequency of risk exposure (time variance) and to acknowledge the uncertainty in parameter values in a structured way to avoid the pitfalls of worst-case analysis. The procedure is based on combining Monte Carlo probabilistic modelling techniques with predictive models.

The quantification of the uncertainty of the system as a whole is carried out by the following steps:

- Step 1: information about the probability distribution of each input parameter and variable in the system is assigned.

- Step 2: for every calculation, the simulation uses a value for each input parameter randomly selected by the Monte Carlo engine from the probability density function for that variable. Over multiple calculations, the Monte Carlo engine produces a range of values for the input parameters and variables, reflecting the probability density function of each input parameter and variable. The set of samples ('shot') is entered into the deterministic model.

- Step 3: the conceptual model is then solved for each shot, as it would be for any deterministic analysis, static or dynamic.

- Step 4: the model results are stored and the process is repeated until the specified number of model iterations is completed. The output can now be expressed as a probability density function or cumulative probability density function (Fig. 3.1).

3.2.1 Uncertainty and variability

The probabilistic simulation takes into account both input and parameter uncertainty, thereby dealing with the difficulties in estimating model parameters and taking into account the inherent uncertainty in specific phenomena. (Variability represents heterogeneity or diversity, which cannot be reduced through further measurement or study. Uncertainty represents ignorance about a poorly characterised phenomenon, which can sometimes be reduced through further measurement or study.) In the approach set out in Figure 3.1 the variability is assumed to be completely captured by the introduction of dynamic mechanistic simulations, and uncertainty is captured by the Monte Carlo simulation. Therefore, there is no need for a second-order Monte Carlo analysis that would simulate variability and uncertainty in two loops, as illustrated in Grum and Aalderink 1999.

3.2.2 Time-series analysis of the results of the model

This iterative process generates a probability density function or cumulative density function of the output (Rousseau *et al.* 2001). Based on the distribution of the output, a risk exposure level representing the high end (e.g. 95th percentile), central tendency (median or mean) or any other desired level of probability can be identified. It is therefore possible to represent uncertainty in the output of a model by generating sample values for the model inputs and running the model repetitively. Instead of obtaining a single-value result, as is the case with a deterministic simula-

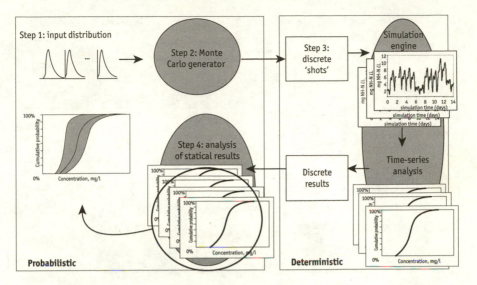

FIGURE 3.1 Layout of the probabilistic methodology

tion, a set of results is obtained (Cullen and Frey 1999). This set represents the cumulative effect of the given uncertainties of the input items.

This procedure and the pertaining software was originally developed in collaboration with the University of Ghent and used to evaluate compliance costs in upgrading waste-water treatment plants towards higher standards (Bixio *et al.* 2001). We have now extended it for balancing cost implications and health risks in the supply of recycled municipal waste-water. A case study limited to the QRA of nitrite and nitrate in drinking water supply will be shown to illustrate the benefits enjoyed with the proposed method. Results are compared with traditional procedures.

3.3 Example: quality risk assessment applied to household waste-water

At a Belgian sewage treatment plant (STP), 2,500,000 m³ of effluent per year is treated in a re-use water unit and, after a residence time of four to seven weeks in the aquifer, it is re-used for potable water production (see Fig. 3.2).

Nitrogen and its components are an example of the many compounds that are ubiquitously present in domestic waste-water in concentrations higher than the acceptable concentration for potable re-use. Nitrite ions, and to a lesser extent nitrate ions, originally not present in domestic waste-water but generated as an intermediate product of nitrogen removal from waste-water treatment, can reach the receiving water body at concentrations up to 10 times higher than those allowed for drinking-water consumption.

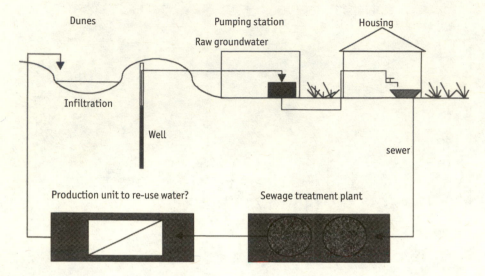

FIGURE 3.2 Water re-use scheme

As the STP has been in operation for a number of years the statistics of the measured concentrations in the effluent could be directly compared with the drinking-water standard. It is worth mentioning that the drinking-water standard for nitrite and nitrate refers to the no-observed-adverse-effect level (NOAEL) of the most critical toxic effect (methemoglobinemia) in the most sensitive human sub-population (infants) based on studies on human data (US EPA 2002).

Figure 3.3 sets out the frequency and cumulative distribution of oxidised nitrogen in the STP effluent (24h composite samples) as well as the NOAEL. The data, which were collected at regular intervals in the period 1996–2002, are expressed in nitrite equivalents (E-NO_2N), with the conservative assumption that a maximum of 10% of nitrate can be reduced to nitrite within the human body (US EPA 2002). In other words, the E-NO_2N is calculated by adding 10% of the nitrate concentration, [NO_3N], to the concentration of nitrite, [NO_2N]:

$$\text{E-}NO_2N = [NO_2N] + 0.1 \times [NO_3N] \qquad [3.1]$$

Figure 3.3 shows that the effluent values are below the NOAEL for more than 95% of the cases and that they never exceed the threshold of 1.5 mg per litre E-NO_2N (for 428 data points).

If the STP had not already been in operation the effluent concentrations could have been calculated by fate models (i.e. by taking a deterministic approach). The analyst could use, for instance, a modified IAWQ (International Association on Water Quality) Activated Sludge Model No. 1 (Henze *et al.* 1987) that includes two-step nitrification (see e.g. Ossenbruggen *et al.* 1996). Exogenous factors such as influent loading, temperature, pH and so on as well as process kinetics and stoichiometric parameters should then be estimated and introduced in the models.

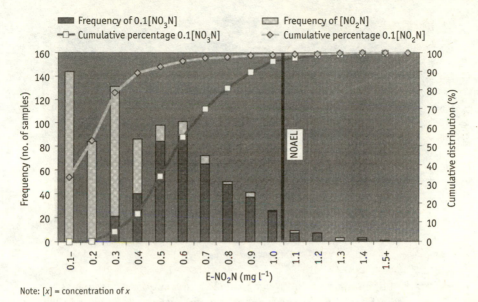

Note: [x] = concentration of x

FIGURE 3.3 Frequency diagram for the nitrite equivalent, E-NO$_2$N, in milligrams NO$_2$N per litre, in the effluent from a sewage treatment plant (STP) in Belgium, showing the no-observed-adverse-effect level (NOAEL)

Traditional methods would have obtained a margin of safety on the predictions by compounding conservative assumptions on flow (no dilution) and load (high percentile values), characteristics of the waste-water (limited carbon source for the denitrification process), temperature, pH and so on. However, a lot of useful information, especially concerning the uncertainty or conservatism of the assumptions, would then have been lost. By contrast, with Monte Carlo techniques, all relevant information of the historical data series—dynamics, the important correlation between parameters and variable as well as the data uncertainty—can be retained, thus limiting arbitrary judgements. To illustrate this point Figure 3.4 shows the measurement and statistics of the nitrogen concentrations in relation to the inflow at the STP.

As the Monte Carlo technique can retain information about low-boundary, median and high-boundary regression curves, as well as their probability distribution (see Fig. 3.4), it avoids compounding overly conservative boundary regression curves or values and can maintain the causal link between risk and uncertainty.

Figure 3.5 illustrates the results of the cumulative probability distribution curve of nitrite at a waste-water treatment plant outlet during a representative summer period as an example. (We have considered a summer period because the aquifer recharge is carried out only during that season.) The 5th percentile, 50th percentile and 95th percentile uncertainty boundary profiles are plotted against the NOAEL.

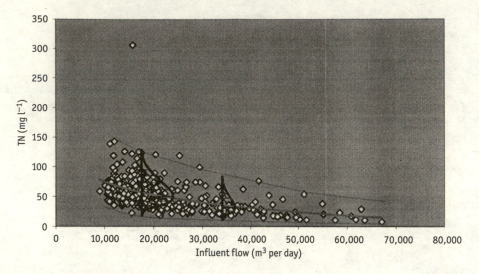

FIGURE 3.4 Plot of influent total nitrogen load (TN), in milligrams nitrogen per litre, against daily flow at a sewage treatment plant inlet in Belgium (428 data points)

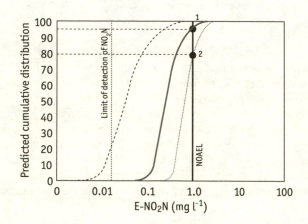

Concentration of activated sludge effluent

----- 5th percentile

——— 50th percentile

·········· 95th percentile

FIGURE 3.5 Predicted percentage cumulative distribution of predicted environmental concentration (PEC) against nitrite equivalent, E-NO₂N, in milligrams nitrogen per litre, showing the no-observed-adverse-effect level (NOAEL): simulation results for secondary effluent, summer period

Figure 3.5 shows that with 50% certainty the secondary effluent is for more than 95% of the time below the NOAEL value and with 95% certainty for more than 80% of the time (points 1 and 2, respectively). Dilution (a third reclaimed waste-water plus two-thirds natural groundwater) and removal in soil passage reduce further the nitrate + nitrite concentrations below the NOAEL.

QRA with traditional methods (worst-case analysis) would indicate that the STP effluent concentrations are not sufficient to achieve 'acceptable risk' levels for drinking water and an additional downstream pollution barrier with a removal efficiency higher than 75% would be removed (SVW 2002). This seems overly conservative, especially considering that conservatism is also applied from the regulator. The NOAEL relies on a series of conservative assumptions. More recent studies hint that historic nitrate contamination was merely an indicator of bacterial contamination and that the NOAEL of 10 mg NO_xN per litre or 1 mg NO_2N per litre is in all probability overly protective (Avery 1999).

The worst-case risk analysis significantly impacts the cost of the project and does not add any beneficial protection against nitrite exposure. The construction and operation of the additional pollution barrier increase the operating costs by approximately € 0.7 per cubic metre.

The proposed procedure shows a clear path forward to provide the best opportunities for balancing cost implications and benefits of compliance.

3.4 Discussion

3.4.1 Strengths and advantages of the probabilistic approach

First, decisions are made with a healthier understanding of the factors influencing that decision. By explicitly incorporating uncertainty and variability in the model-based risk analysis one can simplify the risk managers' decision or increase his or her 'comfort factor' by pointing out dangers in a more realistic fashion—that is, by putting the accent on where the uncertainty or indeterminacy actually is and/or by providing a sort of guarantee (to the manager and to outside overseers) that an impartial systematic search has been conducted. The procedure is more transparent to stakeholders, as the measure of the risk of a particular course of action is grounded on a rational analysis of the available imperfect information and the expert judgement is made explicitly. A transparent process with all the assumptions and parameters clearly stated can partly settle possible controversies between water utilities, government and environmentalists.

Second, the methodology can enhance the probability of meeting standards while reducing the disbursement of capital in excess of what is required. The approach informs the risk manager about the degree of conservatism that would result from the compounding of conservative assumptions employed in conventional projects and proposes a robust and transparent way of avoiding such an eventuality. In the conventional approach, the poor link between the cause–effect relationship of risk and uncertainty makes it necessary to calculate a overly conservative point estimate of input variables and/or parameters. The uncertainty of each input variable and parameter can now be explicitly introduced into the model-based analysis and will contribute to the calculation of the overall uncertainty of the system.

Last, the procedure provides a platform on which the systematic evaluation of the input uncertainties can help the risk manager to rationalise the acquisition of the new measurements. Because uncertainty can be reduced (at a cost!), but not eliminated, proper quantitative information about the causal link of the input uncertainty and the overall uncertainty in the system can enhance the probability of properly allocating limited financial resources to decreasing the overall uncertainty in the system. The risk assessor may wish to reduce the uncertainty of a particular situation by gathering additional information. This implies a reallocation of the investment resources, implying higher costs for monitoring and personnel in the early phase of the project. The risk assessor can justify the potential value of acquiring additional information based on an objective utility function.

3.4.2 Weaknesses and disadvantages of the probabilistic approach

First, it is clear that, in principle, the concepts introduced in this chapter are potentially of great significance in the decision-making process. However, the risk analysis is basically a mathematical tool and can only be of practical use if predictive models are available and quantitative estimates of the probability distribution of the sensitive input parameters and variables can be made. Thus, the importance of information cannot be understated. Results are dependent on the willingness and ability of the risk assessor to invest time and resources searching valid and relevant information. On the one hand, the availability of information plays a central role, reducing the space for arbitrary judgement. On the other hand, it also implies that the effective use of the Monte Carlo simulation technique depends heavily on such information being available.

Second, it is worth noting that this approach does not eliminate risk; it merely helps risk assessors and managers identify and deal with imperfect information. Because of the increased level of complexity and the underlying assumptions this approach should never be applied in a mechanistic fashion, and any conclusions it suggests must be carefully considered in light of sound technical judgement and experience. In fact, although this methodology can serve as a more objective basis for risk characterisation, this does not mean that expert judgement is abandoned altogether! On the contrary, expert input is required more than ever and should play a major part in the setting of an acceptable level of risk.

Where probability drawn from past or present experience is not available, 'subjective' probabilities are considered; these are based on the risk assessor's own expectations, preferences, experience and judgement. These expectations can provide some assistance, but it is clear that subjective probabilities assigned over the uncertainty can be a dangerous guide in decision-making. Risk assessors and managers may have an unjustified overconfidence in the modelling approach, and expert judgement must be used with caution.

Last, modelling must be applied keeping in mind its limitations. Models are generally built around some specific narrow boundary conditions. Moreover, the risk assessor must not confuse mathematical rigour with reality, forgetting the limitations of the scientific knowledge or the real-life technical challenges. The results are only as good as the science and the available data.

3.5 Conclusions

The case study clearly illustrates that the ability to identify, manage and share risks can greatly reduce costs for projects with certain types of risk profile. Procurement procedures that present a more balanced approach to risk allocation, by tailoring liabilities and process guarantees to meet specific project needs, will benefit from significant cost reductions.

The starting point is a clear understanding of the costs, potential liabilities and benefits of risk assignments—obtainable only when an explicit link between risks and uncertainties that generate those risks is maintained. This is generally not the case for conventional risk assessment methods.

The probabilistic risk characterisation method illustrated in this chapter appears to be a promising approach for business and public administrations for balancing project costs and risks, allocating risks to an acceptable social, economic and environmental level. The approach provides an explicit way of calculating the level of risk, avoiding the problems of compounding conservative, more arbitrarily defined, assumptions.

Although the predicted environmental concentration (PEC), potential daily intake (PDI) and the predicted no-effect concentration (PNEC) should be based only on scientific and public health considerations, without regard to economic cost considerations, the risk management action, and therefore the margin of safety, should take account of economic cost considerations and technical feasibility.

The costs of risk management measures (risk reduction) must be balanced against the level of risk reduction those measures aim to achieve. The case study illustrated in this chapter hints that the assignment of a clearly enunciated level of risk in the commercial terms of the contract to reduce potential liabilities and share risks can lead to the implementation of recycling schemes that traditional approaches fail to identify due to the heavy costs of compliance.

References

Anderson, J., and R Iyadurai (2003) 'Integrated Urban Water Planning: Big Picture Planning is Good for the Wallet and the Environment', *Water Science and Technology* 47.7–8: 19-23.

——, A. Adin, J. Crook, C. Davis, R. Hultquist, B. Jimenze-Cisneros, W. Kennedy, B. Sheikh and B. van der Merwe (2001) 'Climbing the Ladder: A Step by Step Approach to International Guidelines for Water Recycling', *Water Science and Technology* 43.10: 1-8.

Avery, A.A. (1999) 'Infantile Methemoglobinemia: Re-examining the Role of Drinking Water Nitrates', *Environmental Health Perspectives* 107.7: 583-86.

Bixio D., G. Parmentier, D. Rousseau, F. Verdonck, J. Meirlaen, P.A. Vanrolleghem and C. Thoeye (2001) 'Integrating Risk Analysis in the Design/Simulation of Activated Sludge Systems', in *Proceedings of the 74th WEF Annual Conference and Exposition (WEFTEC), 15–19 October 2001; Atlanta, USA.*

Cullen, A.C., and H.C. Frey (1999) *Probabilistic Techniques in Exposure Assessment: A Handbook for Dealing with Variability and Uncertainty in Models and Inputs* (New York: Plenum Press).

Grum, M., and R.H. Aalderink (1999) 'Uncertainty in Return Period Analysis of Combined Sewer Overflow Effects Using Embedded Monte Carlo Simulations', *Water Science and Technology* 39.4: 233-40.

Henze, M., C.P.L. Grady Jr, W. Gujer, G.V.R. Marais and T. Matsuo (1987) *Activated Sludge Model No. 1* (Scientific and Technical Report 1; London: International Association on Water Quality [IAWQ]).

NRC (National Research Council) (1998) *Issues in Potable Re-use: The Viability of Augmenting Drinking Water Supplies with Recycled Water* (Washington, DC: National Academy Press).

Ossenbruggen, P.J., H. Spanjers and A. Klapwik (1996) 'Assessment of a Two-step Nitrification Model for Activated Sludge', *Water Research* 30.4: 939-53.

Rousseau, D., F. Verdonck, O. Moerman, R. Carrette, C. Thoeye, J. Meirlaen and P.A. Vanrolleghem (2001) 'Development of a Risk Assessment Based Technique for Design/Retrofitting of WWTPs', *Water Science and Technology* 43.7: 287-94.

Schijven, J.F., and S.M. Hassanizadeh (2000) 'Removal of Viruses by Soil Passage: Overview of Modelling, Processes and Parameters', *Critical Review of Environmental Science and Technology* 30.1: 49-127.

Shuval, H., Y. Lampert and B. Fattal (1997) 'Development of a Risk Assessment Approach for Evaluating Waste-water Re-use Standards for Agriculture', *Water Science and Technology* 35.11–12: 15-20.

SVW (Studie Voor Water) (2002) *Health Risk by Re-use of Treated Waste-water: Final Report* (Confidential Study 4-7, 2002; Antwerp, Belgium: SVW; in Dutch).

US EPA (US Environmental Protection Agency) (1998) *Drinking Water Contaminant Candidate List: Federal Register Notice about the Contaminant Candidate List* (63 FR 10273; Washington, DC: US EPA, 2 March 1998).

—— (2002) 'Integrated Risk Information System (IRIS) Data Base Access', www.epa.gov/iris, accessed May 2002.

WHO (World Health Organisation) (1989) *Health Guidelines for the Use of Waste-water in Agriculture and Aquaculture* (Geneva: WHO).

—— (1996) *Guidelines for Drinking Water Quality. II. Health Criteria and Other Supporting Information* (Geneva: WHO, 2nd edn).

4

Environmental management with the balanced scorecard
A CASE STUDY OF THE BERLIN WATER COMPANY, GERMANY

Carl-Ulrich Gminder

Institute for Economy and the Environment, Switzerland

It is strategically important for a waterworks company to devote resources to the environment. The quality and availability of its main resource—water—is crucial for the successful and responsible business in the mid and long term. But waterworks are increasingly focused on short-term revenues: the private companies feel the pressure of shareholders; the public companies are squeezed by the financial crises in the public sector.

- How can positive environmental strategies be set and implemented taking these conditions into account?

- How can positive environmental strategies be translated into real substantive action and not just paid lip service?

These issues are examined in this case study about the Berlin Wasserbetriebe (hereafter referred to as the BWC [Berlin Water Company]). The BWC, which is the largest water supply and waste-water treatment company in Germany, serves 3.4 million people. It has a monopoly on the water supply and waste-water treatment business in its service area. In 1999, 49.9% of the company was sold to Vivendi and RWE (Rheinisch-Westfälische Elektrizitätswerke), but the remaining 50.1% is still state-owned. The partial privatisation brought tremendous changes in management and organisation. Strategic goals were implemented that focused only on the shareholders, the customers and the employees and not on societal needs and the environment. Indeed, environmental management was in danger of being entirely removed from the agenda. A new management tool, the balanced scorecard, was launched in order to translate these the new strategic priorities into action.

The case study[1] presented here shows how, as a result of a project involving the company's environmental manager and the University of St Gallen, the strategic importance of the environment was enhanced, primarily by integrating sustainability into the main management tool, the balanced scorecard. A sustainability balanced scorecard was first developed for the environmental department of the BWC; then, using this, as well as actively participating in the first rework cycle of the existing balanced scorecard of BWC, the environment was discussed and reintroduced as a strategic concern. A company-wide environmental goal was developed, introduced and translated into indicators and measures (see Gminder and Bergner 2002).

4.1 Using the balanced scorecard for managing sustainability

The concept of the balanced scorecard (BSC) was developed in the beginning of the 1990s by Kaplan and Norton (Kaplan and Norton 1996) in order to bridge the gap between strategic management and operational daily management. The BSC became successful because of its simple yet intelligent design, ease of communication and flexibility of application. It can be applied at the corporate, business unit, department or even employee level. Its potential for use as a management tool for corporate sustainability has been discussed for a number of years, and although the existing approaches primarily emphasise the financial aspects it has been found that the BSC approach can successfully integrate other sustainability aspects such as the societal and environmental (see Bieker et al. 2001; Epstein 1996; Epstein and Wisner 2001; Figge et al. 2002; Gminder and Bieker 2002; Hockerts 2001; Johnson 1998; Schaltegger and Dyllick 2002; SIGMA 2001; Zingales and Hockerts 2002).

4.1.1 What is the balanced scorecard?

The term 'balanced' refers to a balance between soft facts of organisational development and hard facts of finance, a balance between internal and external stakes and a balance of leading and lagging indicators. The BSC approach has two main components. One of these is a management tool that is built up from three aspects:

- Objectives

- Key performance indicators (KPIs) that measure progress in achieving the objectives (so-called leading indicators and strategic projects, such as the number of customer orders)

- KPIs that measure the results (so-called lagging indicators and targets, such as profit or turnover)

---

1   The study was carried out within the research project 'Sustainability Balanced Scorecard' (SBSC) of the Universities of St Gallen (Switzerland) and Lüneburg (Germany), funded by the German Ministry for Education and Research (BMBF).

The other part of the BSC is a management methodology for translating strategic goals into action and supporting the 'management by objectives' idea. The traditional BSC comprises four perspectives: financial, customer, process, and learning and development. The perspectives are established in order to manage the concerns of the shareholders, customers and employees and also to address aspects of business processes, finance and corporate development. Each organisational unit that applies the BSC can choose the number and naming of the perspectives. A recent development is the recommended inclusion of a fifth perspective, that of sustainability. Within each perspective, objectives, indicators and measures are all defined.

A sustainability balanced scorecard (SBSC) is a type of BSC specifically designed to reflect the issues and objectives of corporate sustainability. In order to clarify appropriate sustainability strategies and translate them into action, it is generally recommended that managers first design a separate SBSC. This must then be integrated into the traditional BSC in order to ensure a holistic view of sustainability. This process will help overcome the distinction between a traditional financially oriented management approach and one emphasising sustainability or environmental management concerns. Figure 4.1 shows how the SBSC can be integrated either completely or partially. It also shows the option of creating a further perspective applicable to societal management (for an explanation, see Gminder *et al.* 2002: 121).

Where a traditional BSC does not yet exist, the development of the BSC and the integration of sustainability can be done in one step (see the case study of Volkswagen, in Bieker *et al.* 2002). Even where a traditional BSC exists, the development of a separate SBSC may not be necessary. Instead it may be sufficient to develop new environmental or societal goals, then enrich them with indicators and measures and integrate them into the traditional BSC in the course of the next review cycle, as was done in the case study of the BWC discussed here.

An important structural element of the BSC is the strategy map. This is a diagram that shows all perspectives and all objectives at a glance. The objectives are linked by arrows expressing the cause–effect relationships between the different objectives. It is a rule in a traditional BSC to place the financial perspective at the top and follow this with all links in that perspective. This rule may need to be reappraised when the orientation is skewed toward sustainability. In addition, the links between the objectives may be contrary, and the earlier a contrary relation is made clear the better the company can seek ways to resolve potential conflicts. If this is not done, management may be unaware of problems that will become apparent to employees responsible for implementing the BSC at the operational level.

4.2 Integrating the environment into the balanced scorecard of the Berlin Water Company

The case study focuses on integrating environmental protection into the BSC at a company level. The first step is to evaluate the existing company situation. Once this has been done the task is to explain how environmental objectives, indicators and measures can be developed and integrated into the company BSC. The final step is to examine the results and draw conclusions.

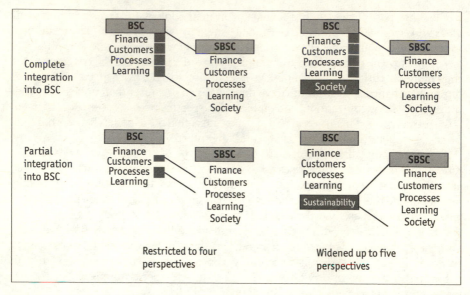

FIGURE 4.1 The possibilities for integrating a sustainability balanced scorecard (SBC) into the balanced scorecard (BSC)

Source: Gminder *et al.* 2002: 123

The research methodology that was used for this case study was 'action research'. Document analysis, combined with evidence gained from interviews with company employees at all levels, from the CEO to workers in a sewerage maintenance team, was used to understand the company's structure and function and to allow identification of a way to manage environmental and societal issues. Four workshops were then held to further develop the company's BSC. Finally, the results were written down and presented for validation throughout the company.

4.2.1 The Berlin Water Company

As noted in the introduction, the BWC is the largest water supply and waste-water treatment company in Germany; in 2001 its 5,500 employees produced a turnover of €982 million and an operating profit of €269 million. One activity of the BWC is the supply of drinking water, almost all extracted from the ground in Berlin itself. Seven waterworks extract 220 million m³ water from the ground each year and pump it through a 7,800 km pipe network. Each of the waterworks is certified to ISO 14001.[2] The quality of the water is extremely high for a large city, and no disinfection or chlorination is necessary. The other activity is the treatment and discharge of waste-water, which also occurs in the city. Seven sewage works treat 240 million m³ waste-water each year, transported through a 9,000 km sewerage network. Two of these

2   For more details of ISO 14001, see www.iso.ch/iso/en/prods-services/otherpubs/iso14000/index.html.

works are ISO 14001-certified. In order to preserve the lakes and rivers within the city where the treated waste-water is discharged, several measures of monitoring and treating the lake and river water quality are carried out.

The waste-water treatment is a state-run task and a non-profit business, in contrast to the water supply business, which is run for profit. Both parts have a monopoly, but their tariffs are determined by municipal law.

4.2.2 The management of the Berlin Water Company

The formal organisation structure starts at the top with the board and a group of 'shared service' departments, followed by 14 business units, departments, works and maintenance units, with various groups and teams below them, down to the single employee.

In 2000, the board publicised a company vision and its corporate objectives. The vision comprises four areas. One of these addresses the major tasks of supplying water and the careful, environmentally friendly treatment of sewage. The other three address stakeholder interests, including those of the shareholders, the customers and the employees, for each aspect of which five to six company objectives are stated. However, the environmental and societal interests are not operationalised by specific objectives, and many employees do not see why this would be necessary, because they recognise that a clean environment with clean water is necessary for the sound economic operation of the company. In fact, the omission of environment was a deliberate decision by the board because of the dominating financial interests of the private and the state shareholders.

The company objectives are the strategic input of the company's BSC. They also serve as objectives for the individual business units. Within the units the objectives are translated into personal agreements for all departmental or team leaders. This recently implemented approach of 'management by objectives' is reported to be viewed very positively by the employees.

Explicit business strategies do not exist but, implicitly, there are two main strategies. First, the profit orientation strategy emphasises the importance of reducing costs and enhancing distribution (water use declined in the 1990s). Second, the customer orientation strategy places importance on customer satisfaction and on the training of employees. Measures to implement the strategies are taken within a framework of projects. Many different types of indicators are used within the company, and the BSC has the benefit of pointing out those that are really important.

The management and control of the BWC involves regular internal reporting, which triggers activities if necessary. The management system is in transition from the old state-oriented planning system towards the new system with a business-oriented focus, and institutional controlling processes are not yet set up. The budget plan for the coming years is still the most important management tool. The BSC is one of the tools for changing existing systems along with a risk-management approach, the principle of management by objectives and new reporting to the board, but all struggle to gain acceptance given the power of the old structures, rules and plans.

The BSC has been in use since July 2001 on a company level, operated through the Shared Service Department for Corporate Development (the VUE [Vorstandsabteilung Unternehmensentwicklung]). The company's objectives are directly integrated as goals of the BSC, each specified by between two to four indicators and by a range of measures. The reporting cycle of the BSC is not monthly as usual, but quarterly. Individual business units have also established BSCs. All BSCs are still in the trial phase and need to be completed and enhanced through application and evaluation, and in interviews most employees claimed that the BSCs were still too weak and subordinate to the budget plans.

4.2.3 The management of environmental protection

The strategic importance of environmental protection for the BWC is clear. Groundwater is the crucial resource for the core business of the BWC (i.e. selling clean drinking water), and the purer the groundwater the lower the cost of treating it to drinking-water standards. Strong treatment processes for waste-water are of similar importance, because exploitation and discharge is done in the same geographical area, so the quality of the discharged water influences the quality of the ground water. Environmental protection is also critical in the mechanical processes of the works, the burning of sewage sludge and eco-efficiency in the administration.

The task of environmental protection is decentralised across the business units, where it is the responsibility of environmental managers, co-ordinators and skilled workers. Central support and co-ordination is provided by the Shared Service Department for Operations Officers and Environmental Affairs (VBU [Vorstands-abteilung Beauftrage und Umweltschutz]). The VBU is in charge of environmental organisation and legal compliance, providing environmental training, checking the environmental performance of the works and identifying potential societal and legal trends. It has 14 employees whose tasks are determined mostly by the legally defined officers for waste, water protection, emissions, accidents and radiation protection.

Since the partial privatisation the main focus of the company has been to optimise the formal protection of the environment, as shown in Figure 4.2. Indicators are used to guide the framework of internal environmental data surveys (e.g. the results of water analysis; some 480,000 analyses are made from 78,000 samples each year). The costs and quantity of waste are managed by means of the SAP software, and data from the water and sewage works are reported monthly. The BWC does not publish an environmental report but supplies data for the reports of its private co-owners—Vivendi and RWE.

4.2.4 The integration of environment into the balanced scorecard

To enable the integration of environmental protection into a BSC it is important to develop objectives, indicators and measures according to the structure of the BSC. Apart from the formal structure it is also essential to integrate environmental protection into the organisational processes (e.g. the review processes of the BSC) and into

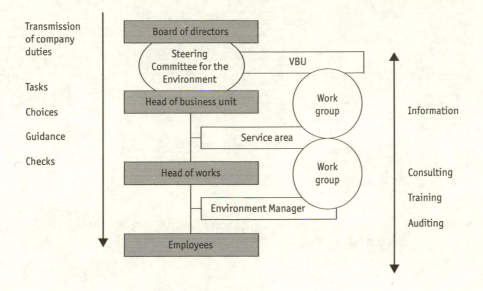

VBU = Shared service Department for Operations Officers and Environmental Affairs

FIGURE 4.2 Organisation of environmental protection at the Berlin Water Company

Source: Gminder and Bergner 2002: 205

the organisational hierarchy and the minds of the employees. To achieve this it is necessary to co-operate with the department that manages the BSC and get support from the board or the CEO. 'Soft' processes, such as talking to people, convincing them and including them in development activities, are far more important for the success of a BSC than 'hard', more formal actions such as defining objectives, indicators and measures, but both have a role to play. The head of the VBU department at the BWC was well aware of the importance of 'soft' processes, though sound 'hard' action was guaranteed by the support of the VUE, which manages the BSC. In this organisation the company level was considered to be the most appropriate for integration of environmental protection; Figure 4.3 shows the steps taken in the integration process.

Before starting training workshops, strategic clarification of the value of environmental protection was necessary at the board level. This clarification was not easy because the company was struggling with the operational change from non-profit bureaucracy to profit management, and the opinions of the four board members differed. After three months of uncertainty, the shared service departments responsible for the BSC (the VUE) and for the environment (the VBU) took action themselves and decided to start with four workshops and to develop proposals for the company objectives as well as operationalising them for the BSC.

Participants in the workshops were employees of VUE and VBU, together with those from the department of water and the sewage works co-ordination. First, the

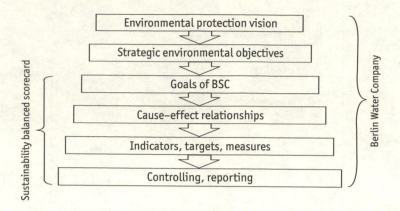

FIGURE 4.3 Process of integrating environmental protection into the balanced scorecard of the Berlin Water Company

Source: Gminder and Bergner 2002: 215

term 'sustainability' needed to be clarified, and the group decided to focus on environmental protection and excluded societal and economic sustainability. The aim of the group was to develop usable results, rather than 'dreams' that would stress the company too much in the current situation. Although this aim was perhaps necessary in order to produce acceptable results, it turned out to be a constraint when it eliminated some valuable and progressive proposals too early.

After the clarification of the meaning of 'sustainability', environmental objectives were developed in a brainstorming session, then bundled, grouped and reduced. The reduction was one condition of acceptance. The results were a mixture of objectives and measures; thus a separation was also necessary. During this process a new strategic objective was identified—'protection of natural resources (water, soil, air)'—and this was listed alongside the other 15 company objectives.

The next step was to link the environmental objectives to the other perspectives in the BSC. In addition to the perspective of the employees ('learning'), each of the perspectives was discussed, as it was argued that protection of natural resources serves the financial wealth of the company in the long term. It also benefits customers through ensuring good water quality and is a goal achieved by good process practices. The creation of a separate sustainability perspective was deemed to be unnecessary as it involved only a single goal. Finally, the process perspective was chosen as the most pragmatic solution. Other environmental goals could be subordinated to other company objectives and therefore automatically to the relevant perspectives. Most of the other objectives were also put into the process perspective—for example, the objective 'enhancing material and energy efficiency' related to the objective 'increasing productivity'.

Clarification on the strategic level was emphasised at the same time. The defensive attitude towards environment was found to change during the case study, and by spring 2002 the CEO defined increased 'environmental awareness' as one of the five necessary changes for the year. Given the definition of the strategic 'natural resource' objective and the ongoing discussion about sustainability, it became obvious that, for political reasons, environmental protection could not be excluded from consideration. As a result, it was proposed that an SBSC working group be incorporated into the strategic planning and review process. This suggestion was presented to the annual conference for upper management, where the board and the heads of the business units decided that it should be integrated into the BSC, even though the number of goals was reduced from 16 to 12 and one board member was still strongly opposed to it. There was still no update to the vision for the company, though the board agreed to undertake this and to clarify new company objectives, after 2004.

To assist the process, new indicators needed to be defined and discussed. A prerequisite was to limit the number to an average of one to three per goal, but aggregation was possible. For example, for the objective 'increasing productivity' (where eco-efficiency is subsumed) the costs per m^3 water and waste-water must be measured. In doing this, the working group determined that waste costs, energy costs, waste-water fee and compliance penalties should all be taken into account. Another way in which aggregation could be done is through the construction of an index. Hence an environmental pollution index was designed, including emission figures for several pollutants, such as carbon dioxide (CO_2), sulphur dioxide (SO_2) and methane (CH_4), mercury and so on, and was used as one of the five indicators for the 'natural resource' objective. Other indicators in addition to the index included:

- An approved average daily extraction rate for the drawing of raw water (in order to control the quantitative use of groundwater)

- The amount of cleaned groundwater in relation to the amount of polluted groundwater (in order to control the qualitative use of the groundwater)

- The number of works certified according to ISO 14001 or the EU Eco-Management and Audit Scheme (EMAS)[3]

- Expenditure on research and pre-emptive measures for resource protection, groundwater management, soil protection as well as lake and river management

The process proved controversial. The vice head of the VUE complained that 'no other objective has so many indicators'. The head of the VBU objected to the aggregation: 'Does this number tell us anything?'. It seems that the pressure of reducing goals or indicators is inevitably a painful one, yet it increases the clarity and simplicity of the controlling process. It also forces more detailed management on lower hierarchy levels.

The last step was the construction of the strategy map. Here, the cause–effect relationships were discussed and determined, and all objectives related to sustainability were identified and linked. An interesting picture of the corporate sustainability of the BWC evolved from all perspectives, as shown by Figure 4.4.

3   For more details of EMAS, see www.europa.eu.int/comm/environment/emas/index_en.htm.

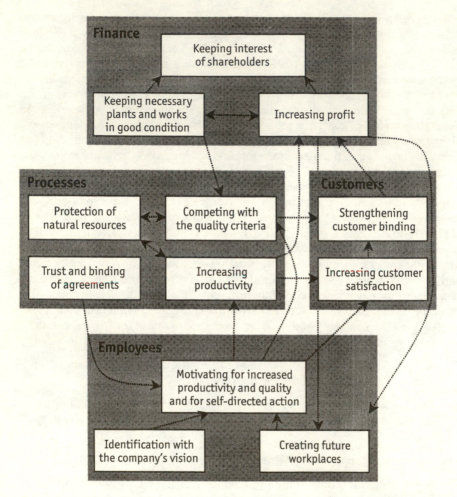

FIGURE 4.4 Sustainability-oriented strategy map of the Berlin Water Company (BWC)

Source: Gminder and Bergner 2002: 223

4.3 Conclusions

At the BWC, an acceptable solution was developed for managing environmental protection by using the BSC, and the results of the case study work had high practical benefit for the company.

From a theoretical point of view, the case study has shown that the BSC is a management tool that is flexible enough to deal with environmental and societal issues. It offers a method to translate the strategies of corporate sustainability into action and integrate them into the general management of a company, so that sustainability no longer has to be managed apart from other management tasks and systems. It has also shown that environmental protection is only one of several strategic objectives of a company. It does not provide the amount of detail that an environmental manager would need; thus a company SBSC neither substitutes for environmental management nor removes the need for there to be an effective environmental management system (such as ISO 14001 or EMAS) in place.

The SBSC can be a good way to bring discussions about corporate sustainability issues to the attention of general management, but it is only a tool to get people to sit down and talk about the issues. The real integration takes place in the minds of the employees, especially the top management. The BSC enables workshops, discussions, meetings and communication to clarify the importance of corporate sustainability. It also encourages the translation of corporate sustainability policies into action by integrating them into general management rather than simply paying lip service to the issues.

Waterworks management is under enormous financial pressure at the moment, whether it be under private or municipal ownership; thus other issues may seem far more important than sustainability. In a situation where all thoughts and actions are checked against profitability, environmental protection is quickly filed under 'costs or expenses', where it may be incorrectly suggested that in order to reduce costs it is necessary to reduce environmental protection. Although this may bring short-term gain, the mid-term and long-term costs are liable to be far higher: 'In Paris they need 18 steps for purifying the drinking water', the vice head of VUE reported, 'in Berlin we just need two because our groundwater is still so clean'. The importance of a clean environment and clean water resources for a water company was a permanent topic in workshops and interviews for this study. Most employees acknowledged a need, and even demand, for a pro-environment policy from top management, arguing that environmental protection should never be subordinated to productivity and quality for political reasons.

This case study shows that the discussion of environmental protection leads to a revaluation of the 'new' (profit-only) management way of thinking. The 'new' management tool BSC places the topic firmly on the agenda. Without it, environmental protection may be reduced to the minimum level that allows for legal compliance, an approach that undervalues the strategic importance that pro-environment policies have in the business of water supply and waste-water treatment. As summarised by a member of the workshop team:

> The research project was helpful to discuss with the board, to get clarification about just how important a clean environment is for a clean product. And that this issue should be not neglected, just because the current focus is on profit.

References

Bieker, T., T. Dyllick, C.U. Gminder and K. Hockerts (2001) 'Towards a Sustainability Balanced Scorecard: Linking Environmental and Social Sustainability to Business Strategy', in *Proceedings of the 10th Business Strategy and the Environment Conference, September 2001, Leeds* (Shipley, UK: ERP Environment): 22-31.

——, S. Herbst and H. Minte (2002) 'Nachhaltigkeitskonzept für die Konzernforschung der Volkswagen AG', in S. Schaltegger and T. Dyllick (eds.), *Nachhaltig managen mit der Balanced Scorecard* (Wiesbaden, Germany: Gabler): 315-42.

Dyllick, T., and K. Hockerts (2002) 'Beyond the Business Case for Corporate Sustainability', *Business Strategy and the Environment* 11.2 (March/April 2002): 130-41.

Epstein, M.J. (1996) *Measuring Corporate Environmental Performance: Best Practices for Costing and Manageing an Effective Environmental Strategy* (Chicago: Irwin Professional Publications).

—— and P. Wisner (2001) *Good Neighbours: Implementing Social and Environmental Strategies with the BSC* (Balanced Scorecard Report 3.3; Cambridge, MA: Harvard Business School).

Figge, F., T. Hahn, S. Schaltegger and M. Wagner (2002) 'The Sustainability Balanced Scorecard: Linking Sustainability Management to Business Strategy', *Business Strategy and the Environment* 11.5 (September/October 2002): 269-84.

Gminder, C.U., and M. Bergner (2002) 'Die Weiterentwicklung der BSC bei den Berliner Wasserbetriebe', in S. Schaltegger and T. Dyllick (eds.), *Nachhaltig managen mit der Balanced Scorecard* (Wiesbaden, Germany: Gabler): 199-229.

—— and T. Bieker (2002) 'Managing Corporate Social Responsibility by Using the Sustainability Balanced Scorecard', in *Proceedings of the Contribution to the 10th International Conference of the Greening of Industry Network, June 2002, Gothenburg, Sweden.*

——, ——, T. Dyllick and K. Hockerts (2002) 'Nachhaltigkeitsstrategien umsetzen mit einer Sustainability Balanced Scorecard', in S. Schaltegger and T. Dyllick (eds.), *Nachhaltig managen mit der Balanced Scorecard* (Wiesbaden, Germany: Gabler): 95-148.

Hockerts, K. (2001) 'Corporate Sustainability Management: Towards Controlling Corporate Ecological and Social Sustainability', in *Proceedings of Greening of Industry Network Conference, 21–24 January 2001, Bangkok.*

Johnson, S.D. (1998) 'Identification and Selection of Environmental Performance Indicators: Application of the Balanced Scorecard Approach', *Corporate Environmental Strategy* 5.4 (Summer 1998): 34-41

Kaplan, R.S., and D.P. Norton (1996) *The Balanced Scorecard: Translating Strategies into Action* (Boston, MA: Harvard Business School Press).

—— and —— (2001) *The Strategy-Focused Organisation* (Cambridge, MA: Harvard Business School).

Schaltegger, S., and T. Dyllick (eds.) (2002) *Nachhaltig managen mit der Balanced Scorecard* (Wiesbaden, Germany: Gabler).

SIGMA (2001) 'The SIGMA Sustainability Scorecard', in *The SIGMA Project Guidelines*, Chapter 6.4, www.projectsigma.com, accessed 12 March 2002.

Zingales, F., and K. Hockerts (2002) 'Nachhaltige Balanced Scorecard: Beispiele aus Literatur und Praxis', in S. Schaltegger and T. Dyllick (eds.), *Nachhaltig managen mit der Balanced Scorecard* (Wiesbaden, Germany: Gabler): 151-66.

Part 2
Privatisation

5

The private sector and service extension

David Lloyd Owen

Envisager, UK

In this chapter I describe how private-sector services are being mobilised to deliver water and waste-water services by water-sector organisations in the developed economies to countries with economies that are in a developing phase. Their needs are different because the policy contexts (politics and governance), standards and risks experienced by entities installing and improving water services in the two are different. It will be shown that the international water-sector companies have evolved a diverse suite of financial and contractual arrangements, often in association with international financial institutions (e.g. the World Bank). I will also examine how the water sector is evolving, as new companies shape their financial and technical competence to operate and compete internationally.

The role of private-sector participation (PSP) in delivering services and extending them is examined in terms of mobilising new sources of finance, the populations served and how services have been extended once PSP contracts have started. Although the role of PSP in developing economies is a relatively recent phenomenon, its record has demonstrated that certain types of contracts, along with attitudes to risk and operational management, have material advantages over other approaches. The capacity for PSP to deliver services and new sources of funding is set within the context of the water and sanitation targets set in The Hague (2000) and Johannesburg (2002) processes. The emergence and performance of locally based PSP players is compared with that of the traditional internationally based operators, and current and potential synergies between the two are considered.

5.1 Financing universal service provision

5.1.1 The cost of universal service provision

According to figures developed by the World Bank in the late 1990s (for basic services) and various sources in the EU, USA and Japan (for enhanced services) the funding needs over the next decade for providing basic water and sanitation services (driven by public health concerns) range between US$325 billion and US$680 billion, and those for enhanced water and sanitation services (driven by environmental standards) range between US$600 billion and US$800 billion (Owen 2003).

The World Water Council's 'World Water Vision for 2025' (Vision 2025), launched at the Second World Water Forum at The Hague in March 2000, was designed to represent a multilateral and multinational consensus as to the best ways to address water problems by 2025. Vision 2025 seeks to address the current lack of access to water provision, sewerage and sewage treatment by 2025 (Cosgrove and Rijsberman 2000: 53). In order to provide universal access to water and sewerage services, Vision 2025 calls for investment in new water and sanitation assets to rise from US$30 billion in 1995 to US$75 billion per year from 2000 to 2025 and for investment by industry, and for environmental protection, to increase from between US$10 billion to US$15 billion in 1995 to US$75 billion per year between 2000 and 2025 (Cosgrove and Rijsberman 2000: 60). Vision 2025 anticipates that nationally based private companies will contribute 45% of this investment, against 15–21% in 1995, with international finance increasing from 5–6% to 24% (Cosgrove and Rijsberman 2000: 64). Such a financial commitment will not take place unless adequate investment conditions exist, and these require private-sector participation in the management of these services (Cosgrove and Rijsberman 2000: 61).

Table 5.1 outlines the overall aims of Vision 2025 and its projected costs. In Table 5.2 these are applied to water and sewerage provision and treatment.

5.1.2 Is Vision 2025 affordable?

There are three main elements in financing water service extension: the cost of acquiring and installing new assets, the cost of maintaining them and the cost of repaying the debt taken on. It is the financial cost of each of these in relation to the cost of the new assets to be provided that determines the affordability of service extension. This is a material concern, as Vision 2025 assumes that access to water and sewerage services will cost 'conservatively' an average of US$500 per capita in urban and rural areas in the developing countries. In all, Vision 2025 assumes that between US$2,050 billion and US$2,300 billion needs to be invested over a 25-year period. The affordability of Vision 2025 as it currently stands will clearly pose problems, given the limited scope for new overseas development assistance (ODA) flows into developing economies. I have not been able to identify any quantitative analysis of the costs of operating and maintaining new assets or servicing and repaying the debt finance that is to be raised. Currently, total ODA runs at US$53 billion a year, with water and sewerage being given a relatively low priority.

5.1.3 The private sector and affordability

There are two principal drivers for PSP. In the developed economies of North America, Western Europe and South-East Asia, PSP is primarily utilised in order to shift the financial burden of upgrading and extending municipal water and sewerage services from central and local government to the private sector. This spending

	2000	2025
Population	4,760 million	6,530 million
Population lacking safe water	1,300 million	330 million
Population lacking sanitation	2,600 million	330 million
Forecast investment (US$ billion per year)	70–80	180

TABLE 5.1 Vision 2025: water, sewerage and sewage treatment access in developing countries, 1995–2025

Source: Adapted from Vision 2025, in Owen 2002

Area of spending	Spending (US$ billion per year)	
	1995	2000–2025
Drinking water	17	17
Sanitation	1.5–2.5	15
Waste-water treatment	11.5	50–60
Total	30–31	82–92

TABLE 5.2 Water and sewerage spending in developing countries, 1995–2025

Source: Prynn and Sunman 2000

is driven mainly by demand for higher service quality, aesthetics (taste, colour and odour) and environmental considerations.

In developing economies, PSP is being employed to finance and manage the development and operation of the water and sewerage infrastructure on commercial lines and as a means of mobilising funding from a variety of sources. The principal drivers are public health (access to potable water) and security of supplies (prevention of source contamination, ability to meet growing demand and ability to deliver water supplies on a consistent basis).

5.2 The private sector and the MDGs

5.2.1 From vision to action: Johannesburg and Kyoto

The 2002 Second Earth Summit in Johannesburg saw an agreement that the World Water Vision's targets for halving the number without access to water or sanitation by 2015 should be formally adopted. No significant progress was made on developing these targets on a country and regional level at the 2003 Third World Water Forum in Kyoto apart from recommendations in the Camdessus Report (Winpenny 2003) for the development of suitable overseeing and reporting mechanisms by 2006.

5.2.2 The politics of private-sector participation and service extension

A common political argument against privatising water and sewerage services is that it will mean that water will be too costly for poorer people. In fact, pricing policies based on charging more per unit of water for households who use water for non-essential purposes have been used to make private water provision both more affordable and financially viable. Cross-subsidies and social provisioning lie at the core of service extension, with water and sanitation services being provided for less than 2% of household income in 85% of projects funded by the World Bank or Asian Development Bank (Tynan and Kingdom 2002: 2). Questions about affordability and private-sector involvement in developing economies tend to ignore the fact that, under the current arrangements, it is the poorer people living in urban areas who have to pay over the odds to water vendors for supplies of distinctly dubious quality (see Table 5.3). People are willing to pay an economic price for water services if it comes with guarantees of quality and availability (Cowen and Tynan 1999; Nigam 1996; Tynan 2000).

5.2.3 The practicalities of delivering service extension

What can the private sector offer to the unserved urban poor? For multilateral institutions, governments, municipalities and the private sector, PSP in service extension can be an effective tool where projects are delivered more cheaply, new sources of finance are mobilised and existing assets are operated more efficiently. These benefits apply to all water and sewerage PSP projects but are particularly pertinent here. United Utilities' water and sewerage contract in Manila (Philippines) reduced prices by 65% in 1997 and is performing satisfactorily in terms of finances and service delivery. The 24-hour water delivery increased from 22% of the network in 1997 to 80% by 2001, with 99.7% water quality compliance; 50,000 low-income households were connected by 2004 (United Utilities 2004) with a further 19,285 households (115,700 people) in the first six months of 2003 (Platts 2003).

Raising finance has become problematic, with the project finance market currently running at perhaps 25% of the peak capacity seen in the late 1990s.[1] The private sector has two real strengths: mobilising existing assets to optimise their efficiency and developing new assets so that they provide a given level of performance at the lowest price. The challenges in arranging finance stem from poor risk management and concerns about foreign currency exposure.

A mix of foreign and international debt can help to ameliorate this, as is being used in Malaysia and China.[2] Multilateral institutions, development banks, politicians and international aid agencies need to create the right conditions to encourage these capital flows. Assurance of cost recovery in the medium to longer term is essential, and it is vital to get the cost of service provision down to affordable levels by using an appropriate and upgradeable infrastructure.

1 David Suratgar, Member of the Board, BMCE, Morocco, personal communication, 2002.
2 Suratgar, personal communication, 1998.

City	Cost (US$ millions)		Ratio, *D/V*
	For domestic use, *D*	From informal vendors, *V*	
Vientiane, Laos	0.11	14.68	135.92
Faisalabad, Pakistan	0.11	7.38	68.33
Bandung, Indonesia	0.12	6.05	50.00
Manila, Philippines	0.11	4.74	42.32
Cebu, Philippines	0.33	4.17	12.75
Phnom Penh, Cambodia	0.09	1.64	18.02
Ulaanbaatar, Mongolia	0.04	1.51	35.12
Hanoi, Vietnam	0.11	1.44	13.33
Ho Chi Minh City, Vietnam	0.12	1.08	9.23
Karachi, Pakistan	0.14	0.81	5.74
Dhaka, Bangladesh	0.08	0.42	5.12
Jakarta, Indonesia	0.16	0.31	1.97

Note: Ratio, *D/V* calculated from original, unrounded data

TABLE 5.3 Comparing the cost of water supplied from household connections and informal vendors

Source: Mcintosh and Yniguez 1997

The Camdessus Report (Winpenny 2003), released at the Kyoto Summit in 2003, outlines the current challenges facing the private sector and makes some general pointers towards improving conditions by 2006. Converting good intentions into an effective reality will be challenging.

5.2.4 The role of the private sector

Experience in the USA, England and Wales, and Germany since the 1990s has demonstrated that the privatisation of water and sewerage services can reduce capital spending by 20–45% and, through economies of scale and efficiency measures, service provision costs by 10–25% (Owen 2002). Capital spending costs can be reduced by managing construction work on a performance-related basis. In Chile, water utilities have become more efficient than their state-held peers since privatisation in 1998 (Bitran and Valenzuela 2003). Cost reductions in that country are driven by competitive tendering whereby the competing bidders are motivated to find the most cost-effective ways of delivering a set of service criteria for a satisfactory rate of return. This approach creates incentives for the bidders to identify areas where they can drive operating costs down while at the same time improving service quality. Often the two will be linked. People are more willing to pay when they receive a reliable service, with demonstrable improvements in water quality. Reducing distribution losses allows more water to be provided to the customer without the need to mobilise new resources. Progressive tariff policies, allied with effective billing and the removal of illegal connections, drive down the overall cost of water provision for the less well-off, allowing social equity to be improved.

At the start of 2003, Suez Ondeo (France) served 46.5 million people in developing economies, including 8.7 million people classified by the company as being among the urban poor (Suez Ondeo 2002:20), at the same time as extending water services to 7 million people within its concession areas (Suez Ondeo 2003: 13). Veolia Environnement (France), United Utilities, UK), Bouygues (France, parent company of Société d'Aménagement Urbain et Rural [SAUR]) and RWE (Germany, parent company of Thames Water), among others, also provide services to the urban poor where there were no such services prior to privatisation. The emphasis lies in developing a new infrastructure that meets current needs (piped water and sewerage) but is suitable for upgrading as and when higher standards of service delivery are needed. By mobilising local labour, costs of developing these services can be greatly reduced. Suez has been able to reduce the cost per household connection in Buenos Aires from US$600 to US$120 for water, and from US$1,000 to US$120 for sanitation (Suez Ondeo 2002: 26). Rural service provision is appreciably cheaper, concentrating on ensuring the ready availability of water within a short distance from each house, along with sanitation and effluent recovery and composting systems.

5.3 Differing levels of private-sector involvement

Because of the ambiguous nature of definitions at present, the forms of privatisation outlined below should be regarded as indicative. It is evident that a contract could offer elements from the differing categories. The difficulty is that such elastic contract definitions incur material costs when defining each contract.

5.3.1 Commercialisation

- Time-horizon: open
- Customer: retail
- Cash-flow profile: n/a
- Construction risk: n/a
- Regulatory risk: n/a
- Ownership: public
- Investment: public
- Operation: public
- Tariff collection: public

Commercialisation, a first move towards privatisation, calls for the municipal water and/or sewerage entity to be operated as a free-standing concern that does not involve cross-subsidies with other municipal services and runs on a self-financing basis.

A commercialisation strategy has already been adopted in a number of countries either as an end into itself or as a prelude to more extensive private-sector participation. Prior to the current privatisation programme, Chile used commercialisation allied with short-term service contracts, delegating responsibility to the private sector for a narrow range of services such as meter installation. Santiago's Aguas Andinas is the most notable example, having been commercialised in 1989 and sold in 1999. Other examples of entities operating on a commercial basis include South Africa's Umgeni Water and Thailand's municipal and provincial water authorities, which remain under public control.

A hybrid privatisation has emerged from a number of these commercial entities where the municipality floats some of the shares of the entity while retaining majority ownership and therefore management control. The best example is in Brazil, where Rio's Companhia de Saneamento Basico do Estado de São Paulo (SABESP) is actively traded on the National Bourse, while the municipality for the time being retains 72% of the company's equity.

5.3.2 Operations and maintenance (O&M) and lease contracts

The next step up involves awarding operations and maintenance (O&M) or lease contracts. These two types of contract do not delegate full financial responsibility to the private operator, especially with regard to private capital investments.

Operations and maintenance contract

- Time-horizon: 2–5 years, up to 10 years
- Customer: government or municipality
- Cash-flow profile: fixed fee for service
- Construction risk: none
- Regulatory risk: none
- Ownership: public
- Investment: public
- Operation: public
- Tariff collection: public and private

O&M contracts usually operate on a fixed-fee basis. They do not address problems of municipal inefficiency, and their short-term nature means that political stability can be poor and there is limited scope for the private sector to improve the performance of the utility. Examples include metering as well as leakage reduction and systems management for Mexico City (Mexico), with four contracts held (by Suez [2], Veolia Environnement and United Utilities), and water management for Antalya (Turkey), by Suez.

Lease contract

- Time-horizon: 10–15 years, up to 25 years
- Customer: retail customer
- Cash-flow profile: subject to market risk

- Construction risk: none
- Regulatory risk: medium
- Ownership: public
- Investment: public
- Operation: private
- Tariff collection: private

Lease contracts typically involve asset operation and tariff collection, with the municipality controlling the assets and capital expenditure. Risk elements start emerging, with the private sector now dealing directly with the customers, and thus this can be the focus of discontent. Examples include water and sewerage management in urban areas of Guinea, by the Société d'Electricité et d'Eau du Gabon, Bouygues and by Veolia Environnement, and water services for Dakar and other major urban areas of Senegal, by Senegalaise Des Eaux and SAUR.

5.3.3 Concessions

Concessions involve the private-sector operation of assets in order to pay for new facilities and upgrading work. Build–own–operate (BOO) and build–operate–transfer (BOT) contracts sell some services to the municipality in relation to a specific programme of capital improvements, while the full utility concession contract embraces all aspects of service provision and capital spending. These contracts require a much more specific regulatory environment so as to account for the elements of risk involved. In many cases the concession award takes place with the splitting of the water and sewerage entity into a service-provision entity and an asset-owning entity. The concession winner gains control of at least a significant proportion of the service provision entity's equity, along with management control. The municipality in turn retains at least a controlling stake in the asset-owning entity, which is subsequently responsible for the extant assets, and new assets are vested into this entity at an agreed date.

Build–operate–transfer and build–own–operate concessions
- Time-horizon: 10–30 years, up to 95 years
- Customer: government or municipality
- Cash-flow profile: payment on completion
- Construction risk: high
- Regulatory risk: low
- Ownership: public
- Investment: private
- Operation: private
- Tariff collection: public

The cash flows of a BOO or BOT project are usually contractually predetermined, and often with government backing. There is an element of construction risk, but the absence of market risk means that the project can have more debt loaded in than in a full utility privatisation. The construction risk of the project can be mitigated whereby a facility already generating a cash flow gets taken over for expansion by the private sector. Therefore BOT and BOO projects can be an effective means of rapidly organising private capital and management towards a narrow range of services. However, some of the simpler project-oriented contracts do not affect the utility's management and operation, and thus underlying problems such as leakage (and illegal interception), over-staffing and poor tariff collection may not be addressed. In these cases, the underlying utility remains uncreditworthy, and it can be argued that a BOO or BOT contract may in fact delay system-wide improvements.

Concession contracts call for a full understanding of the financial risks involved with the project. These concession contracts can be regarded as the classic water privatisation model. Examples include bulk water provision through BOT for Chengdu (China), by Veolia Environnement, water treatment through BOO for Riverland (Australia), by United Utilities and Bechtel, and a sewage treatment works through BOT for Puerto Vallarta (Mexico) by Cascal.

Full utility concession

- Time-horizon: 20–30 years
- Customer: retail
- Cash-flow profile: subject to market risk
- Construction risk: low
- Regulatory risk: high if politics are volatile
- Ownership: public
- Investment: private
- Operation: private
- Tariff collection: private

Here, the private sector is responsible for operating services while developing new assets for handing over to the municipalities in the longer term. There have been mixed results to date. Examples include water and sewerage operations for Buenos Aires (Argentina) by Aguas Argentinas, water provision for Malacca (Malaysia) by Veolia Environnement, and water provision in Johor (Malaysia) by RWE (starting as an O&M contract and designed to evolve into a full concession).

In full utility concessions, existing revenues can be used immediately to service debt, thereby mitigating construction risk. Over a period of time, a utility can benefit from a steady flow of revenues from a diversified customer base and, if it integrates horizontally, from a diversified asset base. A more robust balance sheet can be created, allowing for internal finance as well as the use of capital markets to sell long-term debt.

Asset sale

- Time-horizon: in perpetuity
- Customer: retail
- Cash-flow profile: subject to market risk

- Construction risk: very low
- Regulatory risk: very high
- Ownership: private
- Investment: private
- Operation: private
- Tariff collection: private

Problems of public perception and changes in regulatory priorities have meant that, with the exception of Chile and one contract each in the Czech Republic and Belize, the 'British model', as asset sales have been dubbed, has not been copied abroad.

5.4 PSP in reality

5.4.1 The current extent of private-sector participation[3]

In 1988, PSP was in effect restricted to its 'traditional' markets in the USA (asset-owning companies), England and Wales (the statutory water companies), France, Italy and Spain (concessions and lease contracts), along with some contracts in Africa. The World Bank noted eight PSP water and sewerage contracts in developing economies between 1984 and 1989 (Silva *et al.* 1998: 1) against 97 between 1990 and 1997 (Silva *et al.* 1998: 2).

The total number served by the private sector at the start of in 1988 is estimated at 93 million, mainly in developed economies. Since 1988, it is estimated that PSP has reached a further 369 million people, to cover a total of 462 million people, or 8% of the global population. Table 5.4 presents annualised data for the net increase of people being served by PSP globally between 1988 and 2002.

Until 2000, growth in PSP had been episodic, with peaks in 1989 (privatisation of the water and sewerage companies in England and Wales), 1993 (Latin America, before the 1994 Peso Crisis) and 1997 (South-East Asia, before the 1998 'Asian Flu' currency crisis). Growth has been more consistent since 2000, especially in terms of smaller contract awards and organic growth, which takes place through population growth within an operating area and extending services to people previously unconnected to water or sewerage services.

3　Except where a specific citation has been employed, data on the numbers served by the private sector has been prepared by the author. Its interpretation is based on the author's private databases and information made available by the companies through their websites, corporate publications (annual reports, environmental reports, issue reports and press releases), presentations to the investment community, interviews with the company by the author and verifiable third-party sources, especially the periodicals *Global Water Intelligence* (Oxford, UK: Media Analytics), *Platts Global Water Report* (Maidenhead, UK: McGraw-Hill), *Source* (Netherlands: WSSCC [Water Supply and Sanitation Collaborative Council] and IRC [International Water and Sanitation Centre]; www.wsscc.org/source) and online data provided by Bloomberg LP (www.bloomberg.com).

Type of contract	Number of people served by contracts by period (million)			
	1988–89	1990–94	1995–99	2000–2002
Major awards[a]	23.1	8.3	26.6	30.4
Organic growth, from continuing contracts	1.0	1.4	3.2	5.0
Minor contracts[b]	0.5	0.3	2.4	3.7
Contract losses, handed back to public control	0.0	0.0	−1.0	−0.8
Net increase in population served	24.6	10.0	31.2	38.3

[a] Where direct information is available

[b] Data from indirect reporting by companies

TABLE 5.4 Water or waste-water services privatised per year, 1988–2002

Source: author's surveys, from contract award database, company websites, presentations and interviews

By the start of 2003, 226 million people in developed economies were served to some extent by PSP, compared with 236 million in developing economies. Between 1988 and 2002, 138 million more people have been served by PSP in developed economies and 231 million in developing economies (see Table 5.5).

Region	People served (millions)	People served as a percentage of the population
Western Europe	161.5	42
Central and Eastern Europe	14.1	4
Middle East and Africa	37.6	4
South Asia	0.0	0
Central Asia	1.6	2
South-East Asia	92.3	5
Oceania	5.3	18
North America	65.2	21
Latin America	84.0	16
World total	461.6	8

TABLE 5.5 People served through private-sector participation at the start of 2003

Source: author's surveys, from contract award database, company websites, presentations and interviews

5.4.2 Corporate strategies

A variety of interrelationships has developed both between companies and within companies with regard to global water and sewerage contracts (see Table 5.6). Multi-utility strategies (power, water, waste management) have been implemented in a number of contracts in Africa, most notably the 1997 power and water contract for Casablanca, Morocco, awarded to Suez. The construction of water and waste-water facilities and their operation have always been closely interlinked. In the cases of Veolia Environnement and Suez, the water companies have branched into construction, but more often it is the construction company that is attracted to the services concessions, having built facilities for municipal customers. Joint ventures for water and sewerage contracts typically include a company with experience in the water sector and one with a significant presence in the target market(s). Examples include Sino-French Holdings (Suez and New World Developments), for China, Hong Kong and Macao, and Pro-activa Medio Ambiente (Veolia Environnement and Formento de Construcciones y Contratas), for Latin America.

It is evident that the two companies that developed the international water concession market both in the 1880–1914 period and since 1980—Suez and Veolia Environnement—continue to lead this market, but that dominance is now being challenged by Germany's RWE. There is a general trend that the larger the company in terms of people served, the greater the proportion of people served outside the company's home market.

Company	Home country	Millions of people served			Home (%)[a]
		Home	International	Total	
Suez Ondeo	France	17.0	114.1	131.1	13
Veolia Environnement	France	26.0	87.8	113.8	23
RWE	UK and Germany	27.6	41.5	69.1	40
Aguas de Barcelona	Spain	15.5	20.3	35.8	43
Bouygues	France	6.0	24.4	30.5	20
United Utilities	UK	10.3	10.2	20.5	51
Anglian Water Group	UK	5.8	10.6	16.4	35
Severn Trent	UK	8.3	6.3	14.6	57
FCC (Spain)	Spain	6.1	5.9	12.0	52

[a] The number of people served in the home country as a percentage of the total number of people served

TABLE 5.6 The leading international players (by millions of people served) at the start of 2003

Source: author's survey, from contract award database, company websites, presentations and interviews

5.4.3 New entrants

Initial public offerings (IPOs) of a company take place where all or part of the shares of a water or multi-utility company are listed on the local stock exchange. In addition to 18 companies being launched on stock exchanges in developing economies since 1988 (3 by national governments, 7 by municipalities or state governments and 8 by the private sector, either as spin-offs from parent companies or through their management selling off part of their equity holdings in the company), 8 previously established companies have been identified as having made a strategic move into this sector. In Europe and America (North and South), 27 companies have experienced an IPO during the same period. Market exits take place where companies are taken over by other companies or decide to divest their activities. Table 5.7 summarises the 45 IPOs and 21 market exits I identified as occurring between 1988 and 2003.

The United Kingdom is exceptional. In 1989 the 10 major water and sewerage companies covering England and Wales were privatised, but since 1988 there has been a concerned rationalisation of the 29 statutory water companies (i.e. privately owned companies that provided water to a local area). In one extreme case, Northumbrian Water was privatised in 1989, acquired by Suez in 1996, which combined the company with three statutory water companies it had previously acquired and divested 75% of its holding in Northumbrian Water in 2003.

5.4.4 The performance of private-sector participation

Table 5.8 is based on 97 water and sewerage privatisation awards identified by the World Bank during the first eight years of the 1990s, involving a total investment of US$24.95 billion (Silva *et al.* 1998: 5) from banks and multilateral agencies.

Although there are many O&M and lease contracts, the lack of private-sector investment involved highlights their role as a partial privatisation that does not mobilise new sources of private-sector investment. A number of greenfield contracts have been awarded in areas earmarked to become new housing or industrial zones. This approach has had some popularity in the Philippines. Divestitures have been seen to date in Chile. Given the confusion between contract types, it is not worthwhile at this stage to classify the concession contract types more specifically. The concession approach, allied with the splitting of water and sewerage entities into operating and asset-holding companies, is becoming the favoured approach towards water privatisation in many countries.

Table 5.9 highlights the recent shift towards PSP as a form of financing water assets. With US$4.8 billion in investment in 1990–2004 against US$24.3 billion in 1995–99, it is evident that the pace of investment increased in the latter half of the 1990s, although only US$5.1 billion was invested in 1998–99, as a result of economic problems in Asia during those two years. Typically, equity investment provided by the companies involved in operating the concession is equivalent to 30% of the total investment, indicating that the private sector invested US$12.2 billion during the period 1990–99, giving a total investment of US$41.3 billion.

Because access to water is seen as a right ('a gift from God' is the usual, poetic, term) rather than a luxury (electricity, gas and telecommunication utilities), it is a

Region	Initial public offerings (no.)	Market exits (no.)
North America	2	1
Latin America	2	0
United Kingdom	13	15
Rest of Europe	12	2
Asia	16	3

TABLE 5.7 Water company and multi-utility public offerings and market exits, 1988–2003

Source: author's survey, from Bloomberg LP and corporate databases

	Percentage of total	
Type of contract	Projects	Total investment
Concession	50	80
Divestiture	6	4
Greenfield project	31	16
Operation and management, and leases	13	0

TABLE 5.8 Private-sector participation in water and sewerage in developing countries, by contract type, 1990–97

Source: Silva *et al.* 1998: 5

	Investment (US$ millions)	
Region	1990–94	1995–99
East Asia and Pacific	4,023	8,631
Europe and Central Asia	16	1,539
Latin America and Caribbean	4,732	8,965
Middle East and North Africa	0	4,106
South Asia	0	0
Sub-Saharan Africa	23	1,054

TABLE 5.9 Investment in water and sanitation with private-sector participation in developing economies

Source: WDI 2001

more politically contentious issue, especially when municipal elections are being contested. Of 202 water and sanitation projects supported by the World Bank that had reached financial closure between 1990 and 2001, 7 (3.5%) had been cancelled, involving 11.3% of the US$39.7 billion in investment committed. This compares with 1.9% of all 2,492 infrastructure (e.g. gas, power, telecommunications, water and sewerage, and roads) projects during the same period, and 3.2% of their value

(Harris *et al.* 2003). In terms of contracts financed by the World Bank between 1990 and 1999, 60% of 400 infrastructure concession contracts were renegotiated within three years, 85% within four years. For water contracts, the average period before a contract was renegotiated was 1.7 years, against an infrastructure-sector average of 2.2 years. Between 1990 and 2001 in Latin America, 71% (63) of 89 concessions supported by the World Bank were renegotiated, 4 by the companies and 59 by the governments. Although 87 of these contracts went through a formal award process, only 12 were subject to independent regulation (Guash *et al.* 2003).

Seven of the more high-profile examples are profiled briefly in Box 5.1. In each case, the contract locality and service is mentioned, the lead concession holder and the date of the contract starting and being terminated as well as an outline of what took place.

The differing perceptions as to why a PSP contract is withdrawn is highlighted by Cochabamba (see Dalton 2001), where a lack of preparation took place prior to the PSP award, allowing for popular discontent to be used by anti-PSP activists (see also Box 5.1). In the three years since the contract was withdrawn, no new investment has been made for the city. Thus PSP is likely to be seen as a necessity in the medium term. In the case of Aguas Argentinas, the Suez and Aguas de Barcelona concession (see Box 5.1), write-downs have been made in response to the devaluation of the peso in 2001–2002 that have been ameliorated through the postponement of agreed-on capital spending work. The economic crisis in Argentina means that the scope for recovering these losses through tariff rises are minimal, obliging the companies to take a long-term view of their involvement in the concession.

5.5 Conclusions: the need for engagement

This chapter has outlined the potential for PSP to play a part in ensuring universal provision of water and sewerage services for urban areas in developed and developing economies on an affordable basis. PSP for these services remains a contentious (for the public and the politicians) and risky (for the companies and multilateral institutions) area. The two sets of interests need to engage to optimise the potential role that PSP can play.

Building on models developed in Britain, France and North America, the private sector has been able to offer a flexible range of PSP options to developing economies. Despite the challenges thrown up by various economic crises, PSP for water and sewerage services in developing economies has become an increasingly robust and attractive proposition. It remains, however, only part of the solution towards attaining universal service provision and retains many of the characteristics of an industry still in its developmental phase.

The private sector has to acknowledge a systemic failure to communicate in a quantitative and rigourous manner the benefits and challenges inherent in having PSP play a leading role in developed economies while at the same time supporting the process of providing universal access to water and sanitation services for urban areas in developing economies. In addition, the private sector needs to address the

Bangkok, Thailand, sewerage
- Education and advertising campaigns
- Concession holder: United Utilities
- Period of contract: 1992–96

Contract workload was materially extended without additional payments. United Utilities withdrew; arbitration is expected in 2004–2005.

Tucumann, Argentina, water and sewerage services
- Concession holder: Veolia Environnement
- Period of contract: 1995–97

There was a tariff dispute after political change in the municipality. Veolia Environnement withdrew; a compensation claim is currently under dispute.

Malaysia, urban sewerage
- Concession holder: Prime Utilities
- Period of contract: 1993–2000

Price cuts were imposed by the government after the 1997–98 recession. The government bought Prime Utilities out of the concession when the company faced bankruptcy.

Cochabamba, Bolivia, water provision
- Concession holder: International Water
- Period of contract: 1999–2000

There were riots against project; these resulted in fatalities. International Water withdrew and is currently suing the government.

Buenos Aries, Argentina, water and sewerage services
- Concession holder: Azurix
- Period of contract: 1997–2001

Poor performance by the company was penalised by the municipality. The parent company handed back the concession to the municipality.

Manila, Philippines, water and sewerage services
- Concession holders: Suez and Benpres
- Period of contract: 1997–2003

There were cash-flow problems after the 1998 peso devaluation. Suez withdrew when tariff changes were constrained. The case is now under arbitration.

Aguas Argentinas; Buenos Aries, Argentina, water and sewerage services
- Concession holders: Suez and Aguas de Barcelona
- Period of contract: 1993 to the present

There were € 650 million in losses after the currency crisis in 2001–2002. The contract is ongoing, but capital spending has been postponed.

BOX 5.1 Seven high-profile examples of problematic private-service participation applicability of its risk-management strategies and to appreciate local social, environmental and market drivers.

Concern has also been expressed about perceived information asymmetries that can favour private-sector companies with a wide experience of market conditions and strategies. This may lead stakeholders to regard the bidding (and renegotiation) process with scepticism. These concerns are best addressed through a capacity-building programme designed to ensure that local and national interests are suitably addressed, while a formal disclosure system before, during and after the privatisation programme will allow stakeholders to have the information they need to be able to engage constructively with the service provider, the private sector and the regulators.

The somewhat tentative nature of much of the data presented in this paper and the bias towards research carried out by the World Bank highlights the relative paucity of non-partisan research carried out either by the private sector or by the academic community. I believe that although corporate publications (see Suez Ondeo 2002; Thames Water 2003) are laudable, they are written from the viewpoint of a single company and are not seen as pieces of independent research. As a result, other information asymmetries exist, whereby interests opposed to PSP are not subject to the degree of scrutiny that would be expected to be the case were a similar research effort carried out on behalf of the private sector.

The industrial and academic communities are perceived to work at different speeds, especially in the dissemination of their findings and the need for access to information for responding to market developments. Even so, there is an identified need for the two communities to engage with each other in developing a research agenda, building on recent work carried out (e.g. see Sohail 2002) on PSP and service extension that would allow for a constructive dialogue between the various interest groups to emerge in a timely manner for working together in seeking to meet the Vision 2025 targets.

References

Bitran, G.A., and E.P. Valenzuela (2003) *Public Services in Chile: Comparing Private and Public Performance* (Public Policy for the Private Sector Note 255; Washington, DC: World Bank).
Cosgrove, W.J. , and F.R. Rijsberman (2000) *World Water Vision* (London: Earthscan Publications).
Cowen, P.B., and N. Tynan (1999) *Reaching the Urban Poor with Private Infrastructure* (Public Policy for the Private Sector Note 188; Washington, DC: World Bank).
Dalton, G. (2001) *Private Sector Finance for Water Sector Infrastructure: What Does Cochabamba Tell Us About Using This Instrument?* (Occasional Paper No 37; London: Water Issues Study Group, School of Oriental and African Studies [SOAS], University of London).
Platts (2003) 'Glowing Success', in *Global Water Report 177* (Maidenhead, UK: McGraw Hill, August 2003).
Guash, J.L., J.-J. Laffont and S. Straub (2003) *Renegotiation of Concession Contracts in Latin America* (Policy Research Working Paper WPS 3011; Washington, DC: World Bank).
Harris, C., J. Hodges, M. Schur and P. Shukla (2003) *Infrastructure Projects: A Review of Canceled Private Projects* (Public Policy for the Private Sector Note 252; Washington, DC: World Bank).
Mcintosh, A., and C. Yniguez (1997) *Second Water Utilities Data Book* (Manila, Philippines: Asian Development Bank).

Nigam, A. (1996) 'Sustainable Financing of WATSAN', paper presented at the *22nd WEDC Conference*, Water, Engineering Development Centre (WEDC), Loughborough University, UK.

Owen, D.A.L. (2002) *Masons Water Yearbook 2002–2003* (London: Masons Solicitors, London).

Prynn, P., and H. Sunman (2000) 'Getting the Water to Where it is Needed and Getting the Tariff Right', paper presented at the *Financial Times Energy Conference*, Dublin, November 2000.

Silva, G., N. Tynan and Y. Yilmaz (1998a) *Private Participation in the Water and Sewerage Sector: Recent Trends* (Public Policy for the Private Sector Note 147; Washington, DC: World Bank).

Sohail M. (ed.) (2002) *Public–Private Partnerships and the Poor* (collection of eight papers; Loughborough, UK: Water, Engineering Development Centre [WEDC], Loughborough University).

Suez Ondeo (2002) *Bridging the Water Divide* (Paris: Suez Ondeo).

—— (2003) *2002 Activities and Sustainable Development Report* (Paris: Suez Ondeo).

Thames Water (2003) *Planet Water* (Reading, UK: Thames Water Plc, 2nd edn).

Tynan, N. (2000) 'Private Sector Participation in Infrastructure and the Poor: Water and Sanitation', paper presented at *Infrastructure for Development: Private Solutions and the Poor*, PPIAF, DFID and World Bank, London, 31 May–1 June 2000.

—— and B. Kingdom (2002) A Water Scorecard: *Setting Performance Targets for Water Utilities* (Public Policy for the Private Sector Note 242; Washington, DC: World Bank).

United Utilities (2004) *Privatisation: Providing Water and Wastewater Services in the Philippines*, www.unitedutilities.com/resources/files/283_Phillipines.pdf, accessed 12 July 2005.

Winpenny, J. (2003) *Financing Water For All: Report of the World Panel on Financing Water Infrastructure* (the Camdessus Report; Geneva: World Water Council).

World Bank (2001) *World Development Indicators 2001* (Oxford, UK: Oxford University Press).

6

Private-sector participation in water and sanitation reviewed
INSIGHTS FROM NEW INSTITUTIONAL ECONOMICS

Dieter Rothenberger and Bernhard Truffer

Swiss Federal Institute for Environmental Science and Technology, Switzerland

Access to sufficient and safe drinking water and sanitation is a key issue of sustainable development. In 2000 the General Assembly of the United Nations established the Millennium Development Goals, which express the need to halve the proportion of people without access to safe drinking water by 2015 (United Nations 2000). This goal was confirmed and extended by the Johannesburg Declaration on Sustainable Development, which also incorporated the issue of access to basic sanitation (United Nations 2002).

One approach to support these objectives might be private-sector participation (PSP) in the provision of water and sanitation. PSP is often perceived as a way to tap new financial sources for rehabilitation and expansion of plants or networks or to improve operational efficiency, since conventional economic analysis states that production efficiency is lower in public than in private enterprises (Boyco *et al.* 1996: 309). This holds true especially for local public providers in permanent monopolies compared with usually large, internationally experienced private operators being awarded contracts in competitive bidding processes.

However, experience gained in recent PSP projects all over the world shows that this argument is too generalised to guarantee high-quality water services in the long term. Conventional analysis focuses on a cost–benefit analysis of the service provision itself; that is, the emphasis is solely on marginal production costs, with the costs and benefits of maintaining and reforming the institutional setting (i.e. the regulatory framework or the allocation of responsibilities) tending to be neglected.

Especially in infrastructure-based economic sectors, with their high up-front investments and long-term investment plans, institutional frameworks are of major importance for high-quality and high-reliability service provision. When opting for a PSP contract the decision should be based on full-cost considerations (i.e. including additional costs for co-ordinating the task). These so-called 'transaction costs' can make up a considerable share of the overall costs of the introduction of a new institutional setting. In the health sector, for example, contracting out usually reduces production costs, but evidence suggests that these savings are often more than offset by transaction costs (Vining and Globerman 1999: 79). Similar experiences have been evident in the UK with the introduction of so-called 'compulsory competitive tendering' procedures for services formerly provided by local authorities. Wilson (1999: 38) notes that 'even if tender prices are lower, the costs of monitoring the contract usually outweigh the savings'.

A specific branch of economics, the so-called 'new institutional economics' (NIE), has increasingly received attention since the mid-1980s. It deals explicitly with the analysis of transaction costs that occur in alternative institutional settings. In this chapter we analyse different contractual alternatives for PSP in the water and sanitation (WATSAN) sector based on the concepts put forward by proponents of the NIE. We begin in Section 6.1 with a brief introduction to the concepts of bounded rationality, asymmetric information and transaction costs. From this foundation we go on in Section 6.2 to evaluate alternative PSP contract forms with respect to their specific strengths and weaknesses for the contracting parties. In Section 6.3 we illustrate some key claims of the theoretical analysis by drawing on recent examples of PSP contract negotiations. We conclude the chapter in Section 6.4 by examining how the NIE approach could help in the selection of more appropriate PSP structures in the future.

6.1 Key concepts of the new institutional economics approach

6.1.1 Bounded rationality and asymmetric information

A major starting point of the NIE approach is the notion of bounded rationality (Simon 1976, 1997). Bounded rationality is seen as an empirically more adequate assumption about the decision capabilities of people than that normally taken for granted in conventional economic analysis. In conventional economics, economic actors use perfect rationality to compare decision alternatives in an unbiased way on the basis of all consequences. Under the argument of bounded rationality, economic actors never achieve fully comprehensive knowledge of all issues relevant to their economic and social behaviour because of time, cost and processing capacity limitations. As a consequence, economic actors will be confronted in the marketplace with substantial information asymmetries between the different parties.

This is highly important for the so-called 'principal–agent settings'. These are characterised by an agreement between at least two parties in which a task is allocated to one partner (the agent) on behalf of the other partner (the principal) against compensation of some kind. Since many efforts under such agreements are non-observable, the agent generally possesses better information about the efforts and the results (e.g. sales and profits). Hence, there is ample scope for the agent to pursue his or her own objectives and not (only) the objectives of the principal. With this background, opportunistic behaviour—that is, the maximisation of personal gain at the expense of the transaction partner (e.g. by post-agreement shirking or pre-agreement information hiding)—is an attractive strategy for the agent. In order to prevent opportunistic behaviour, the principal is keen on defining certain monitoring mechanisms, incentives or penalties in the contract, which might induce considerable transaction costs.

6.1.2 Transaction costs

One of the key concepts for analysing organisational forms in order to minimise overall costs is that of transaction costs. These are costs incurred in searching for the right transaction partner, in elaborating and agreeing on the contract terms, in monitoring performance and in intervening in case of contractual failure. Transaction costs are directly linked to the existence of information asymmetries: the more serious the effects of asymmetric information and the greater the potential for opportunistic behaviour, the more important are safeguards to protect both sides from losses. The need to write more complete agreements on which the transaction is based and to monitor these agreements more closely thus induces higher transaction costs.

Most transactions are based on more or less explicit contracts. The terms of the contracts and thus the negotiation position of the two contracting parties differ in the specific investment required to fulfil the tasks, uncertainty about the context in which the task has to be completed, complexity in the overall setting and contestability (see e.g. Ashton 1998; Vining and Globerman 1999; Williamson 1990). In the following sub-sections we briefly elaborate on these factors, all of which directly influence the level of transaction costs.

Asset specificity and lock-in

In many transactions the partners have to invest in transaction-specific assets. Assets are specific if they are not deployable for alternative uses without major reduction in value (Ashton 1998: 357; Williamson 1991: 281). If they cannot be used for other purposes these assets may create lock-in situations, i.e. they will be perceived as exit barriers for the investors. It is important to note that a high degree of asset specificity may not be confined to physical assets, but may also apply to investments in human resources such as transaction-specific knowledge or the reputation of a company within a environment broader than the project itself.

A potential lock-in situation due to asset specificity increases the vulnerability of the investor to opportunistic behaviour by the other party. After the contract has been signed and the corresponding investments have been made, the power balance between the contracting parties switches, and the competitive market structure of the pre-contract situation is suddenly transformed into a bilateral monopoly. The player with a lower degree of specificity in his investment may try to renegotiate the agreement and thus obtain additional benefits not foreseen in the original contract. Since both actors know about their asset specificity, they will try to protect themselves by arranging a more detailed (and thus more expensive) contract which prevents opportunistic behaviour and prescribes detailed arbitration procedures. This strategy implies that transaction costs tend to rise with increasing asset specificity (Dorward 2001: 61).

Uncertainty and task complexity

The bounded rationality concept implies that information about future circumstances and the outcomes of a specific transaction is accompanied by differing, but high degrees of, uncertainty, so the agreement or contract on which the transaction is based is necessarily incomplete. As a consequence, renegotiations become more likely, and transaction costs may increase in order to prevent opportunistic behaviour. An additional criterion that is, to a certain extent, related to uncertainty is task complexity. Tasks with a low complexity imply relatively little additional cost to negotiate and to monitor the contractual arrangements. Complex tasks, in contrast, involve relatively high uncertainty and may be a source of considerable information asymmetry. This implies high transaction costs, since the definition, negotiations, implementation and monitoring of a contract require more care and time.

Contestability

A market is contestable if firms are immediately available to provide a service. This means that there are no or very low barriers to market entry and that there is sufficient competition to prevent collusion. Contestability can be reduced if the task is relatively complex and a change of contract partners would affect not only the very specific task but also other aspects such as basic societal services in the transition period. Low levels of contestability imply a high potential for opportunism at the contract stage.

6.2 The importance of new institutional economics for private-sector participation contracts in the water and sanitation sectors

In general, WATSAN system operators can be departments of public authorities, public companies or private companies, in charge for the comprehensive operation, maintenance and financing of the system. The operation of the system is a classical example for a principal–agent setting. Hence, the decision about the appropriate organisational form for the provision of WATSAN services is a typical example of one that may lead to high transaction costs.

A great variety of PSP forms is available in the market, but in this chapter we will focus on contractual PSP, leaving divestiture aside. PSP contracts differ with regard to their duration, investment requirements or allocation of risk and responsibilities. This variety results from the different technical or economical circumstances and the specificities of the individual projects. A brief summary of the various contracts is given in Table 6.1 (for a comprehensive description of PSP options, see e.g. World Bank 1997).

Contract type	General characteristics	Possible results	Responsibility (risk)	Reward (remuneration)
Service contract	The private partner has to provide a clearly defined service for the public sector; rather short-term option Duration: 0.5–3 years	Can help to overcome particular problems of the public service provider	Private operator with very limited responsibility	Fixed fee
Management contract	The tasks of the private partner include direct support for core activities such as operation and maintenance of the system Duration: 3–10 years	Can increase production efficiency and overall performance of the existing system	Private partner has no entrepreneurial risks (in terms of collection rates, etc.); consumers remain customers of public entity	Fixed management fee (sometimes with some incentive payment)
Lease contract (or affermage)	The task of the private partner is the full operation and maintenance of the system Duration: 8–20 years	As for the management contracts, but also improved investment planning and finance management	Private partner has entrepreneurial risks; public partner has investment risk; tariff-setting procedure crucial issue	Payment via water fees for operation; add-on for investment goes to public partner
Concession contract	The task of the private partner is the full operation, maintenance and investment in the system Duration: 15–30 years	As for the lease contract, but capital investments should facilitate expansion and rehabilitation of the system	Private partner has entrepreneurial risk and investment risk; tariff-setting procedure crucial issue	Full refinancing via water fees

TABLE 6.1 Summary of contractual options for private-service participation

With reference to the concepts outlined above, NIE examines alternative organisational forms according to their ability to perform a specific transaction in a cost-minimising way, putting special emphasis on transaction costs. Hence, in the following sections we analyse the various PSP contracts with respect to the factors influencing the level of transaction costs.

6.2.1 Asymmetric information

Owing to the limited scope of the service contract in terms of duration and responsibilities, information asymmetry is of little significance. By contrast, in a concession contract, information asymmetry may be a major problem. The adequacy of tariff-setting renegotiations or investment plans can be judged properly by the public authorities only if they have access to the necessary information, which frequently is not the case. Therefore an important PSP problem for public authorities in WATSAN services is how to reduce the information asymmetry to prevent monopolistic rent-seeking (Shirley and Ménard 2002: 39).

6.2.2 Asset specificity

Many WATSAN systems require large capital investment to ensure long-term operation and the expansion of the system to non-connected areas. Combined with long amortisation periods, this implies that asset specificity is relatively high, which is crucial if investments have to be financed by the private sector. A service or a management contract contains only limited investments, such as in cars, customer management systems or metering equipment, all of which are relatively low in specificity. The issue of possible stranded investments is becoming more important in leases and it plays a central role in concession contracts, since they each require major capital investment. This high asset specificity creates 'hold-up' problems, particularly for the private company, since low regulatory or political commitment and the discretionary powers available to the regulator pose major threats to the investments made.

A different kind of specificity is one based on reputation and credibility (Alcázar *et al.* 2002: 84). If a company withdraws from a contract this may damage its reputation and diminish its prospects for future PSP contracts. A public partner may also face this lock-in situation, since PSP projects are often closely monitored, especially by multinational companies and international financial markets (Alcázar *et al.* 2002: 84) as well as international financing institutions. Therefore an early termination of the contract can lead investors in other sectors to fear that their investments are not safe either, resulting in reduced investments or project withdrawals. These kinds of specificities are much greater in more comprehensive contracts such as concessions or leases that attract public attention.

6.2.3 Uncertainty and task complexity

One major factor influencing the level of uncertainty is the contract duration. Service contracts normally have a very short duration and a very clearly defined task, thus uncertainty both with regard to possible changes in contractual conditions or concerning the task itself is relatively low. This is also true for the service operator's remuneration, which is based on a pay-per-service agreement.

Management contracts with an incentive-based payment component allow more uncertainty concerning the operator's remuneration, and the definition of the tasks is more difficult. Furthermore, there are factors influencing the outcome that are not under the control of the private partner.

Task definition in lease or concession contracts is very complex. Issues such as tariff setting often have to be defined with use of poor and unreliable data. In addition, the very long duration of the contracts implies a higher level of uncertainty concerning future political support, acceptance by the population, the national economic situation and so on. Private operators in long-term lease or concession contracts are very vulnerable to unforeseen changes in the regulatory requirements such as new environmental standards or higher levels of connection rates.

A higher level of information asymmetry can be observed either where information disclosure is not foreseen in the contract or where it is not enforced by the public authorities (for an example, see Shirley and Ménard 2002: 39). Furthermore, if a regulatory body is not properly set up or lacks sufficient technical and economic capacity, the ability to use and process information will decrease over time.

6.2.4 Contestability

The market for PSP contracts in WATSAN is dominated by a few multinational operators (see Finger and Allouche 2001; see also Table 6.2). This dominance is becoming even more pronounced where complex contracts such as lease or concession contracts are concerned, when the public authorities are often confronted with a very limited choice of possible operators, and a take-over by a new company after an early termination of the contract is quite difficult. As Klein (1998: 4) points out, 'governments are often reluctant to terminate a concessionaire, because they are afraid that basic services, such as water supply, may be interrupted'.

The selection criteria in an auction process reinforce this oligopoly over time, since comparisons with other international projects with similar characteristics are crucial. Though references are normally an important instrument to overcome information problems because they reveal the experience of the applicant, they can also be barriers to market entry by new entrants interested in concession or lease contracts.

Water division	Sales (4 million)	Customers served worldwide (millions)
Ondeo	10,088	115
Vivendi Water	13,640	110
Thames Water[a]	2,746	37
SAUR	2,494	36
Anglian Water[b]	936	5
Cascal (Biwater)	181	6.7

a Thames Water figures not including shared customers (e.g. in Adelaide, Berlin or Budapest).
b Anglian Water Group announced it would sell the international branch of Anglian Water in 2003.
SAUR = Société d'Aménagement Urbain et Rural

TABLE 6.2 Internationally active private operators in the water and sanitation sector

Sources: company annual reports (all figures 2001)

Concerning the management contract, the situation is slightly different, since more private companies are prepared to enter a contract with lower entrepreneurial risk and no major investments. The portfolio of companies able to deliver management services is much bigger, since consulting and engineering companies might take over these tasks too. Thus, contestability is higher with management contracts than with lease or concession contracts. Service contracts, which involve the least comprehensive capabilities and the lowest involvement in the overall operation, show even higher contestability than management contracts.

6.2.5 Summary

The type of contract chosen for PSP has a clear impact on transaction costs: the more specific the required investments, the longer the duration and the more comprehensive the task, the higher the additional costs. Table 6.3 provides a comparison of the PSP contractual options as analysed here from NIE viewpoints.

Thus many authors argue that, in situations where high specificity, complexity and uncertainty are combined with low contestability, outsourcing under long-term contracts is often less satisfactory than own-production (Lane 2000: 133)—that is, in the case of WATSAN services, outsourcing is less satisfactory than public provision. Long-term concession contracts are normally used to attract private investment and to reap major operational improvements. As a consequence, there is a clear trade-off between minimisation of transaction costs and the mobilisation of private capital with the respective production efficiency gains envisaged with lease or concession contracts.

In the next section we will present anecdotal evidence about cases where information asymmetry and transaction costs either had a major impact on the outcome of PSP processes or were identified as major obstacles to sound co-operation.

6.3 Empirical evidence

PSP has been identified by international funding agencies as an important tool for improving WATSAN service provision in developing countries. Thus we will focus mainly on empirical evidence from developing countries, including a detailed analysis of the Buenos Aires concession. Examples will be analysed from an NIE viewpoint (i.e. with respect to the importance of asymmetric information and transaction costs during the design and implementation of the PSP contract). This will provide an insight into the problems of PSP processes.

In developing countries the provision of WATSAN services has to deal with major difficulties. On the one hand there are technical and organisational systems, which often are on the brink of collapse. PSPs must be evaluated against a background of, among other things, drastic under-investment, an untrained labour force and outdated equipment, all contributing to high losses of water, frequent interruptions to the service, financial losses and so on. Often, the decision whether to implement

Contract type	Information asymmetry	Asset specificity	Uncertainty/ complexity	Contestability	Level of transaction costs (TAC)
Service contract	Meaningless	No investment, low reputation effects	Short-term, clearly defined contract; fixed pay-per-service, low complexity	Very high (contracting out to locals or former employees)	Very low TAC; easy to handle
Management contract	Moderate importance	Low, rather unspecific investment; medium reputation effects	Short- to medium-term; fixed pay-per-service; medium complexity	Moderate to high (greater number of experienced operators; no investment required)	Moderate TAC; renegotiations possible
Lease contract	High importance: private operators benefit from investment in expansion, but do not have to invest	Co-ordinated investment required; high reputation effects	High; medium- to long-term; remuneration from customers' payments; complex contract	Low (few companies with sufficient experience)	High TAC; often renegotiations; often contracts too long (low investments); lock-in
Concession contract	Very high importance: renegotiation on cost and investment require sufficient information	High investment from private sector; very high reputation effects	Very high; long-term; remuneration from customers' payments also for investment; very complex contract	Very low (few companies with sufficient experience and prepared to invest)	Very high TAC; very long contracts, often renegotiations and under-investment; lock-in

TABLE 6.3 Summary of private-sector participation contracts, analysed from the viewpoint of new institutional economics

PSP or not is driven by investment requirements, reflecting a prediction by the World Bank and other international finance institutions that public and donor finance will not be sufficient to fund all required investment (e.g. see Briscoe 1999), especially if the tremendously high figures for achieving the goals mentioned in the opening paragraph of this chapter (see also page 10) are considered (see e.g. Winpenny 2003).[1] Thus, investments in projects with PSP increased tremendously from 1990 to 2001, as Figure 6.1 indicates, but are still very low. Clearly, if a PSP project is to contain private investments, long-term contracts will be necessary to provide sufficient refinancing time for the private partner. This is illustrated in the concession contract in Buenos Aires, which is examined in Section 6.3.1.

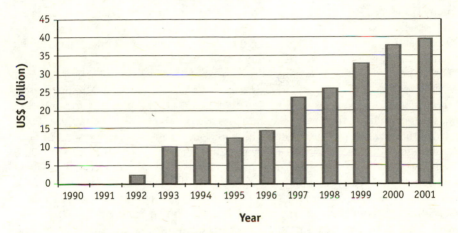

FIGURE 6.1 Cumulative investment in water and sanitation projects involving private-sector participation

Source: Izzaguire 2002: 2

6.3.1 Experiences with the Buenos Aires Concession[2]

In 1993 a consortium called Aguas Argentina headed by Suez-Lyonnaise des Eaux was awarded a 30-year concession contract for Buenos Aires Metropolitan Area. The tender process was pushed forward relatively quickly. The main selection criterion was lowest tariff projection, with the winning bid offering a 26.9% reduction compared with the pre-privatisation tariff level.

The contract was regarded as the flagship of PSP in water and sanitation and thus attracted a lot of public attention from beyond the water sector. The total invest-

1 However, it has to be stated that these figures can be easily reduced if one allows for adapted service and technology levels (Winpenny 2003: 3).
2 The information given in this section is taken from various sources: Alcázar *et al.* 2002, Conte Grand 2000 and Crampes and Estache 1998.

ment required to finance the coverage targets was about US$ 3.5 billion during the lifetime of the contract, with a major investment programme during the first five years. Thus asset specificity played a major role, both with regard to the huge investment and with regard to reputation effects, especially for the country (Alcázar et al. 2002: 84).

Owing to the speedy tendering process, information collection before the bids were handed in was very poor, and the winning bid included four pages describing the weakness of the information. Alcázar et al. (2002: 77) stated that 'bidders might have been misinformed or assumed that they could renegotiate as new information came to light'. In addition, leaving the old, complicated and inefficient tariff regime in place resulted in 'increased government and consumer information asymmetries', which '[opened] the way for opportunistic behaviour by the company' (Alcázar et al. 2002: 78). Since the regulator, ETOSS (Ente Tripartito de Obras y Servicios Sanitarios), was newly established and very inexperienced, strong monitoring that might have helped to reduce information asymmetries did not take place.

High complexity and uncertainty also contributed to the problem. The contract itself ran to hundreds of pages and contained several volumes in an attempt to deal with as many contingencies as possible (Klein 1998: 1). The private partner had to operate and maintain the assets, expand coverage, guarantee water quality and also improve the sewage treatment. All of this took place against a background of poor information at the beginning and a 30-year duration for the contract—this at a time when Argentina had just started to recover from a massive political and financial crisis. In addition, the regulator's role was heavily politicised and the members of the regulator's board had sat for only short terms, there having been a quick rotation—factors that also contributed to the contract's uncertain environment.

Our analysis shows that various factors induced asymmetric information and high transaction costs. Thus, the main selection criterion—'lowest bid for the water price'—was bound to cause opportunistic behaviour and renegotiations, driven from both sides of the agreement. Only one year after the contract was signed, renegotiations took place and an increase of 13.5% in the flexible part of the tariff was agreed. Other tariff elements, such as costs for new connection, also increased tremendously, posing major affordability problems for poor households. For its part, the government accelerated the investment targets.

In 1997 a major renegotiation process started, based on 'lower than expected revenues, non-fulfilment of the investment plan and the growing misunderstandings between the firm and ETOSS' (Conte Grand 2000: 10). In reality the general aspects were more deeply rooted in an inflexible and complicated tariff-setting mechanism and in similarly inflexible and complicated investment targets. The negotiation resulted in a partial shift of the financial burden from new customers to customers already connected, a minor overall price increase and reduced contractual obligations, especially with regard to investment requirement, without penalty. The reduced contractual oblications in particular could be interpreted as a signal to the company that it would not be held accountable for delays (Alcázar et al. 2002: 88). In addition, the costs for expanding the network were paid before the execution of the work, which 'reduced the government's leverage to assure that the works were promptly completed' (Alcázar et al. 2002: 88). In 1998 the company requested an additional tariff increase by 11.7% and was granted 4.6%.

As a consequence of a severe economic and political crisis, in January 2002 the Argentine government ended the fixed parity of the Argentinean peso to the US dollar and blocked any cost overrun-based price adjustments. This created a serious dispute about the future of the contract and possible compensation payments by the Argentine government for the private partner.

Lessons learned

A major flaw in this agreement was the decision, based on the high investment requirements, to design a 30-year concession contract; this ignored the probable inappropriateness of long-term contracts in a climate of political and economic uncertainty and risk. Neither the government nor the company was willing to invest in the collection of more comprehensive information or in a revision of the very complex pricing formula. This reduction in pre-transaction costs directly resulted in very high post-transaction costs. Apart from the pricing issue, all other problems could be attributed to poor information at the beginning and probably also to opportunistic behaviour because of the possibilities for renegotiation. The wording of the loan contract between Aguas Argentinas and the International Finance Corporation (IFC), signed in 1994, supports this claim. This loan agreement was based on the assumption that the tariffs would be increased or the investment requirements reduced, since otherwise Aguas Argentinas would not have been able to meet the debt service requirements (Alcázar *et al.* 2002: 89).

6.3.2 Other examples of regulatory and contractual difficulties

One of the most crucial issues in PSP settings is how to achieve more symmetric information. Here, a strong regulator with competence in defining information requirements and processing obtained data plays a key role. Weak regulatory capacity is seen for example in Abidjan, Côte d'Ivoire, as a major reason for the tremendous information asymmetries. In this case it enabled the private operator to extract excessive additional rents (Ménard and Clarke 2002: 256). Although not bearing any investment and finance risk, the private operator was able to make decisions about investment projects, and implement them, without tendering the construction tasks, and the public agencies with which they were working lacked adequate information to assess the appropriateness of the investment plans. Additionally, the lack of a clear division of roles between various public agencies and the private provider increased the discretionary power of the the private provider and thus the scope for opportunistic behaviour (Ménard and Clarke 2002: 257). However, it is not only private operators that may seize discretionary power: public authorities and regulators also tend to do so when they stand to benefit.

Even in a developed country, such as France, the lack of an effective regulatory body to monitor PSP contracts can lead to severe problems. In 1995, then CEO of Suez Philippe Brongniart pointed out that the elected public bodies were not able fully to comprehend the complicated long-term lease and concession contracts (Bekkada 1995: 11). To improve the situation an association of mayors founded the consulting agency Public Service 2000, which assists the municipalities in information collection and processing and in negotiations with the three big market-dominating players—Ondeo, Vivendi and Société d'Aménagement Urbain et Rural (SAUR). Public Service 2000 was created to reduce transaction costs, facilitating the partnerships by establishing a level playing field between the two partners.

In a PSP process, in addition to a strong regulator, the auction for the contracts is a major source of information about costs and investment requirements in a competitive process. However, the outcomes of auctions may be unreliable, since the auctions are prone to strategic bidding by the private companies. As described in Sections 6.1.2 and 6.3.1, the transaction costs for collecting information and for writing complete contracts are often prohibitively high, resulting in incomplete and sometimes vague contracts. On the one hand, this provides ample scope for renegotiations from the public side and may also put undue pressure on the private operator. On the other hand, incomplete information due to high transaction costs also limits the success of the auction process. Private companies might hand in bids with lower-than-appropriate water prices and renegotiate them soon after the contract is awarded, stating incorrect information in the tender documents as a reason. This obviously weakens the pressure for efficiency improvements, especially with an inexperienced government as negotiation partner (Harris 2003: 9).

Another example of strategic bidding is the frequent failure of private operators to provide staff as outlined in its application. The company tackles the uncertainty of winning a competitive tender by proposing the same key staff in more than one tender process at the same time. Inevitably, then, either the key members of staff proposed will not be part of the project at all or they will be available for only a short period and then be replaced by other, probably less experienced, staff. Owing to the special situation of long-term-contracts this behaviour is reasonable from the perspective of the private partner. Nevertheless, the public partner often cannot successfully intervene and has to accept the changes. Although contractual penalties such as fines, forfeiture of bonds or contract revocation may exist, governments are often very reluctant to enforce these. On the other side, international arbitration procedures to protect the private operator are also common, but can be seen only 'as a last resort and are not very effective in resolving ordinary disputes' (Shirley and Ménard 2002: 17).

Thus, renegotiations are very common in long-term contracts: researchers analysing the renegotiation of concession contracts in Latin America found that more than 70% of the 89 water and sewerage concession in Argentina, Brazil, Chile, Colombia and Mexico that were signed between 1989 and 2000 were renegotiated (Guasch et al. 2002: 23) and thus induced high transaction costs.

Renegotiations are sometimes not the end of the line. The results of a World Bank analysis show that 3.5% of all PSP projects in water and sewerage projects reaching financial closure between 1990 and 2001 were cancelled (Harris et al. 2003: 4).[3] Although this seems to be a relatively small figure, the cancelled projects in fact accounted for more than 11% of the investment value of all PSP projects in water and sewerage. Indeed, this sector had the highest failure rate compared with the energy, telecommunications and transport sectors (see Fig. 6.2). The survey also found that among the cancelled projects the average time before cancellation was four and a half years (Harris et al. 2003: 3), and more than a third (in terms of

3   As projects where the private partner terminated the contract by handing it over to a competitor were not included, the numbers might be higher.

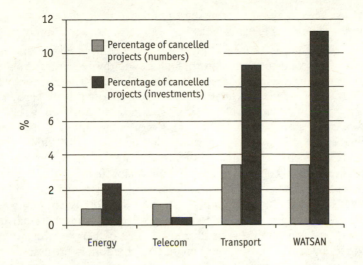

WATSAN = water and sanitation

FIGURE 6.2 Cancellation ratios in developing countries for infrastructure projects with private-sector participation, 1990–2001

Source: Harris *et al.* 2003: 4

investment volume) of the water and sewerage projects reached financial closure between 1999 and 2001 (Izaguirre 2002: 2). A future increase of the overall cancellation ratio might thus be expected.

6.4 Conclusions

The idea of tendering long-term PSP contracts may seem attractive for indebted countries or municipalities trying to attract private capital for major investments. However, as can be seen from the example of Buenos Aires, opportunistic behaviour and transaction costs arising from information asymmetries, asset specificity and uncertainty can pose major problems for the contracting partners. Post-agreement transaction costs in terms of renegotiations could be at least partly avoided, as 'the difficulty is often related to poor initial efforts to assess the sources of demand fluctuations' (Estache and Quesada 2001: 2). Nevertheless, with long-term and complex contracts, renegotiations will remain a major problem. Guasch *et al.* (2002: 5) state:

> While some renegotiation is desirable, appropriate and is to be expected, this high incidence appears to be beyond expected and reasonable levels, and raises concerns about the validity of the [concession contract] model. It might indicate poor design or excessive opportunistic behav-

iour by the new operators, or by the government, in detriment of the efficiency and the overall welfare.

It can be argued that, in order to limit the impact of asymmetric information problems and transaction costs, short-term and easy-to-define contracts should be used where possible to improve the performance of inefficient public service providers. This holds especially true for contracts where the private partner bears no investment risks, a situation that is becoming more widespread, as the international private operators seem to be becoming more reluctant to invest their own money in water and sewerage projects in developing countries (Winpenny 2003: 32). After describing the deep-rooted problems with ability to pay, the chief executive of SAUR International concluded that, without major financial support in terms of subsidies and soft loans by international donors, private operators will not be able to deliver services, especially to poor areas in developing countries (Talbot 2002). Although the share of investment financed by the international private sector has always been relatively small and is estimated at roughly 10–15% in WATSAN (Winpenny 2003: 6), this could mean that the donors or the users themselves have to provide much more of the investment money in most of the developing countries.

Hence, the nature of the contracts has to change as well. If all the capital funds are provided by the public partner or by international financing institutions such as the World Bank, service contracts, management contracts or short-term lease contracts will become more appropriate than long-term lease or concession contracts. Phased approaches (i.e. starting with short-term and clearly defined tasks and increasing the responsibility of the private partner over time) may help to overcome the problems of long-term contracts by generating information as the project progresses. This approach, which provides for more flexibility and can help to create trust between the contractual parties, was chosen for example in Mexico City (Haggarty et al. 2002: 139; Johnstone and Wood 2001: 223).

Obviously, production efficiency improvements may be lower with these small-scale or phased contracts, since they can not reap the full efficiency potential of more comprehensive contracts (Harris 2003: 40) and put aside important and difficult decisions such as issues of prices, investments and staffing (Haggarty et al. 2002: 184). These disadvantages have to be balanced against the lower transaction cost, and especially the often higher-than-expected prices charged after renegotiations—price increases that often pose considerable problems for the poor. Estache and Quesada (2001), using an empirical model, conclude in a study by the World Bank Institute that if renegotiations are likely efficiency should not be the only criterion for awarding concession contracts. Instead, acceptance of a reduction in expected efficiency levels could prove appropriate, 'since lower probabilities of firm-driven renegotiations (due to demand shocks for instance) are associated with higher welfare levels' (Estache and Quesada 2001: 23). This conclusion is consistent with the findings of our analysis that conventional economics, with its focus on production efficiency as indicated by the 'lowest bid for water price' criterion, is too narrow to form the basis for overall welfare improvements. Instead, use of an NIE approach can provide valuable insights into how to improve organisational structures for the provision of WATSAN services.

References

Alcázar, L., M.A. Abdala and M.M. Shirley (2002) 'The Buenos Aires Water Concession', in M.M. Shirley (ed.), *Thirsting for Efficiency: The Economics and Politics of Urban Water System Reform* (Oxford, UK: Elsevier): 65-102.

Ashton, T. (1998) 'Contracting for Health Services in New Zealand: A Transaction Cost Analysis', *Social Science and Medicine* 46.3: 357-67.

Bekkada, Z. (1995) 'Lyonnaise Puts its Case as French Water Corruption Crisis Deepens', *Water Services* 99.1: 10-11.

Boyco, M., A. Shleifer and R.W. Vishny (1996) 'A Theory of Privatisation', *The Economic Journal* 106.1: 309-19.

Briscoe, J. (1999) 'The Changing Face of Water Infrastructure Financing in Developing Countries', *International Journal of Water Resources Development* 15.3: 301-308.

Conte Grand, M. (2000) 'Regulation of Water Distribution in Argentina', in Organisation for Economic Co-operation and Development (OECD) (ed.), *Privatisation, Competition and Regulation* (OECD Proceedings of the AGP [Advisory Group on Privatisation]'s 12th meeting 1998; Paris: OECD).

Crampes, C., and A. Estache (1998) 'Regulatory Trade-offs in the Design of Concession Contracts', *Utilities Policy* 7.1: 1-13

Dorward, A. (2001) 'The Effects of Transaction Costs, Power and Risk on Contractual Arrangement: A Conceptual Framework for Quantitative Analysis', *Journal of Agricultural Economics* 52.2: 59-73.

Estache, A., and L. Quesada (2001) *Concession Contract Renegotiations: Some Efficiency vs Equity Dilemmas* (Working Paper; Washington, DC: World Bank Institute).

Finger, M., and J. Allouche (2001) *Water Privatisation: Transnational Corporations and the Re-regulation of the Water Industry* (London/New York: Spon).

Guasch, J.L., J.J. Laffont and S. Straub (2002) *Renegotiation of Concession Contracts in Latin America* (Research Paper C02-22; Los Angeles: Centre for Law, Economics and Organisation, University of Southern California).

Haggarty, L., P. Brook and A.M. Zuluaga (2002) 'Water Sector Contracts in Mexico City, Mexico', in M.M. Shirley (ed.), *Thirsting for Efficiency: The Economics and Politics of Urban Water System Reform* (Oxford, UK: Elsevier): 139-87.

Harris, C. (2003) *Private Participation in Infrastructure in Developing Countries: Trends, Impacts and Policy Lessons* (Working Paper 5; Washington, DC: World Bank).

——, J. Hodges, M. Schur and P. Shukla (2003) *Infrastructure Projects: A Review of Canceled Private Projects* (Public Policy for the Private Sector Note 252; Washington, DC: Private Sector and Infrastructure Network, World Bank Group).

Izzaguirre, A.K. (2002) *Private Infrastructure: A Review of Projects with Private Participation, 1990–2001* (Public Policy for the Private Sector Note 250; Washington, DC: Private Sector and Infrastructure Network, World Bank Group).

Johnstone, N., and L. Wood (2001) 'Conclusions', in N. Johnstone and L. Wood (eds.), *Private Firms and Public Water: Realising Social and Environmental Objectives in Developing Countries* (Cheltenham, UK: Edward Elgar): 214-23.

Klein, M. (1998) *Bidding for Concessions: The Impact of Contract Design* (Public Policy for the Private Sector Note 158; Washington, DC: Private Sector and Infrastructure Network, World Bank Group).

Lane, J.E. (2000) *New Public Management* (London/New York: Routledge).

Ménard, C., and G.R.G. Clarke (2002) 'Reforming Water Supply in Abidjan, Côte d'Ivoire: A Mild Reform in a Turbulent Environment', in M.M. Shirley (ed.), *Thirsting for Efficiency: The Economics and Politics of Urban Water System Reform* (Oxford, UK: Elsevier): 231-72.

Shirley, M.M., and C. Ménard (2002) 'Cities Awash: A Synthesis of the Country Cases', in M.M. Shirley (ed.), *Thirsting for Efficiency: The Economics and Politics of Urban Water System Reform* (Oxford, UK: Elsevier): 1-41.

Simon, H.A. (1976) 'From Substantive to Procedural Rationality', in S. Latsis (ed.), *Methods and Appraisals in Economics* (Cambridge, UK: Cambridge University Press): 129-48.

—— (1997) *Administrative Behavior: A Study of Decision-Making Processes in Administrative Organizations* (New York: The Free Press, 4th edn).

Talbot, J.F. (2002) 'Is the International Water and Sanitation Business Really a Business?', paper presented at the *World Bank Water and Sanitation Lecture Series*, 13 February 2002, available at www.worldbank.org/watsan/lecture/talbot.ppt, accessed 21 February 2003.

United Nations (2000) *United Nations Millennium Declaration: Resolution adopted by the General Assembly* (New York: United Nations Publications).

—— (2002) *Report of the World Summit on Sustainable Development* (New York: United Nations Publications).

Vining, A.R., and S. Globerman (1999) 'Contracting-out Health Care Services: A Conceptual Framework', *Health Policy* 46.2: 77-96.

Williamson, O.E. (1990) *Die ökonomischen Institutionen des Kapitalismus: Unternehmen, Märkte, Kooperationen* (Tübingen, Germany: Mohr).

—— (1991): 'Comparative Economic Organisation: The Analysis of Discrete Structural Alternatives', *Administrative Science Quarterly* 36.2: 269-96.

Wilson, J. (1999) 'From CCT to Best Value: Some Evidence and Observations', *Local Government Studies* 25.2: 38-52.

World Bank (1997) *Selecting an Option for Private Sector Participation: Part 1 of the Toolkit for Private Sector Participation in Water and Sanitation* (Washington, DC: World Bank).

Winpenny, J. (2003) *Financing Water For All: Report of the World Panel on Financing Water Infrastructure* (the Camdessus Report; Geneva: World Water Council).

7

Ownership and performance of water utilities*

Steven Renzetti and Diane Dupont

Brock University, Canada

There is growing concern about the operations of the municipal agencies responsible for supplying potable water and treating sewage (Easter *et al*. 1993; Renzetti 1999). In particular, the focus is on an examination of whether the ownership of water utilities is a factor explaining their behaviour and whether changing the ownership of municipal water providers will lead to improvements in their operations. In a recent survey of the empirical literature related to the impacts of privatisation, Megginson and Netter (2001: 347) conclude that 'privatisation appears to improve performance measured in many different ways, in many different countries'. Megginson and Netter do not, however, report any studies related to privatising water utilities and they acknowledge that 'the justification for privatisation is less compelling in markets for public goods and natural monopolies where competitive considerations are weaker' (2001: 330). Since it is commonly acknowledged that water has both private and public goods characteristics and that urban water supply is characterised by economies of scale, these considerations would appear to weaken the case for privatisation of water utilities compared with other industries.

The purpose of this chapter is to critically assess what is known regarding the relationship between the ownership and performance of municipal water utilities. We first examine the theoretical models predicting that private firms will outperform public ones. We turn next to the empirical literature and ask: (1) whether there is empirical evidence that public water utilities perform worse than comparable private water utilities; and (2) whether there is evidence that privatising water utility operations (either entirely or in part) improves their performance.

* This chapter was completed while the authors were visiting scholars at CSERGE, University of East Anglia. The authors would like to thank Karen Bakker for comments and their research assistants, Jenna Sudds and Meghan Ihrig, and to acknowledge the financial support of the Canada Donner Foundation. All errors and omissions remain the sole responsibility of the authors.

7.1 Ownership and performance: economic theory

There are many reasons why two firms might differ in their performance, including differences in the scale of operations, the degree of competition faced, managerial skills, agency objectives, discriminatory government policies and ownership. Because of the growth in the number of nationalised firms after the Second World War and the subsequent growth in concerns regarding the performances of these firms, the particular importance of ownership in determining performance has attracted attention (Vickers and Yarrow 1989; Hodge 2000). It has been commonly argued that, holding all other factors constant, privately owned firms will outperform publicly owned firms (Megginson and Netter 2001). The theoretical basis for this contention derives from three perspectives, which are discussed here.

Principal–agent (PA) theory is a useful starting point in trying to understand the influence of ownership on the performance of water utilities. In a PA relationship, the task of the owner is to design a contract that provides the manager with the incentive to choose the strategy that maximises the owner's welfare. The challenge for the owner is that, in a world of asymmetric information and uncertainty, the manager's effort cannot be monitored and contracts cannot be enforced costlessly. A significant issue, then, in comparing public and private ownership is their relative efficacy in providing managers with incentives to act consistently with the enterprise's goals.

One of the factors that may be expected to influence owners' desire to monitor the actions of managers is the potential pay-off to them from improving managerial effort. Property rights (PR) theory argues that private-sector owners, as residual claimants, have more clearly defined incentives to push for efficient decision-making by managers. The same logic applies to the firm's creditors and also to owners of other firms considering a potential takeover. In contrast, politicians, senior bureaucrats and taxpayers have attenuated property rights to the gains associated with improved public-sector agency performance and, as a result, have diminished incentives to push for improvements. Public choice (PC) theory emphasises the potential for inefficient behaviour on the part of public-sector managers since they are assumed to act in their own self-interest: for example, by seeking to expand the size of their own budget.

Taken together, these theoretical perspectives predict that public-sector owners have less incentive to provide oversight and discipline while public-sector managers have more incentive to pursue goals other than those of their agency. The lack of costlessly enforceable contracts that anticipate every contingency means that public agencies will exhibit poorer performance compared with their private counterparts.

These arguments have been challenged on both theoretical and empirical grounds. First, one must be very careful to separate the roles of ownership and the degree of competition faced by a firm when assessing its performance (Rees 1998). Namely, performance may depend as much on the structure of the product market as it does on ownership (Vickers and Yarrow 1989). This counter-argument suggests that, since water utilities operate largely under monopolistic conditions, mere privatisation of these firms is unlikely to lead to better performance.

Second, the presence of regulations, incomplete information and transactions costs may imply that capital markets are not fully efficient sources of discipline. This means that threats of takeover and bankruptcy do not always provide perfect incentive mechanisms for efficient choices by managers (Hodge 2000; Saal and Parker 2001). For example, it has been suggested that England's water industry regulator, OFWAT, discouraged, at least for a period of time, mergers of recently privatised water utilities because it needed to have a sufficient number of firms to provide data for its 'benchmarking' form of price regulation (Cowan 1998; Sawkins 2001).

Finally, there is relatively little empirical evidence of bureaucrats behaving in a manner predicted by public choice theory (Martin and Parker 1997). Taken together, these counter-arguments suggest that economic theory does not unambiguously predict a clear and simple relationship between ownership and performance. As a result, we now turn to the empirical literature concerned with the measurement of performance.

7.2 Ownership and performance: measurement issues

In describing the performance of a firm, there are a number of different aspects that have been considered. While economists have tended to focus on the particular goal of efficiency, a number of other performance indicators such as productivity, profitability, impact on the environment and quality of output have also been used. As the review of the literature in the next section shows, all of these perspectives have been used in assessing the impact of changing the ownership of water utilities. In this section, we restrict our attention to discussing economic efficiency, as this is the measure used most commonly to compare the performance of firms.[1]

Efficiency can be described along a number of dimensions. A firm is technically efficient if it either produces the largest level of output possible given the quantity of input used or if it employs the smallest quantities of those inputs necessary to produce a given level of output. Furthermore, if information regarding input prices is available, then a firm's allocative efficiency can be assessed. A firm is said to be allocatively efficient if it produces a given level of output at minimum cost.

Let us consider an example to make these concepts more concrete. Suppose a firm could choose from three technologies (A, B and C), all of which are capable of producing output Q^0. Suppose A uses 3 units of labour and 3 units of capital, B uses 4 units of labour and 3 units of capital and C uses 2 units of labour and 4 units of capital. In a comparison of A and B, it is clear that B is technically inefficient since it uses more labour and the same amount of capital as A to produce the same quantity of output. With additional information on input prices, we can relate the impact of being inefficient to the cost of production. Namely, if the firm is using more input than is necessary to produce a given output, its cost of production will be higher than the cost of production for the best-practice or more efficient firm. Thus, when compared with B, A is allocatively efficient.

---

1   A comprehensive description and comparison of the alternative methods of efficiency measurement can be found in Coelli *et al.* 1999.

What can we say about A and C? They are both potentially technically efficient, but are they both allocatively efficient? Suppose we know that the prices of capital and labour are $6 and $1, respectively. Then, in order to produce Q^0 using A's input mix costs $21 ([$6 × 3] + [$1 × 3]) while producing Q^0 with C's input mix costs $26 ([$6 × 4] + [$1 × 2]). Thus, we would conclude that C is allocatively inefficient. That is, by rearranging the mix of inputs (moving from C to A), we could reduce the cost of producing a given level of output.

The first way to measure efficiency is the econometric or parametric approach, which is based on a stochastic representation of the production function (these techniques are reviewed in Kumbhakar and Lovell 2000). Unlike the usual econometric model of production, a model that incorporates inefficiency has two error terms. The first is the normal error component that reflects the presence of unobservable factors. It can be positive or negative. The second term is the technical inefficiency error term. This can only be positive since it represents the distance a firm is from the best-practice production level (i.e. the most efficient firm). In order to implement this approach, the researcher must choose between a primal approach (estimating the production frontier to obtain estimates of technical efficiency) and a dual approach (estimating either a cost or a profit frontier in order to obtain estimates of allocative efficiency). The extent to which a firm's costs (profits) are greater (smaller) than those identified by the frontier indicates the extent of inefficiency.

An alternative approach uses data envelopment analysis (DEA) (Dupont *et al*. 2002). The DEA model uses linear programming to define a frontier of most efficient firms and then compares all other firms' performance relative to this frontier. One important feature of DEA is that, in its calculations of the efficiency index, it assigns weights to individual outputs and inputs so that the best possible efficiency score is achieved. As Cubbin and Tzanidakis (1998: 78) note, 'this is sometimes expressed as putting the company "in the best possible light"'. However, the researcher is unable to undertake hypothesis testing of the significance of the results or of the appropriate set of variables to be included to explain firm performance (in a regression model statistical tests can be used to determine whether to include, for example, an index of raw water quality or population density in a model of water utility costs).

7.3 Ownership and performance: empirical evidence

Three developed countries provide us with most of the empirical studies conducted to date. These are the United States, England and Wales, and France. We examine the literature that has compared public and private utilities in America and France and study the impacts of the privatisation of water utilities in the UK.[2] Table 7.1 provides a summary of the studies discussed below.

2   Evidence of the relationship between ownership and performance from low-income countries is not considered in this chapter because of the significant differences in the legal and social contexts in which these water utilities operate. Interested readers should consult Rivera 1996 and Orwin 1999.

Author	Country	Method	Results
Morgan 1977	US	Cost function	Private has lower costs
Crain and Zardkoohi 1978	US	Cost function	Private has lower costs
Bruggink 1982	US	Cost function	Public cost lower by 20%
Feigenbaum and Teeples 1983	US	Hedonic cost function	No difference in costs
Fox and Hofler 1986	US	Combined production–cost function	Cost 'over-runs' of 46% and 43% for private and public, respectively
Byrnes et al. 1986	US	DEA	No difference in efficiency
Teeples and Glyer 1987	US	Hedonic cost function	No cost difference in most general model
Byrnes 1991	US	Cost frontier	No differences in costs
Lambert et al. 1993	US	DEA	Public more efficient
Raffiee et al. 1993	US	Cost function	Public and private exhibit 17% and 22% deviation from minimum cost, respectively
Lynk 1993	UK	Cost frontier	Private and public are 11.5% and 2% above respective cost frontiers
Bhattacharyya et al. 1994	US	Cost function	No difference in overall efficiency but private are technically more inefficient
Bhattacharyya et al. 1995a	US	Cost frontier	Public and private exhibit 10% and 19% deviation from minimum cost, respectively
Bhattacharyya et al. 1995b	US	DEA	Private are 91% efficient while public are 85–90% efficient
Shaoul 1997	UK	Financial analysis	Privatisation raised profits but little else
Cubbin and Tzanidakis 1998	UK	Cost function and DEA	Methods yield different rankings of relative efficiency
Ashton 2000	UK	Cost function	Post-privatisation average efficiency is 85% and range is 77–100%
Saal and Parker 2000	UK	Cost function	Tightened price regulation lowered costs but privatisation didn't
Ménard and Saussier 2000	France	Regression model	No difference in compliance with water quality regulations
Saal and Parker 2001	UK	Productivity analysis	Privatisation increased profits but not productivity

DEA = data envelopment analysis

TABLE 7.1 Empirical water utility performance studies

7.3.1 The American experience

The US provides a potentially valuable environment for comparing the performance of water utilities, as there are a number of jurisdictions in the US where public and private water utilities operate under comparable regulatory environments.

The earliest studies examining the link between ownership and performance estimated an aggregate cost function for water utilities and usually included a dummy variable to test for ownership effects. The results of these efforts were mixed. Morgan (1977) and Crain and Zardkoohi (1978) find that private water utilities have, on average, lower costs. Conversely, Bruggink (1982), Feigenbaum and Teeples (1983) and Teeples and Glyer (1987) find either no cost difference or that public utilities have lower costs. However, as McGuire and Ohsfeldt (1986) point out, a problem with these studies is that they assume cost-minimising behaviour by both public and private utilities. However, the theoretical arguments presented in the section describing economic theory indicate that public utilities may, in fact, not engage in cost-minimising activities. As a result of this type of criticism, researchers began to make use of measurement techniques that allowed them to relax the assumption of cost minimisation. Lambert *et al.* (1993) and Bhattacharyya *et al.* (1994), for example, use a DEA approach to estimate a production frontier for a sample of public and private US water utilities. The latter authors find that public utilities display higher overall and higher technical efficiency while the latter study finds private utilities to be slightly more efficient than public ones (91.3% versus 90%).

Other researchers have employed econometric methods to estimate stochastic cost frontiers. Byrnes (1991) estimates a cost frontier and finds no statistical difference in cost frontiers for public and private utilities. Bhattacharyya *et al.* (1995a) also estimate a stochastic cost frontier for private and public utilities and find that the impact of ownership on performance interacts with the scale of the utility. Thus, large public utilities are less inefficient than comparable private utilities while the reverse is true for small utilities.

Unfortunately, no recent large-scale studies have been conducted to identify the determinants of water utility performance (including ownership) in the US. Thus, it would appear that the most conclusive statement that can be made regarding the American experience is that there is no strong evidence that private water utilities are demonstrably more productive than public water utilities. Having said this, it is important to be mindful of the relatively small number of studies available and the possibility that past studies have not fully accounted for the differing tax rules and regulations under which private and public utilities operate (Seidenstat *et al.* 2000).

7.3.2 The English and Welsh experience

The privatisation of water and sewage utilities in England and Wales has been the largest effort so far to sell off public water agencies (Cowan 1998). As such, it provides a natural experiment for the impacts of a change in ownership on the performance of water and sewage utilities. At the time of the privatisation, the British government argued that the change in ownership was necessary to improve the agencies' performance (Littlechild 1988). The privatisation effort involved several components. The most important component, of course, was the sale of the water and sewage utilities themselves.

Once privatised, the water utilities were subject to a variety of environmental and financial regulations. In particular, the firms were faced with the recently adopted and stringent EU water quality regulations. It is widely believed that these regulations were the primary reason for the significant increase in capital spending undertaken by the privatised water utilities (Cowan 1998; Ashton 2000). The other important form of regulation concerned the adoption of a RPI + K form of price regulation where the aggregate price for a bundle of the utilities' outputs was allowed to rise by the retail price index plus a K factor (Littlechild 1988; Cowan 1994). From the point of view of providing incentives for efficient behaviour, the most important feature of the adopted price regulation is the fact that any individual firm's allowed rate of price increase is a function of the cost performance of its competitors. This 'benchmark' feature of price regulation was supposed to provide the firms with an incentive to innovate and reduce costs, as each firm's allowed price is related to the average of the other firms' unit costs. The second phase of the British government's water sector policy was aimed at promoting competition in the output market. Legislative changes allowed for inset appointments, common carriage agreements and prohibited anti-competitive agreements and abuse of dominant market positions (Rothenberger 2001). Inset appointments allow one water firm to sell its output to customers within another firm's jurisdiction. Common carriage agreements facilitate the delivery of one firm's output through another water firm's network infrastructure.

The empirical evidence on the impacts of the British privatisation is definitely mixed. On the one hand, there is little evidence that the change in ownership, per se, has led to measurable improvements in performance. Shaoul (1997) conducts a financial analysis of the UK water industry pre- and post-privatisation. The author finds higher costs, prices and profits but little improvement in the level of net investment or service quality (the latter being measured by frequency of customer complaints and of utility-mandated water use restrictions). Saal and Parker (2001) conduct a productivity analysis of the privatised industry. The authors find that while labour productivity improved after privatisation, total factor productivity declined. The authors conclude that privatisation resulted in higher profits but few efficiency gains. In contrast, there is some evidence that the combination of environmental and price regulation did improve performance especially after a review and tightening of the price regulation in 1995. More stringent environmental regulations have led to improved drinking and river water quality (Saal and Parker 2001). In addition, the British government's recent downward revisions of the allowable rate of price increases appear to have induced cost reductions and improved efficiencies. Saal and Parker (2000), for example, estimate a cost function for the UK water industry and include time dummy variables in order to test whether either privatisation or tightened price regulation has affected industry costs. The privatisation dummy is insignificant but the price regulation dummy's coefficient is negative and significant. These results suggest that only price regulation has had a discernible influence on costs.

The reforms aiming to introduce greater output market competition have also met with limited success in promoting such competition. There have been a limited number of inset agreements because of complexities and delays in the application procedure. Furthermore, the recent trend towards mutualisation in the English and Welsh water industry suggests a move away from privatisation (Bakker 2003).[3]

7.3.3 The French experience

In France, municipalities (*communes*) have the legal authority to supply water or to delegate that responsibility to another party (Chret 1994). Prior to the Second World War, most local water supply was carried out directly by public agencies. However, an important post-war innovation has been the development of contractual relationships ('delegated management') between communes and private firms in which the latter participate in local water supply. By 1992, 75% of the French population was supplied by some form of a public–private joint operation although these partnerships are concentrated in large and medium-sized municipalities (Petitet 2000; Guérin-Schneider 2001).

There were originally two forms of delegated management. The first, a lease contract (*affermage*), specifies a relatively short-term relationship (10–12 years) in which the firm is responsible for operating a facility while the commune is responsible for building and financing any facilities. The second, a concession contract, is a longer-term relationship in which the firm not only operates a facility but is also involved in financing and building the facility. The contracts also specify how prices are to be determined and what form of payment is to be paid to the private firm. Over time, however, a variety of hybrid, intermediary forms of relationship has developed (Elnaboulsi 2001).

There are few studies comparing the relative performance of French water suppliers under alternative forms of ownership and contractual relationships. Despite this, the theoretical arguments presented above would suggest that the possibility of having a number of private firms bidding for the right to run a municipal water system should introduce a strong degree of competition and, thus, efficiency, into the local water supply system. There are several factors, however, that reduce the potential benefits of private participation in the French water supply industry and potentially reduce the municipality's power to set terms of contractual relationships. These include restrictions on the participation of foreign firms, a lack of transparency in bidding processes and the distorting effects of large subsidies from senior levels of French government (Orwin 1999). In his assessment of the benefits of delegation in the French water market, Elnaboulsi (2001: 532) concludes: 'Therefore, the 1980s showed that, instead of the promised competition, the private finance and less bureaucratic, local municipalities faced cartels, combines and corruption, and the financial risks left to the public sector.'

Another important problem stems from the sovereignty of French communes in decision-making related to water supplies. Garcia and Thomas (2001) demonstrate

---

3   A mutualised water firm is owned by its customers (and, possibly, workers) and run as a not-for-profit co-operative.

the presence of both scale and scope economies for small, local water systems and argue that the failure of small communes to amalgamate their supply networks leads to significantly higher costs. The councils of these small communities may also experience an imbalance in bargaining power between themselves and the large private firms that dominate the French water industry (Buller 1996). Finally, under French law, a mayor may not protect him- or herself from the liability arising from damages caused through the negligent operation of a directly managed supply network. If the operation of that network is delegated to a private firm, however, then the mayor's personal liability is removed (Clark and Mondello 2000). This situation creates a potential conflict of interest for mayors in their choice between direct and delegated operations and may distort their decision-making. It may also decrease the credibility of a threat to revoke a firm's contract when the municipality is dissatisfied with a firm's performance.

There is limited empirical evidence regarding the relative performance of alternative forms of French local water agencies. For example, Orwin (1999) presents evidence that demonstrates that private suppliers have higher prices than directly administered (i.e. public) systems, but Buller (1996) argues that this may be due to the higher frequency of privatised systems in areas where costs of supply are higher (because of, for example, reliance on groundwater supplies). Ménard and Saussier (2000) examine the factors influencing the direct versus delegated administration decision and compare the performance of the two forms of organisation. The authors find that, once differences in raw water quality are accounted for, there is no difference in performance between direct and delegated management.

7.4 Summary and conclusions

This chapter has discussed how the theoretical economic literature predicts that private ownership will exhibit higher levels of efficiency than public ownership. An important qualifying factor, however, is that changes in ownership need to be matched with efforts to introduce competition in capital and output markets. The chapter has also demonstrated that the empirical literature is lacking in conclusive evidence that privately owned water utilities are more efficient than comparable publicly owned water utilities (this is also the conclusion reached by Sepälä *et al.* 2001). Nonetheless, it is worth remembering that many of the empirical studies do not test the predictions of a specific theoretical model for performance differences. As a result, it is difficult to determine which of the theoretical models predicting the superiority of private firms has been rejected.

One might argue that, in practice, we rarely see a purely private or purely public firm since the potential range of public–private partnerships is wide and this makes the assessment of these types of arrangement difficult. And, while there is some anecdotal evidence that public–private partnerships may lower the costs of constructing and operating new facilities (Seidenstat *et al.* 2000), whether these arrangements are welfare-improving depends crucially on the details of the partnership. Particularly important are issues related to the structure of incentives, price-setting rules and risk sharing. It is clear that more research is needed into the variety of forms of public–private partnerships (Seidenstat 2000; Roumasset 2000).

It is worth considering the possible reasons for our inability to find strong empirical evidence to support theoretical predictions regarding the impact of ownership on utility performance. First, the regulatory environment in which firms must operate has a large influence on choices and behaviour: for example, in instances where public and private utilities operate under the same regulatory environment. Health and safety, financial and environmental regulations may prove to be the determining factors in choice of technology and capital.

The final factor that may provide a piece of the puzzle is the fact that water utilities have unique features not found in other industries that have been privatised. In particular, we argued earlier about the importance of a competitive environment for achieving efficiency gains. In other sectors (telecommunications, airlines, railways), privatisation has been accompanied by deregulation (Rothenberger 2001). In the case of water, it is difficult to imagine how municipal water utilities could be compelled to compete in the output market. As discussed above, OFWAT's efforts to promote competition in the English water industry have met with limited success (Sawkins 2001). A more valuable alternative may be to promote increased competition in water utilities' input markets through enhanced use of transparent and competitive tendering and contracting out (as seen in recent French legislation; cf. the discussion in Elnaboulsi 2001). In addition to allowing private firms to bid for one-time construction contracts, water utilities may contract out non-core areas such as billing, plant maintenance, meter installation and monitoring, and water quality testing on a continuing basis.

References

Ashton, J. (2000) 'Cost Efficiency in the UK Water and Sewerage Industry', *Applied Economics Letters* 7: 455-58.

Bakker, K. (2003) 'From Public to Private to . . . Public? Re-regulating and "Mutualising" Private Water Supply in England and Wales', *Geoforum* forthcoming.

Bhattacharyya, A., E. Parker and K. Raffiee (1994) 'An Examination of the Effect of Ownership on the Relative Efficiency of Public and Private Water Utilities', *Land Economics* 70.2: 197-209.

——, T.R. Harris, R. Narayanan and K. Raffiee (1995a) 'Allocative Efficiency of Rural Nevada Water Systems: A Hedonic Shadow Cost Function Approach', *Journal of Regional Science* 35.3: 485-501.

——, ——, —— and —— (1995b) 'Specification and Estimation of the Effect of Ownership on the Economic Efficiency of the Water Utilities', *Regional Science and Urban Economics* 25: 759-84.

Bruggink, T. (1982) 'Public versus Regulated Private Enterprise in the Municipal Water Industry: A Comparison of Operating Costs', *Quarterly Review of Economics and Business* 22.1: 111-25.

Buller, H. (1996) 'Privatization and Europeanization: The Changing Context of Water Supply in Britain and France', *Journal of Environmental Planning and Management* 39.4: 461-83.

Byrnes, P. (1991) 'Estimation of Cost Frontiers in the Presence of Selectivity Bias: Ownership and Efficiency of Water Utilities', in G. Rhodes (ed.), *Advances in Econometrics* 9: 121-37.

——, S. Grosskopf and K. Hayes (1986) 'Efficiency and Ownership: Further Evidence', *Review of Economics and Statistics* 65: 337-41.

Chret, I. (1994) 'Managing Water: The French Model', in *Valuing the Environment: Proceedings of the First Annual International Conference on Environmentally Sustainable Development* (Washington, DC: World Bank): 80-92.

Clark, E., and G. Mondello (2000) 'Resource Management and the Mayor's Guarantee in French Water Allocation', *Environmental and Resource Economics* 15: 103-13.

Coelli, T., D.S. Rao and G. Battese (1999) *An Introduction to Efficiency and Productivity Analysis* (Boston, MA: Kluwer Academic Publishers).

Cowan, S. (1994) 'Privatization and Regulation of the Water Industry in England and Wales', in M. Bishop, J. Kay and C. May (eds.), *Privatization and Economic Performance* (Oxford, UK: Oxford University Press): 112-37.

—— (1998) 'The Water Industry', in D. Helm and T. Jenkinson (eds.), *Competition in Regulated Industries* (Oxford, UK: Oxford University Press): 160-75.

Crain, W.M., and A. Zardkoohi (1978) 'A Test of the Property-Rights Theory of the Firm: Water Utilities in the United States', *Journal of Law and Economics* 21: 385-408.

Cubbin, J., and G. Tzanidakis (1998) 'Regression versus Data Envelopment Analysis for Efficiency Measurement: An Application to the England and Wales Regulated Water Industry', *Utilities Policy* 7: 75-85.

Dupont, D.P., R.Q. Grafton, J. Kirkley and D. Squires (2002) 'Capacity Utilization Measures and Excess Capacity in Multi-Product Privatized Fisheries', *Resource and Energy Economics* 24.3: 193-210.

Easter, K.W., G. Feder, G. Le Moigne and A. Duda (1993) *Water Resources Management* (Washington, DC: World Bank).

Elnaboulsi, J. (2001) 'Organization, Management and Delegation in the French Water Industry', *Annals of Public and Cooperative Economics* 72.4: 507-47.

Feigenbaum, S., and R. Teeples (1983) 'Public versus Private Water Delivery: A Hedonic Cost Approach', *Review of Economics and Statistics* 65: 672-78.

Fox, W., and R. Hofler (1986) 'Using Homothetic Composed Error Frontiers to Measure Water Utility Efficiency', *Southern Economic Journal* 53.2: 461-78.

Garcia, S., and A. Thomas (2001) 'The Structure of Municipal Water Supply Costs: Application to a Panel of French Local Communities', *Journal of Productivity Analysis* 16.1: 5-29.

Guérin-Schneider, L. (2001) *Introduire la mesure de performance dans la régulation des services d'eau et d'assainissement en France-Instrumentation et organisation* (PhD thesis; l'Ecole Nationale du Génie Rural, des Eaux et Forêts Centre de Paris dans la Spécialité Gestion).

Hodge, G. (2000) *Privatization: An International Review of Performance* (Boulder, CO: Westview Press).

Kumbhakar, S., and C.A.K. Lovell (2000) *Stochastic Frontier Analysis* (Cambridge, UK: Cambridge University Press).

Lambert, D., D. Dichev and K. Raffiee (1993) 'Ownership and Sources of Inefficiency in the Provision of Water Services', *Water Resources Research* 29.6: 1,573-78.

Littlechild, S. (1988) 'Economic Regulation of Privatised Water Authorities and Some Further Reflections', *Oxford Review of Economic Policy* 4.2: 40-68.

Lynk, E. (1993) 'Privatisation, Joint Production and the Comparative Efficiencies of Private and Public Ownership: The UK Water Industry', *Fiscal Studies* 14.2: 98-116.

Martin, S., and D. Parker (1997) *The Impact of Privatization: Ownership and Corporate Performance in the UK* (New York: Routledge).

McGuire, R., and R. Ohsfeldt (1986) 'Public versus Private Water Delivery: A Critical Analysis of a Hedonic Cost Approach', *Public Finance Quarterly* 14.3: 339-50.

Megginson, W., and J. Netter (2001) 'From State to Market: A Survey of Empirical Studies on Privatization', *Journal of Economic Literature* 39.2: 321-89.

Ménard, C., and S. Saussier (2000) 'Contractual Choice and Performance: The Case of Water Supply in France', *Revue d'Économie Industrielle* 92.2-3: 385-404.

Morgan, D. (1977) 'Investor Owned vs Publicly Owned Water Agencies: An Evaluation of the Property Rights Theory of the Firm', *Water Resources Bulletin* 13.4: 775-81.

Orwin, A. (1999) *Privatization of Water and Wastewater Utilities: An International Survey* (Toronto: Environment Probe).

Petitet, S. (2000) 'Faut-il parler d'un "modèle français des services urbains"?', *Economies et Sociétés* 34.2: 99-123.

Raffiee, K., R. Narayanan, T. Harris, D. Lambert and J. Collins (1993) 'Cost Analysis of Water Utilities: A Goodness-of-Fit Approach', *Atlantic Economic Journal* 21.3: 18-29.

Rees, J. (1998) *Regulation and Private Participation in the Water and Sanitation Sector* (Technical Advisory Committee Background Paper no. 1; Stockholm: Global Water Partnership).

Renzetti, S. (1999) 'Municipal Water Supply and Sewage Treatment: Costs, Prices and Distortions', *Canadian Journal of Economics* 32.2: 688-704.

Rivera, D. (1996) *Private Sector Participation in the Water Supply and Wastewater Sector: Lessons from Six Developing Countries* (Washington, DC: World Bank).

Rothenberger, D. (2001) 'Deregulation in Water Management: Cross Country Comparison and Lessons Learned from the Electricity Sector', in D. Moody and P. Wouters (eds.), *Globalisation and Water Resources: The Changing Value of Water. Proceedings of the American Water Resources Association/University of Dundee International Conference*, Dundee, Scotland, 6–8 August 2001.

Roumasset, J. (2000) 'Rapporteur's Report on Privatizing Water and Wastewater Systems', in J. Boland (ed.), *Water Resources Update* 117 (Carbondale, IL: Universities Council on Water Resources): 40-43.

Saal, D., and D. Parker (2000) 'The Impact of Privatization and Regulation on the Water and Sewerage Industry in England and Wales: A Translog Cost Function Model', *Managerial and Decision Economics* 21: 253-68.

—— and —— (2001) 'Productivity and Price Performance in the Privatized Water and Sewerage Companies of England and Wales', *Journal of Regulatory Economics* 20.1: 61-90.

Sawkins, J. (2001) 'The Development of Competition in the English and Welsh Water and Sewerage Industry', *Fiscal Studies* 22.2: 189-215.

Seidenstat, P. (2000) 'Emerging Competition in Water and Wastewater Industries', in J. Boland (ed.), *Water Resources Update* 117 (Carbondale, IL: Universities Council on Water Resources): 6-12.

——, M. Nadon and S. Hakim (2000) *America's Water and Wastewater Industries: Competition and Privatization* (Vienna, VA: Public Utilities Reports).

Sepälä, O., J. Hukka and T. Katko (2001) 'Public–Private Partnerships in Water and Sewerage Services', *Public Works Management and Policy* 6.1: 42-58.

Shaoul, J. (1997) 'A Critical Financial Analysis of the Performance of Privatized Industries: The Case of the Water Industry in England and Wales', *Critical Perspectives on Accounting* 8: 479-505.

Teeples, R., and D. Glyer (1987) 'Cost of Water Delivery Systems: Specification and Ownership Effects', *Review of Economics and Statistics* 69.3: 399-408.

Vickers, J., and G. Yarrow (1989) *Privatization: An Economic Analysis* (Cambridge, MA: The MIT Press).

8

The involvement of the private sector in water servicing

EFFECTS ON THE URBAN POOR IN THE CASE OF AGUASCALIENTES, MEXICO

Leslie Morris

Consultant, Canada

Luis Fernando Gallardo Cabrera

IMPLAN, Mexico

Adequate access to safe water that is affordable has long been identified as an important factor in lessening poverty and leading to inclusive sustainable development. In recent years, a significant trend has been the transfer of water management from public to private operation (Gleick *et al.* 2002). The privatisation process, which was principally instigated in the early 1990s as a tool for economic change in the Latin American region (Hardoy and Schusterman 2000), has led to significant concern that tariff adjustments have profound implications for the poor. There is a very close relationship between access to water servicing and the standard of living in lower-income households; many of these communities received services free of charge before privatisation (Hardoy and Schusterman 2000).

This chapter seeks to examine the challenges that the urban poor typically encounter in meeting their household water needs when the private sector has responsibility for service provision. Specifically, it will look at how private-sector participation[1] in water servicing, a process where water is treated as an economic good, affects its distribution as a human rights-based necessity to the urban poor. There will be particular reference to the city of Aguascalientes, Mexico, located in a water-scarce area situated in the central-north region of Mexico. The chapter will

---

1 The term 'private-sector participation' (PSP) is used here as a narrower definition of privatisation. In this case, full privatisation did not occur through the complete transferral of system ownership but rather a concession was granted where the private operator was charged with delivering the service and carrying operation and maintenance costs while collecting profits (Barlow and Clarke 2002).

then identify potential opportunities within the privatisation process to better facilitate a sustainable and sensitive basis for serving the urban poor and allowing such groups to achieve household water security in the context of changing service administration and increasing resource depletion.

8.1 Background: water scarcity and PSP in Aguascalientes

Aguascalientes, a regional capital city of approximately 650,000 people, is considered to be a success story due to its high rate of economic growth in the 1980s. In recent years, one of the greatest challenges in local governance and development of the city has been a dramatic lowering of groundwater levels. This is a critical problem as groundwater is being extracted from aquifers at a much greater rate than it is being replenished. The city itself is now facing serious water scarcity.[2]

The annual precipitation rate of 522 mm is substantially below the national average of 777 mm (Saade Hazin 2001). In years of drought, this level can be reduced to 300 mm. Eighty per cent of the state's supply is extracted from one aquifer, Valle de Aguascalientes, which is seriously over-exploited and is facing a deficit of 95.3%. The water level of this aquifer has decreased at an average rate of 2.7 m per year (see Table 8.1).

Until 20 years ago, groundwater had been extracted at a depth of 10–50 m; now it is extracted at an average of 150 m, and in some areas up to a depth of 500 m. Groundwater is the only effective source of fresh water because of the lack of surface water. Water scarcity has caused irreversible damage to the environment through land subsidence resulting in structural damage to buildings, and increased risk of water contamination through cracks.

The lowering of the groundwater supply has occurred because of a low natural availability due to the aridity of the region, and is compounded by the growing population which has led to an explosion in water use for industrial, agricultural and residential purposes (see Table 8.2). In the 1980s, Aguascalientes had one of the highest growth rates in Mexico, resulting in a tripling of the urban population since 1960. This change coincided with increased levels of investment and, within ten years, Aguascalientes saw the establishment of approximately 300 new industries, including a number of multinationals, which reflects the changes resulting from liberalised trade patterns after the adoption of the North American Free Trade Agreement (NAFTA). Poor management has also contributed to the problem as intensive groundwater development was permitted before any type of integrated water resource management was addressed.

2   Mexico as a country is not classified as being water-scarce, yet uneven distribution of the country's resources highlights a growing scarcity problem for the industrial north. Over 76% of the population and 70% of Mexico's industry, including the city of Aguascalientes, lie in the northern part of the country where only 20% of the water resources exist. Of the 647 aquifers identified in Mexico, approximately 100 are severely over-exploited, representing 51% of total national abstraction (Saade Hazin 2001).

Aquifer	Extent (km²)	Hydrological balance
Valle de Aguascalientes	1,250	Deficit of 95.3%
Zona del Llano	550	Deficit of 4.1%
Valle de Chicalote	250	Deficit of 62.0%
Valle de Calvillo	200	Deficit of 220.0%
Valle de Venadero	100	Positive

TABLE 8.1 Aquifers supplying groundwater in the state of Aguascalientes

Use	Volume (m³ millions)	
Agriculture	437	(74.6%)
Residential use	107	(18.2%)
Livestock watering and other combined uses	34	(5.8%)
Industrial	8	(1.4%)
Total	587	(100%)

TABLE 8.2 Uses of extracted water in the state of Aguascalientes (annual)

These transitions and the range of factors influencing water scarcity emphasise the complexities that emerge for local governance structures when faced with such challenges. There is potential for more sustainable management practices to be used as a valuable tool in equitably allocating existing resources and safeguarding what little resources are left, so it is therefore important that problems are addressed immediately before they become progressively unmanageable in the context of private-sector participation.

8.2 The involvement of the private sector in the case of Mexico

According to Ozuna and Gomez (1999), the privatisation process in Mexico was instigated for various reasons. First, by the 1980s, the provision of water servicing had come to the forefront as a major social problem in Mexico: in 1990, approximately 16.7 million people lacked potable water, and this was partly due to the several financial, technical and institutional problems of the central water utilities. Second, in many urban areas such as in Aguascalientes, the average cost of providing water services to the fast-growing population was rising rapidly.

To confront these issues, the central government shifted its focus to privatisation of state-owned enterprises, and in 1989 the National Water Commission (CNA) was established to co-ordinate efforts (Saade Hazin 2001). In 1992 the National Water Law (*Ley de Aguas Nacionales*) was enacted; its main focus was to allow for greater private-sector involvement in the water industry (Saade Hazin 2001). These actions also occurred in the context of the central government's economic restructuring policies, resulting from pressure from the International Monetary Fund (IMF)'s Structural Adjustment Programmes. The IMF required reforms to open up recipient economies to private investment, while international aid agencies such as the World Bank pushed the process of privatisation in their efforts, but 'without a common set of guidelines and principles' (Gleick *et al.* 2002). Thus, a process of 'rolling back the state' in many countries of Latin America resulted in local authorities having greater responsibility in the delivery of services such as water and sanitation, which very often resulted in greater private-sector involvement in utilities.

In Aguascalientes, private-sector involvement began in 1989 when a service contract was signed with a consortium of the Mexico-based company, Grupo ICA, and Compagnie Générale des Eaux, based in France,[3] known locally as CAASA,[4] to provide water and sanitation services to the population, with revenues granted to the water operator (Saade Hazin 2001). In May 1992, the contract was modified so that the private consortium would be responsible for the administration of revenue. In 1993, Aguascalientes signed a 25-year concession contract with the consortium, with no bidding process. The contract included three phases: a study of the city's situation; marketing activities; and operation and maintenance activities. By the end of 1996, a new concession contract was signed to extend the contract to 30 years.

8.3 Changes in the water sector after private-sector participation

After the introduction of PSP, a number of factors resulted in changes to water tariffs in Aguascalientes. The macroeconomic crisis of 1995 and subsequent fourfold increases in interest rates which limited CAASA's financial capacity (Saade Hazin 2001), combined with increasing extraction costs associated with water scarcity, resulted in explicit challenges to low-income households in funding residential water supplies:

- An increasing block tariff (IBT) structure was implemented, under which all connected users were to pay a fee for a designated block of water.[5]

---

3 A French subsidiary of Vivendi Environment.
4 Concessionária de Agua y Alcantarillado de Aguascalientes Socieda Anonima.
5 Increasing block tariffs (IBTs) are tariffs under which customers pay a certain charge per cubic metre of water until a specified volume is consumed. Above this amount, a higher charge is paid until a second specified volume is reached, and so on (Bellamy 1999).

- Tariffs rose by an average of 60% as many poor households were receiving water servicing free of charge before PSP due to high levels of subsidy.

- Currently, 300 cuts to servicing occur daily because of a strict price recovery policy under which water is cut off if the bill is not paid within two months. A reconnection charge is applied at a cost of US$4, which is approximately the average minimum daily salary.

Under the IBT, each household is subdivided into three categories based on its location, and is charged for water use based on 10 m³ blocks: Category A includes the poorest areas (and rural areas), Category B includes the middle-class areas, and Category C encompasses the most affluent communities. Considerable financial poverty exists in Category A communities: 9.3% of the population earns equal to or less than US$4 a day (which includes 3.5% who have no income), and 27.9% earns US$8 or less (2000 INEGI Census statistics).

8.4 Analysis of present allocation and pricing policy

In this chapter we evaluate water pricing and allocation policy in the case of Aguascalientes, particularly highlighting two key themes that commonly appear in sustainable development frameworks, and which also substantiate significant principles within the Rio Declaration on Environment and Development, reaffirmed at the 2002 World Summit on Sustainable Development: the importance of lessening poverty and reducing disparities in living standards as a means of achieving balanced sustainable development; and the safeguarding of resources for future generations so that future developmental and environmental needs are not undermined.

Information for the following analysis was gathered from interviews with local government, including the Aguascalientes Water and Sanitation Commission (CAPAMA),[6] and also through an informed household survey within Category A communities. Thus, this analysis is largely focused on how these changes affect the end-user, drawing from specific evidence of changes occurring in household water use.

8.4.1 Pricing and subsidies

The issue of water pricing is one of the most critical aspects in the equitable allocation of water and encouragement of conservation. In the case of Aguascalientes the added dimension of water scarcity ensures further complexities as the high cost of extracting groundwater obscures the determination of an adequate tariff level for poorer populations. Many economists and environmentalists argue that, in areas where extraction costs are high due to water scarcity, the 'true cost' of water should be levied to promote conservation. Obvious conflicts are thus created: poor house-

---

6   Comisión de Agua Potable y Alcantarillado del Municipio de Aguascalientes.

holds must have the ability to meet their water demands despite the rising cost of provision related to resource depletion.

In Aguascalientes, the change in water pricing was the most contentious change that resulted from privatisation, leading to substantial protest from poorer populations, ensuring that water servicing has become one of the most highly politicised issues in local politics. The inability of the IBT policy to effectively meet the needs of the population is demonstrated by the high number of poor households falling into arrears and being disconnected from the network. Although the conventional wisdom behind promoting these tariffs is that the differentiated pricing structure will help the poor, the following attempts to demonstrate its shortcomings in practice.

The true cost of water is set at US$8.94 (minus the rate of 20% which is taken by the concession), the price paid by the Category B 'middle' households. Category C communities then pay US$13.65, which represents close to twice the level paid by Category A for the initial 10 m³ block, at US$7.05 (see Fig. 8.1). This pricing proportion is comparable to situations in other parts of Latin America. For instance, in Cordoba, Argentina, there is a 'zone coefficient' where poorer households pay slightly more than 50% of the monthly charge of wealthier households (Johnstone *et al.* 1999).

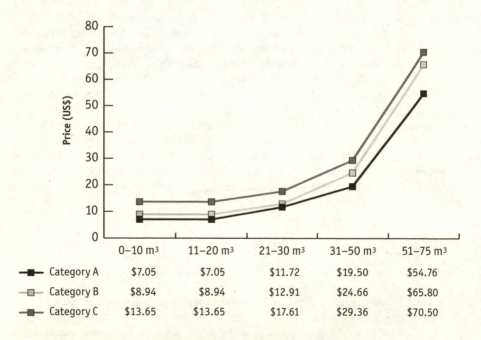

	0–10 m³	11–20 m³	21–30 m³	31–50 m³	51–75 m³
Category A	$7.05	$7.05	$11.72	$19.50	$54.76
Category B	$8.94	$8.94	$12.91	$24.66	$65.80
Category C	$13.65	$13.65	$17.61	$29.36	$70.50

Per block unit of water

FIGURE 8.1 Increasing block tariff rates up to 75 m³ (in US$, January 2003 rates)

Market-based approaches, such as the 50% price reduction for targeted poor communities, are often not successful in making water affordable to all, as they do not take into account the fact that many households are disproportionately poor. Because water is a basic need, typically lower-income households spend a large proportion of their disposable household income paying for water (Johnstone *et al.* 1999). In Mexico City, the lowest-income households typically spend just over 5% of their total expenditure on water services, relative to just over 1.5% for the highest (Johnstone *et al.* 1999). Extreme disparity between household incomes demonstrates potential conflicts in pricing policies such as the IBT and the difficulty in co-ordinating the needs of the population in one policy.

The argument that the use of subsidies is necessary in order to include a social component in tariffs (Hardoy and Schusterman 2000) is valid in the case of Aguascalientes due to the high cost of extraction. Generally, subsidies that could facilitate payment structures in Aguascalientes include (1) a direct subsidy that would involve payment by the government to supplement tariffs or other water charges for residential customers; and (2) methods of indirect subsidy in which the higher tariffs are used to supplement lower tariffs.

Direct subsidies are typically successful in that they target poor residents transparently, and they also give concessions an incentive to serve the poor. Additionally, this method is effective as the government is responsible for co-ordinating social welfare measures; it is argued that actions for incorporating social objectives are best taken at government level. The 'water stamps' scheme in Santiago, Chile, where low-income households are simply and directly subsidised for water needs, can be viewed as a successful example of this (Gleick *et al.* 2002). In this case, vouchers are allocated to cover a portion of the purchase of the first block of water consumption to households requesting the subsidy, whose socioeconomic condition is verified by the local authority. After verification, households are classified, providing priority for the poorest.

A similar but more complicated system operates in Aguascalientes. The system targets pensioned, retired or elderly customers, but is also solicited to supplement poor households' tariffs. The method of targeting households is similar to the Santiago case; however, subsidies in this case are given for a set amount of time; CAASA gives a discount on the water bill, and the corresponding amount is then ultimately reimbursed from the municipal budget. The use of this programme to assist Category A customers is minimal (35% of the funds of the programme is given to poor households, despite a very high number of requests) and the inability of the scheme to meet the needs of the poor effectively is evident through the number of cuts made daily to water connections for non-payment.

One possible explanation why this programme is not expanded could be because indirect subsidy methods (such as through cross-subsidisation through IBT use) are more heavily relied on to meet the needs of customers. The assumption that richer customers' higher water consumption habits at the higher priced blocks can effectively subsidise low-income groups has been criticised for various reasons (Boland and Whittington 1997). A limitation to this view is that maximum possible subsidies arising from this process are likely to be small and are highly dependent on the poor household using the first block of water (Boland and Whittington 1997), which may not occur. In Garn's discussion, as referenced in Hardoy and Schusterman 2000, it was found that cross-subsidies are risky for various reasons: their use obscures the true cost and thus distorts the tariff; they have the potential to hamper economic activity because the additional costs of covering the cross-subsidy are borne by business and industry; they lead to distortions in the use of water and conflicting messages put to the user; and high-income groups will find ways of not paying for these subsidies.

An opportunity for a more 'pro-poor' approach to pricing water would be reflected in a process that generates clear information on poor households' typical water use before tariffing policies are implemented, with the role of local government as regulator in social priorities clearly outlined. This comprehensive approach would involve obtaining specific details that define the situations and conditions typically representative of a poor household. These include researching proportions of household income spent on water compared with household demographic information, and the realities of water use in poor households, which may include shared connections and supplements from outside vendors. A process of information generation on poorer households' socioeconomic conditions would also promote an informed method of defining eligibility criteria for households that request direct subsidies.

8.4.2 Determining the volumes to be tariffed

The ability of an IBT to deliver on its promise of effectively targeting the poor depends on the tariff designer's success in setting the volume of water of the initial block equal to a household's essential water needs (Boland and Whittington 1997). A successful process should be flexible to reflect different domestic uses for water, including a consideration of livelihood aspects, combined with household demographics of such groups. By assigning the same volume to all households, the IBT does not reflect this flexibility and the fact that the size of the first block is the same for a household of two or ten demonstrates further its inability to meet the essential needs of each household it is meant to serve.

Despite this, for the purposes of comparison, a basic consumption requirement of 4–5 m^3 per month will be used; most international surveys suggest that this amount is required to sustain a household of five people in the South (Bellamy 1999).[7] Hence, the first block of 10 m^3 represents twice the daily requirement for basic water consumption for the average household. In many cases the volume of the first block is in excess of essential needs, demonstrating potential conflicts for politicians and the private operator to restrict the size of the initial block in an IBT structure. A larger volume benefits upper-income households who have more intensive water needs such as operating household appliances, watering gardens and washing cars.

The fact that IBT structures do not adequately take into account household demographics and water use is important when evaluating how this system allows for cross-subsidy to occur and also creates implications for water efficiency. These two

---

7   This figure was chosen because in Aguascalientes in 2000 the average family size was actually 4.5 people (INEGI [Institute Nacional de Estadistica Geografia e Informatica], 2002), although in poorer households the average may be slightly higher.

aspects are the strong points in the promotion of an IBT structure, so their evaluation is essential. If the first block is only partially consumed by a poor household, while richer households consume the full block of the cheapest tariff, then the poor households do not take advantage of the full cross-subsidy provided by the higher tariffs paid by Category C households. This structure could prompt customers to use more water than is necessary to consume the entire first block, which would contradict principles of sustainability.

8.4.3 Incorporating efficiency incentives

Promoting water conservation has the potential to contribute significantly to sustainable water management, and this aspect of policy is an area in which the criticality of water scarcity issues is effectively addressed. Typically, managers of water, whether they are public or private, have had weak and ad hoc means to promote water efficiency. In fact, the idea of efficiency—to reduce water consumption—would also reduce revenues, so there is often very little incentive to promote water efficiency (Johnstone and Wood 2001).

Mechanisms put directly to the private company, which encourage the concession to treat water efficiently, often result in this value being passed on to the residential customer so that all users are ultimately prompted to conserve scarce resources. However, in many water-scarce areas, water providers are not required to pay the full scarcity value of water, which means that service providers have little incentive to ration or allocate based on scarcity (Johnstone *et al.* 2001). CAASA pays a rate of US$26.52 for each 1,000 m³ unit of water extracted, to the National Water Commission (CNA), a rate that is based on a national system of poverty grading, not on water availability, despite the fact that the price of extraction is higher in zones of scarcity. Such a minimal rate is not restrictive to the private sector, although this does highlight the potential conflict between poverty and efficiency incentives.

Another approach for promoting efficiency is to reduce unaccounted-for water (UAW); it is reported that 50% of water extracted from aquifers is lost due to failing and obsolete infrastructure and poor maintenance. This goal is addressed in the concession contract, which includes a specific target to reduce UAW from 50% in seven years. This gives an incentive to the private sector to improve infrastructure, although it is recognised that the municipal government has the responsibility to work together with the concession to reduce this level. Despite this ambitious initiative, the crisis of failing infrastructure persists. In addition, it was stipulated in the original contract that the concession would treat waste-water for re-use, but this had not occurred at the time of writing. A public education campaign has been undertaken, but in order to address fundamental behaviour change these actions must occur in a supportive policy environment where wasteful use is discouraged consistently.

8.5 Quality of servicing

There are many ways in which overall quality can be defined and hence evaluated, as the term encompasses a range of concepts and is often relative. However, typically within service contracts, quality of service can address such elements as water pressure, continuity of supply and water quality (Rivera 1996). The issue of quality, most effectively being judged by the customer, was directly addressed to a number of poor households located in Category A communities. Overwhelmingly, it was found that, in a high proportion of households visited by the authors, the service provider was not known, although all customers in these communities felt that the water price was too high, and could identify when their households encountered difficulties paying for water around the time that PSP occurred. This aspect is supported by a formal study initiated by the Municipality of Aguascalientes in which it was found that 42.8% of the population did not know what entity is responsible for water services. This alludes to a clear lack of presence and client–service provider relationship, and that to date the privatisation process has not been accountable to the citizens it serves, a very common argument against privatisation.

Although increased information generation would better inform the process of designing local water pricing policies, a participatory approach should also be heavily promoted in order to enhance sustainability aspects. A very significant aspect of poverty is related to the ability of people to express and empower themselves with respect to local political issues, and inadequate service provision further deepens poverty as insecure household conditions lead to inadequate living conditions.

Respondents also had concerns about continuity and reliability of supply; households in poor areas typically only receive water in the mornings, and because of this several households responded that they were not receiving sufficient water to sustain their families. This is despite the large first block of water allotment, which is thus not available at all times to many poor households who are not able to fund storage devices to allow for continuous water supply when services are cut.

Deteriorating water quality has also created increased challenges for the poor, and is directly related to scarcity. Increased drilling depths at which water is extracted have led to very high concentrations of fluoride in aquifers; some local samples have yielded concentrations higher than that permitted by the Official Mexican Guidelines (Norma Oficial Mexicana).[8] There are very few incentives to the private company to address long-term health problems associated with this naturally occurring contaminant. In Aguascalientes, water quality is deteriorating despite increasing costs. This has a direct effect on the poor in particular, as the additional cost required to purify water with the household, or, alternatively, to buy drinking water from private vendors, is prohibitive and consequently many use the water for household purposes without treating it first.

---

8   The average concentration of fluoride is 1.6 mg/l; however, some samples have been found containing up to 4 mg/l. Mexican guidelines warn against concentrations higher than 1.5 mg/l.

Another important aspect of service quality is billing, as these arrangements greatly affect how customers attain water under private servicing. Typically, billing arrangements corresponding to IBT accommodate those with secure financial arrangements, as they are based on a system of monthly payments, a system that does not accommodate many poorer households with insecure incomes. In order to pay monthly bills, there must be some sort of financial security in the form of savings. Billing arrangements need to reflect a reduced time-frame which more realistically allow households living in poverty to fund supplies.

8.6 Conclusion: a strategy for sustainable water management

Overall, the question of whether privatisation has been successful in the case of Aguascalientes is relative. In certain respects, the involvement of the private sector has led to increases in efficiency and access—both substantial achievements. Despite this, it is evident that, based on the aims stated at the outset of this chapter, PSP in the case of Aguascalientes has not adequately addressed sustainability: environmentally, users are locked into a cycle of wasteful water use and, socially, PSP enhances the widening gap between rich and poor. Especially under conditions of monopoly, and including the added dimension of water scarcity, there is great potential for the poorest populations to suffer adverse consequences and for the perspective of long-term sustainable management of resources to be overlooked.

A substantial achievement in measuring social effects is based on the argument that water is a human right and a basic need, which affirms that populations should be ensured a minimum amount of safe water. It is obvious that substantial challenges occur frequently among marginalised populations, evidenced in the frequency of cuts to poor households due to the high price, and the poor quality of service.

Based on the experiences of Aguascalientes, there are many opportunities presented where operations can be improved according to the principles of sustainability. Some of those addressed include:

1. Recognise water as a fundamental **human right**, and ensure a basic amount of good-quality water is guaranteed to all households. This amount should be clearly defined and guaranteed as a high-priority use before more water is provided to other customers for non-essential uses. To address this, the IBT structure could either accommodate poor households through free or low-priced first block.

2. Only beyond this amount may water be **priced**, but with improvements to the pricing policy. Processes should strongly adhere to principles of water conservation and equitable allocation during all stages. More-innovative strategies could be explored such as adjusting prices according to household size and income level.

3. The concession contract should clearly reflect **environmental and social objectives**. The local government should have enhanced abilities to regulate and intervene when these priorities are compromised.

4. When the basic amount cannot be paid by certain groups because of poverty, then the use of **subsidies** to supplement payment for basic amounts should be analysed and discussed in public (Gleick *et al.* 2002). This should be an open and visible process, clearly targeting stakeholders and should be designed to give a strong incentive to make it profitable to serve the poor.

5. Cuts to water servicing should be reserved for delinquent customers, and not to households that are simply unable to pay because of restrictions inflicted by poverty. The **billing period** should be changed to a timeframe shorter than one month if necessary.

6. The regulatory body (i.e. the municipality) should have a stronger mandate to ensure sustainability. There should be identified areas for **public–private-sector participation** in achieving shared goals, such as in the example of reducing unaccounted-for water.

7. Identify areas where **public participation** in the privatisation process can occur, where citizens can identify concerns and methods of providing a better service. This would create a stronger customer–service provider relationship, and would enhance service quality, as well as substantiate an important step for the private service provider to demonstrate accountability.

8. **Generate information** on household demographics, income patterns and household consumption in water use, in order to better inform pricing and allocation policy. In many cases, tariff policies tend to be based on inadequate knowledge (Yepes 1999). Specialised research would support an understanding of how the three different income groups utilise water and a demonstration that low-income households typically use a fraction of the first block would stimulate incentives to reframe allocation policies.

A very unfortunate outcome of PSP in Aguascalientes has been the inability of the local government to react against the concession with respect to these very obvious faults. Further, to break the contract is virtually impossible as the very high cost of the penalty is prohibitive. It is apparent that the lack of competition resulting from the monopoly has also contributed greatly to these flaws. The extent to which CAASA can adequately address harmful effects on marginalised populations and the rapidly depleting resource base depends to a great extent on its ability in the future to address 'local' needs. Only through a more comprehensive process of determining tariffs, widespread use of subsidies, allowing for efficiency incentives to be incorporated into policies, and more attention paid to quality of servicing of the poor could they ultimately contribute to a wider development framework in Aguascalientes. It is critical that, if PSP is to continue, different paradigms are developed in order to provide for a more equitable distribution of existing resources in the most sustainable manner possible.

Bibliography

Adams, W.M. (2001) *Green Development: Environment and Sustainability in the Third World* (London: Routledge, 2nd edn).

Anton, D.J. (1993) *Thirsty Cities: Urban Environments and Water Supply in Latin America* (Ottawa: International Development Research Council).

Appleton, B., and B. Chatterjee (2001) 'Innovative Strategies for Water and Sanitation for the Poor: Access and Affordability', thematic background paper, *Bonn International Conference on Freshwater*, Bonn, Germany.

Barlow, M., and T. Clarke (2002) *Blue Gold: The Battle against Corporate Theft of the World's Water* (Toronto: Stoddart).

Bellamy, R. (1999) 'Rethinking Municipal Water Tariffs', International Development Research Council, Ottawa, www.idrc.ca/reports/read_article_english.cfm?article_num=328.

Boland, J.J., and D. Whittington (1997) 'The Political Economy of Increasing Block Tariffs in Developing Countries', in A. Dinar (ed.), *The Political Economy of Water Pricing Reforms* (New York: Oxford University Press).

Brooks, D.B. (2002) *Water: Local Level Management* (Ottawa: International Development Research Council).

Calder, I.R. (1999) *The Blue Revolution: Land Use and Integrated Water Resources Management* (London: Earthscan Publications).

Dinar, A. (ed.) (2000) *The Political Economy of Water Pricing Reforms* (New York: Oxford University Press).

—— and A. Subramanian (1997) *Water Pricing Experiences: An International Perspective* (World Bank Technical Paper No. 386; Washington, DC: World Bank).

Gleick, P.H., G. Wolff and E.L. Chalecki (2002) *The Risks and Benefits of Globalization and Privatisation of Fresh Water* (Oakland, CA: The Pacific Institute).

Gutierrez, E. (2001) *Framework Document: A Survey of the Theoretical Issues on Private Sector Participation in Water and Sanitation* (London: WaterAid and Tear Fund).

Haggerty, L., P. Brook and A.M. Zuluaga (2001) *Thirst for Reform? Private Sector Participation in Providing Mexico City's Water Supply* (World Bank Policy Research Working Paper 2654; Washington, DC: World Bank Development Research Group).

Hardoy, A., and R. Schusterman (2000) 'New Models for the Privatization of Water and Sanitation for the Urban Poor', *Environment and Urbanization* 12.2 (October 2000): 63-75.

Idelovich, E., and K. Ringskog (1995) *Private Sector Participation in Water Supply and Sanitation in Latin America* (Washington, DC: World Bank).

IDRC (International Development Research Council) (2002) Local Water Management Program, www. idrc.ca/water.

Johnstone, N. (1997) *Economic Inequality and the Urban Environment: The Case of Water and Sanitation* (London: International Institute of Environment and Development).

—— and L. Wood (eds.) (2001) *Private Firms and Public Water: Realising Social and Environmental Objectives in Developing Countries* (Cheltenham, UK: Edward Elgar).

——, —— and R. Hearne (1999) *The Regulation of Private Sector Participation in Urban Water Supply and Sanitation: Realising Social and Environmental Objectives in Developing Countries* (London: International Institute of Environment and Development).

Kemper, K.E., and D. Olson (2000) 'Water Pricing: The Dynamics of Institutional Change in Mexico and Ceara, Brazil', in A. Dinar (ed.), *The Political Economy of Water Pricing Reforms* (New York: Oxford University Press).

Nickson, A., and R. Franceys (2001) 'Tapping the Market: Can Private Enterprise Supply Water to the Poor?', *Insights* 37 (June 2001).

Ozuna, T., Jr, and I.A. Gomez (1999) 'Governance and Regulation: Decentralization in Mexico's Water Sector', in *Spilled Water: Institutional Commitment in the Provision of Water Services* (Washington, DC: Latin American Research Network, Inter-American Development Bank).

Pablos, N.P. (1999) 'Actores sociales y distribución de costos y beneficios en la privatización del agua potable en Aguascalientes', *Ciudades. Revista Trimestral de la Red Nacional de Investigación Urbana* 43 (July–September 1999): 57-63.

Rivera, D. (1996) *Private Sector Participation in Water Supply and Sanitation: Lessons from Six Developing Countries* (World Bank Directions in Development; Washington, DC: World Bank).

Saade Hazin, L. (2001) 'Private Sector Participation in Water Supply and Sanitation: Realising Social and Environmental Objectives in Mexico DF', in N. Johnstone and L. Wood (eds.), *Private Firms and Public Water: Realising Social and Environmental Objectives in Developing Countries* (Cheltenham, UK: Edward Elgar).

Savedoff, W., and P. Spiller (1999) *Spilled Water: Institutional Commitment in the Provision of Water Services* (Washington, DC: Latin American Research Network, Inter-American Development Bank).

Swyngedouw, E.A. (1995) 'The Contradictions of Urban Water Provision: A Study of Guayquil, Ecuador', *Third World Planning Review* 17.4: 387-403.

Yepes, G. (1999) *Do Cross-Subsidies Help the Poor to Benefit From Water and Wastewater?* (UNDP– World Bank Water and Sanitation Program).

9

Joint-use municipal–industrial infrastructure

AN INNOVATIVE APPROACH TO EXPANDING URBAN WATER SERVICES IN THE DEVELOPING WORLD

Jennifer Bremer

University of North Carolina at Chapel Hill, USA

Steven Nebiker

HydroLogics Inc., USA

The urgent need to expand water and waste-water services for the world's growing cities makes it imperative to seek new and creative solutions for the mobilisation of water services investment. The core barriers facing such investment are not technical but financial: whether the implementor is a municipality or a private company, municipal water services, particularly waste-water, have proven extremely difficult to finance.

Innovative approaches are needed to mobilise investment to fill this gap. One such approach is joint-use municipal–industrial (JUMI) infrastructure. This approach calls attention to the existence of a wealth of opportunities to incorporate water and/or waste-water services for nearby municipalities within private industrial facilities or to facilitate such services as an adjunct to, or as a substitute for, treatment within the industrial operation. By taking advantage of these opportunities on a systematic basis, private-sector industry can help meet the shared need of municipalities and major industrial facilities to increase the security of water supply, expand water treatment and ensure the sustainability of towns, industries and their surrounding environments.

JUMI has not been recognised as a specific approach, but applications combining industrial and urban services have been used extensively in a wide variety of settings, as the examples in this chapter demonstrate. Although these JUMI applications have been ad hoc, their success indicates that JUMI merits consideration as a valuable adjunct to the principles of 'green design'. The JUMI approach makes companies proactive partners with municipalities in meeting the water needs of their communities. By applying JUMI principles in the development of new industrial facilities and retrofits, major industrial users of water have an opportunity to make a major contribution to enabling the world's cities and towns to meet water treatment and sanitation needs that would otherwise not be served for many years.

Although the JUMI approach cannot be implemented in every project, by every company or in every city, preliminary research presented here shows that it could readily be used in a variety of settings, if two sets of measures are implemented. First, if JUMI were to be systematically documented, recognised as a standard component of 'green design' and actively considered when new industrial facilities or plant upgrades are being designed, then, in this way, many economically and technically attractive opportunities to apply the JUMI approach would be identified. Second, major corporations should make a commitment to take advantage of such opportunities whenever technical and economic considerations favour their use. If these two measures are implemented, water and waste-water treatment services could be made available to many urban residents who now suffer a lack of such services.

JUMI is far from a 'silver bullet' to close the investment gap. In view of the huge shortage in water and sanitation services in the developing world, however, no approach that can help to close the gap should be overlooked. Neither the public sector nor the private sector can meet the challenge of providing water services to the world's cities. Only the combined impact of many different approaches, applied creatively in different circumstances across the globe, can make a dent in the huge backlog of needed investment. It is in this context of diversified and situation-specific response that an approach such as JUMI can have the potential to make an important contribution.

In the next section we introduce the JUMI concept; in Section 9.2 we review experience with a number of projects identified as using this type of approach and in Section 9.3 we draw lessons learned from this preliminary experience. In Section 9.4 we look at the future for the JUMI approach.

9.1 Joint-use municipal–industrial infrastructure: a promising approach to meeting municipal water service needs

A promising approach to promoting private investment in the water and waste-water sector is to incorporate municipal water and waste-water treatment into large-scale industrial projects or facilities. This co-treatment approach could most readily be included in major water-using industrial facilities, such as refineries, chemical plants, pulp and paper mills, sugar factories, mining facilities, agribusiness plants and beverage facilities.

This approach, which we have termed joint-use municipal–industrial infrastructure, or JUMI, has the potential to be modified to encompass a wide range of commercial and quasi-commercial circumstances.

- At one end of the continuum are projects that can be justified along purely commercial terms, which enable companies to meet waste-water treatment and water supply needs more cheaply than they otherwise would by pairing their efforts with those of the municipality that hosts them.

- At the other end of the continuum are projects that offer an effective and attractive way for a company to comply with expectations for community involvement that cannot be justified on commercial grounds. Given the high cost of treatment facilities and their long-term nature, purely philanthropic projects will be rare, but there would appear to be many opportunities for companies to help meet the water needs of their communities at very low cost to the company. Companies might supply bulk clean water to schools or hospitals, for example, taking advantage of excess treatment capacity in their own systems.

- Somewhere in the middle are projects that generate commercial advantage partly from pure cost savings and partly from their positive impact on community relations. Where companies face pressure from local stakeholders to demonstrate their commitment to the communities' well-being, a JUMI project may offer an attractive way to combine social and environmental responsibility, reduce local opposition to the project and link the industrial facility more closely with the communities' own needs.

Although JUMI has not previously been identified as a coherent strategy, countless examples exist of water initiatives in industry that indirectly benefit the community, such as through the treatment and recycling of industrial effluent in ways that help preserve scarce water resources for other users. By systematically seeking opportunities to use JUMI principles in the design of new facilities and the optimisation of existing facilities, companies could develop an industry initiative that would, taken on aggregate, significantly increase access to water and waste-water services across the world's communities.

One of the most promising areas for such collaboration is in the area of project finance, which is a complex and difficult challenge in municipal water projects. Leveraging industry's creditworthiness to secure financing for municipal treatment projects offers an overlooked means of capitalising on the strong projected growth levels for the industrial treatment market.

Mexico offers a number of concrete examples where JUMI principles have been used to meet local water needs. These experiences, described at greater length in Section 9.2.1, highlight four drivers for industrial water treatment on which municipalities can capitalise to further joint-use projects:

- **Enhanced commercial feasibility.** Compared with municipal project sponsors, private companies providing water services to private clients are able to generate higher revenues from treatment and are more likely to be paid for their services, raising project sustainability and, therefore, financiability.

- **Large projected need for treatment.** Despite the new projects planned for the industrial sector in Mexico (such as those associated with Pemex; see Section 9.2.1), 72% of the total industrial discharges remained untreated as of 1996 (WEEA 1995). Progress in expanding treatment has been rapid but, as of 2001, the vast majority of industrial (and municipal) discharges remained untreated (HDC Consulting 2001).

- **Increased pressure for environmental reform.** Liberalised trade commitments (e.g. the North American Free Trade Agreement [NAFTA]), public relations and regulatory pressures are prompting companies to invest in environmental programmes for their production facilities. Future industrialisation and potential expansion of agrochemical use to achieve food security are likely to have serious future consequences for water quality, including increased toxic contamination of the coastal and marine environment. In Mexico, industry generates three times the biological oxygen demand (BOD) generated by urban areas (HDC Consulting 2001).

- **Cost savings and reliability improvement.** Many of the treatment programmes that enable industrial facilities to reduce the treatment burden on municipalities, such as waste-water re-use, can also improve the reliability of the manufacturer's water supply and lower the overall cost of production. This is especially true when raw water is priced at its economic cost.

There is a need for a systematic effort to identify and document the most effective joint-use approaches, to raise the profile of industrial–municipal projects and to promote more active consideration of such use by municipalities and companies alike.

In this chapter we begin this process. In the next section we briefly document a number of successful applications of industry involvement in co-treatment with municipalities, both in developing countries and in Europe and the USA. The examples shown are in all probability only the tip of the iceberg. There may well be a much larger number of such initiatives that have been undertaken at the local level that the preliminary research reported here failed to identify. Building on these examples, in Section 9.3 we identify lessons learned from the experience to date and suggest additional steps to promote use of JUMI co-treatment strategies to expand coverage of urban water and waste-water treatment needs.

The research reported here grew out of our work with the Environmental Technologies Trade Advisory Committee (ETTAC), a federal advisory committee overseen by the US Department of Commerce (USDC) and with a US firm, Poseidon Resources (in Stamford, CT). Through this work and other professional contacts, we became familiar with Poseidon's successful development of several privately financed waste-water projects in Mexico. Such projects are virtually unknown in the developing world and therefore clearly merited further analysis to identify the model underlying them and to determine whether it had broader application. As further described in the next section, the Poseidon projects were developed jointly with Pemex (Mexico's oil industry parastatal), municipalities hosting Pemex refineries and private investors. These projects are further detailed in Section 9.2.1.

Building on this initial example, we searched for other cases by contacting a number of multinationals and professionals in the industry and reviewing information in the literature and on the World Wide Web. A number of other examples were identified and are also reported below, in Section 9.2.2. This research has only begun the work of identifying experience with JUMI approaches and transforming these ad hoc applications into replicable models, but it suggests the direction in which this work might proceed.

9.2 Joint-use municipal–industrial applications from international and US experience

9.2.1 Pemex and municipal waste-water treatment in Mexico

To address water management concerns, the Mexican government passed major environmental reforms in the mid-1990s. The legislation was in response to pressure from the country's NAFTA partners as well as to increasing competition by industrial users for use of limited local water supplies. Pemex Refinación, the refining subsidiary of Pemex, was one of the first industrial concerns to be directed by the government to conserve water, reduce industrial waste-water discharges and thus minimise water pollution (Sondy and Shah 1999).

Refinación implemented a waste-water treatment programme in 1994 consisting of treatment and recycling of effluent from each of its refineries (Salamanca, Salina Cruz, Cadereyta, Madero, Tula and Minatitlan) as well as collection and treatment of waste-water from selective local municipalities. All six treatment plants are in operation, treating a combined flow of 2,500 litres per second (216 million litres per day) at a total cost of US$174 million.

Most refineries already had in place pre-treatment facilities that were designed to remove hydrocarbons from the effluent by using oil separators and flotation units. After pre-treatment, the waste-stream is treated in oxidation ponds and then pumped into the new treatment facilities for removal of nitrogen, sulphur and organic materials. The treatment goal is to reduce water consumption while enhancing the re-use of the reclaimed waste-water for cooling-tower make-up (which often accounts for a significant percentage of historical water consumption [Baron *et al.* 2000]). By treating municipal waste-water, Refinación assures itself of a reliable water supply. It also avoids discharging effluent into the receiving streams, thus reducing urban pollution.

The project details are summarised in Table 9.1. Refinación submitted five of the required treatment facilities as build–own–transfer (BOT) schemes through competitive bid. The average project cost was approximately US$30 million. The size and complexity of these projects led to the formation of consortia that typically included a local construction firm, a foreign environmental engineering firm and investors. All winners were Mexican-led consortia (Sondy and Shah 1999).

	Refinery					
	Cadereyta	Madero	Minatitlan	Salina Cruz	Tula	Salamanca
Project sponsor	GEMA Consor-tium	GEMA Consortium	Aguas	Degremont	Aguas Tratadas de Tula	Pemex
Cost of plant (US$ millions)	26.5	27.5	39.8	40.6	15.7	24.1
Treatment capacity (litres per second)	655	154	340 + 110[a]	100 + 156[b]	240	495 + 255[a]

a municipal   b seawater   GEMA = Grupo Empresarial de Mejoramiento Ambiental S.A. de C.V.

TABLE 9.1 Project details of Pemex refinery treatment, Mexico

Source: Suarez 2002

In late 1994, however, the Mexican peso was devalued, which forced a restruc-turing of the projects. The contractors' own financial resources were jeopardised because their debts were denominated in dollars and new sources of debt essentially became unavailable. The contractors began looking to international water companies such as Poseidon Resources to participate as partners in order to access international sources of equity and debt. Through this process, Poseidon has become the largest US investor in the Mexican water sector.

Implementation of the waste-water treatment programme has reduced Pemex's raw water consumption by almost 38 million m³ (38 billion litres) per year (Biswas and Tortajada 2001). A significant amount of savings is derived from agreements to use municipal waste-water as an alternative source of raw water. This waste-water is treated at the refinery treatment plant along with the refinery's other waste-water flows. For the Cadereyta plant, untreated waste-water is purchased from the local utilities in Monterrey.[1] Monterrey has the capacity to treat all of its waste-water, but has discovered a mutually beneficial option in selling some of it to the Cadereyta refinery. At the other refineries that receive municipal waste-water, the local utilities are offered no payment. However, the agreement is again mutually beneficial because the city would otherwise be unable to treat the waste-water because of capacity constraints, and Pemex gets a reliable source of water in return.

These projects generally have been viewed as the best investment opportunities available in the Mexican water sector. There are many reasons for this (Sondy and Shah 1999):

- **Pemex has a strong credit rating and experience with risk allocation in project financings.** Its strong credit rating reduced risk to lenders. Also, Refinación structured its treatment outsourcing programme to pro-vide an equitable distribution of risks between itself and the service providers.

---

1   Infante, Lic., Servicio de Agua y Drenaje de Monterrey (SADM), personal communication, 2002

- **The project sponsors were able to minimise risks.** The winning consortium was able to structure the engineering, procurement and construction (EPC), O&M (operation and management) and equity–debt arrangements separately.

- **Refinación assumed a majority of the operating and construction risks.** Refinación's refineries are dependent on the waste-water treatment facilities for treated water to sustain the refinery operations. For this reason, Refinación included in the service agreement a provision whereby, in the event of a material construction or operational failure, Refinación has a right to terminate the service agreement and is then obligated to purchase the facilities.

- **Refinación assumed a currency risk.** As a global exporter of crude oil, Refinación can raise capital in many foreign currencies. This allowed developers to seek out the cheapest debt financing available in the markets and then bid tariffs in the appropriate currencies for reimbursement of debt costs as well as equity returns without requiring the use of long-term foreign currency hedges.

- **Refinación's high standard of management in the bidding process encouraged innovative responses.** To encourage companies to fulfil their commitments, Refinación required security instruments during the bidding and construction phases of the projects. The size of the instruments struck a balance between affording Refinación protection and encouraging bidders to participate. In contrast, some municipal bids in Mexico have required that developers guarantee as much as 100% of project costs to secure their bids.

By harnessing private-sector innovation, Refinación has benefited from lower treatment tariffs and better technological solutions; at the same time, investors and lenders have been able to achieve attractive returns relative to the level of risk they assumed (Sondey *et al.* 1999: 2). Most importantly, Refinación has avoided regulatory action that can lead to stiff financial penalties. Also, Pemex has lowered its fees for water use and discharge (although this has yet to be quantified). In Mexico, water use tariffs cover use from surface water and groundwaters, including utility-provided potable water. Discharge tariffs are determined by volume, BOD and total suspended solids above the standard. By re-using waste-water produced by the refinery and the local community, the refinery (and community) benefit through lower tariffs. (WEEA 1992). Table 9.2 provides an overview of the benefits of the Pemex co-treatment approach.

Whereas Pemex projects have been a success, the municipal water market has struggled, largely because of financing obstacles. The major reason is concern about the creditworthiness of Mexican municipalities. Municipalities are very dependent on federal tax receipts since tax collection in Mexico is centralised. Also, municipal water companies often subsidise their water users, meaning their financial solvency is in turn dependent on federal subsidies. In order to finance water projects, municipal credits are thus heavily reliant on the payment guarantee programme for water projects provided by the National Public Works Bank of Mexico

Pemex Refinación (off-taker)	Community	Government	EPC, O&M and equipment contractors	Project sponsors, investors, and lending agencies
Additional supply of water (increased reliability) cost of disposal	Additional source of revenue and/or lower the cost of treatment	Reduced stress on water supplies	Healthy financial returns	Attractive, stable, long-term financial returns
Environmental compliance	Delayed capital expenditure	Increased sanitation coverage in city	Increased likelihood of payment	Diversification effect
Reduced risk and life-cycle costs through outsourcing	Increased water supply and reduced pollution	Potentially reduced financial support of municipal waste-water utility	Large projects increase opportunity for US participation	Non-recourse financing
Water use and discharge fees		More competitive bidding, greater participation, and better risk sharing		Promotes the needed investment in the water and sanitation sectors

BANOBRAS = National Public Works Bank of Mexico
EPC = engineering, procurement and construction
O&M = operations and management

TABLE 9.2 Direct benefits and assumptions of the Pemex co-treatment approach for different stakeholders

(BANOBRAS; see Sondey *et al.* 1999). This bank offers infrastructure loans and grants and payment-support mechanisms to promote private investment.

9.2.2 Other joint-use municipal–industrial applications

Although JUMI has not previously been identified as a specific approach, interviews with industry representatives and a review of the professional literature indicate that JUMI applications have been used on an ad hoc basis in a number of industries, ranging from agribusiness to oil refineries. The following examples indicate the range of such experience and suggest the potential for expanded use of the JUMI approach to expand capacity for water and waste-water treatment in developing world urban applications.

Agribusiness, Hungary

In 1992 the Swiss agribusiness multinational Nestlé bought a factory in Hungary. At that time, the plant was discharging untreated waste-water into an open pond, creating environmental problems. Rather than building a waste-water plant serving the factory directly, Nestlé helped local authorities to build a waste-water treatment plant serving the whole city as well as the plant. To address the lack of available governmental funds, Nestlé advanced money to the city for construction. The new plant began operation in 1997, benefiting the entire community (Nestlé 2000: 44). Nestlé has also contributed to the local infrastructure serving communities around its factories in Poland and at Avanca, Portugal, making financial contributions to assist in the construction of water piping and sewage systems (Nestlé 2000: 44).

Poultry industry, USA

In Chesapeake Bay the burgeoning poultry industry is under significant pressure to reduce pollution. To address this problem, two poultry processors, WLR (Wampler) Foods and Rocco/Shadybrook (ROCCO) joined with the towns of Broadway and Timberville to replace their conventional waste-water treatment systems with an innovative system, owned and operated by a third firm, Sheaffer International. The system eliminates more than 90,000 kg of nitrogen and phosphorus that would otherwise be discharged each year by the four community waste-water treatment plants into a river system in the Chesapeake Bay watershed, which is already heavily affected by eutrophication as a result of heavy nutrient inflows.

The system uses extended treatment times and natural biological processes to clean the water. This approach eliminates the generation of odours and sludge. The low remaining concentrations of nutrients in the water are compatible with the planned use for irrigation, with the additional benefit of increasing production of crops (some of which are then used to feed poultry, achieving nutrient recycling).

Sheaffer will operate the facility under contract for a minimum of 25 years. The affected towns, rather than facing the cost of building and maintaining new treatment plants to comply with state and federal clean water regulations, will have only to maintain their collection systems and pay a service fee based on their use of the Sheaffer system. The two poultry processors will pay a service fee based on the strength and volume of their waste-water (ACB 1999).

In return for irrigation units, the landowners have given Sheaffer 25-year ease-ments to apply waste-water on their fields. Not only will this arrangement lead to higher crop yields but it will help preserve water in the rivers during low flow periods.

Desalination, USA

The desalination plant in Tampa, Florida, the biggest such facility in the Western hemisphere, is a good example of a private-sector effort to leverage the support and resources of industry to develop a municipal water treatment project. In order to make desalination cost-competitive with alternative sources of municipal water, the private sponsor, Poseidon Resources, used an innovative design that reduces the plant's operating costs by drawing on waste heat from an existing coastal power plant, owned by the Tampa Electric Company (TECO).

Under this innovative approach, TECO will lease an unused portion of its Big Bend power plant site to the project.[2] The desalination project will take as its input stream seawater that has already passed through Big Bend's condensers, enabling it to improve operating efficiency, reduce power consumption, increase the life of the membranes as a result of the lower viscosity of warm (post-condenser) water and reduce harm to fish or other marine life that might be caught up in the intake system. In addition, mixing the salty concentrate, a by-product of the desalination plant, with the large volumes of seawater (5.3 billion litres) discharged from the power plant significantly dilutes the desalination plant's discharge before it is returned to the bay. These planning and design measures have significantly reduced the costs of treatment and facilitated environmental compliance, to the benefit of the consumer and a regional economy heavily dependent on adequate water.

9.3 Lessons learned and issues related to expanded application of the joint-use municipal–industrial approach

Several factors emerge as needing consideration in developing successful JUMI applications, based on literature surveys, correspondence with environmental com-pliance officers at large corporations and project experiences.

9.3.1 Regulatory framework

A strong regulatory environment is needed to require industries to implement and maintain water use and quality targets through treatment. In Mexico, the institu-

---

2 This approach also avoids potential difficulties associated with siting the plant, which can be a major project barrier in today's environment of strong local opposition to large production facilities.

tion of water use and discharge tariffs has perhaps been the most important development in the industrial treatment market (WEEA 1992). At the same time, the regulatory framework should be sufficiently flexible to encourage companies to undertake environmental programmes without these programmes being administratively burdensome, resulting in a win–win situation for all parties. Pemex was able to avoid further regulatory action based on its significant commitment to improved water resource management.

9.3.2. Compatibility of municipal and industrial waste-streams

The characteristics of industrial effluents differ from those of municipal sewage and from industrial sector to another. One key difference is whether the effluents contain heavy metals and/or non-biodegradable organic pollutants that cannot be removed through conventional biological treatment of a typical municipal waste-water treatment plant. In that case, co-treatment of municipal and industrial waste-water may not make economic sense, since separate treatment facilities would be required for each waste-water stream.

JUMI co-treatment approaches are most appropriate for industries with high organic loadings, including the pulp and paper industry, food processors and beverage manufacturers.[3] Metal-based industries, such as those represented by Boeing and Alcoa, have less potential for JUMI approaches. Electronics facilities that are heavy users of highly treated water, however, may offer opportunities for JUMI approaches to potable water treatment. Regardless of water or waste needs, moreover, corporations from any industry can contribute to expanding urban facilities by mobilising financial resources, supporting engineering requirements or by making corporate philanthropic commitments.

An additional factor to consider is the potential for partially treated sanitary waste-water to present health problems for industrial plant workers, particularly in developing countries. Shell Oil, for example, chose not to treat municipal waste-water on its sites for fear of introducing infectious disease through employee exposure to bacteria in the re-used water.[4]

9.3.3 The size of the industrial plant and its proximity to the communities needing service

Most industrial plants that are close to population centres are small to medium in size. In such cases, it may be more cost-effective to discharge industrial pollutant loads to the municipal treatment plants. In the USA municipal facilities receive about 80% of industrial pollutants discharged to sewers (Smith-Vargo 1990). Large-scale industrial facilities, in contrast, are often located far from population centres. The transportation

---

3   Larry Weinberg, Environmental Administrator, Boeing Corporation, personal communication, 2002.
4   Anne Marie Van der Rest, Environmental Administrator, Shell Oil BV, personal communication, 2002.

of treated water or waste-water over long distances could make co-treatment cost prohibitive, particularly if the costs of energy needed for pumping is high.

9.3.4 Urgency of water supply or treatment needs

Corporations are increasingly recognising that access to water is an important strategic factor. It may shape their locational decisions, limit consumer markets for their products or lead to disputes with local communities. Community concern over declining water quality may also raise pressure on companies to expand waste-water treatment or to reduce their water use, regardless of whether the corporation actually accounts for a large share of the community's total water service needs. In such situations, use of JUMI approaches can be effective on technical and political grounds. JUMI has the potential to make municipal projects feasible that otherwise would not be, and to demonstrate that major industrial facilities are prepared to act as full members of the community.

9.3.5 Financial aspects of joint-use municipal–industrial applications

When municipal facilities do not exist (as is often the case in developing countries) or need upgrading industry may be better positioned to provide financial support for co-treatment at the municipal level rather than installing facilities itself. Such support can generate benefits both for the industrial corporation and for the municipality. Potential mechanisms for financial support to municipal projects include up-front financing assistance (as in the Hungarian case outlined in Section 9.2.2.1), co-guarantees of municipal financing or pledge of income and/or payment of higher-than-market user fees for treatment of industrial waste-water (cross-subsidisation).

Where co-treatment is attractive, the success of the approach will depend heavily on the financial arrangement between the different stakeholders:

- First, rational risk allocation among project participants promotes a strong project financial structure. It simplifies credit analysis by the prospective lender and, in a competitive bidding situation, encourages investors to bid aggressively. Risk allocation must address the need for appropriate buy-out provisions in the event of non-performance by one party or another.

- Second, currency protection for debt and equity investors that allow developers to lower the cost of capital may be necessary in developing countries. The Camdessus Commission Report, issued for the Third World Water Forum, calls for a devaluation liquidity facility to address the problem of large currency devaluations, which have crippled several private concession schemes (Winpenny 2003: 6). JUMI approaches may lessen the impact of devaluations, as in the Pemex case, by linking municipal projects to hard currency income sources (oil exports, in this case).

- Third, credit quality of the consumer (off-taker) is often a barrier to financing non-JUMI municipal projects and shapes lender perceptions of the likelihood of payment. In the Mexican and Hungarian examples described in Section 9.2, creditworthy firms (Pemex and Nestlé) provided financial support to the project, either as the customer or by serving as a lender with social as well as commercial concerns. In the Mexican case, the combination of Pemex's high credit rating, its extensive dollar-denominated transactions and its technical dependence on a reliable source of water combined to reduce the risk to investors. Incorporation of municipal treatment into industrial projects may also result in lowered risk, as more than one off-taker would be responsible for payment of services and community-relations risk to the industrial investor—increasingly recognised as a major source of project risk—might be reduced. However, issues of shared liability and differential creditworthiness of the various off-takers must also be considered and may work against the use of JUMI approaches where these differences cannot be resolved.

- Fourth, bilateral and multilateral development banks can help bridge the financing gap for private funding, especially early in the project launch process. In Mexico, for example, resources include the Inter-American Development Bank (IADB), the NADBank (a bilateral bank created by NAFTA) and bilateral or multilateral bank guarantees (Multilateral Investment Guarantee Agency [MIGA], Overseas Private Investment Corporation [OPIC] and so on). The incorporation of municipal services into an industrial project may make such projects more attractive to these public funders. There is increasing recognition that subsidies may be needed to keep water and waste-water tariffs for low-income municipal consumers at an affordable level, and lenders are increasingly willing to address this problem head-on, but JUMI projects may provide a way to reduce such subsidies through direct cross-subsidisation or flexibility on the part of the corporate investor in order to address corporate citizenship and community relations concerns, in addition to purely financial factors.

- Last, sovereign guarantees are often a prerequisite for non-recourse project financing in an emerging market but are difficult to obtain for many municipal projects. In Mexico and Turkey, for example, the federal government will generally not provide such guarantees to municipal projects, reflecting the policy that the project users—whether local governments or private-sector firms—should assume the project risk.[5] The lack of credit or credit enhancements such as sovereign guarantees for weak municipal project sponsors highlights the potential value of an approach such as JUMI, which enables the city to benefit from the high creditworthiness and low risk of corporate partners such as Pemex, Nestlé and Alcoa.

---

5   An exception in Mexico is the limited revolving credit facility through BANOBRAS, a public infrastructure bank, which can provide up to six months of payments to a concessionaire in the event the consumer or off-taker fails to make timely payments. This protection, however, is limited to projects with low credit risk (ITA 1996).

Dispute resolution and renegotiation provisions are critical for project success, particularly in view of the very long-term nature of water projects and the lack of competition inherent in the local water market. This is one of the areas where further work would be important if JUMI applications in developing countries are to grow.

9.4 Next steps for the implementation of joint-use municipal–industrial approaches

The foregoing discussion demonstrates that JUMI approaches hold considerable potential as a tool for making municipal water and waste-water projects both feasible and financially viable. In order to transform JUMI from an ad hoc approach applied by creative project developers, several steps are necessary. First, additional examples and their corporate sponsors should be identified. Second, these experiences should be documented so that other corporations and municipalities can take advantage of these approaches. Third, JUMI should be incorporated into the principles of 'green design', creating a mechanism to develop and disseminate the approach. Fourth, leading corporations might make a commitment to consider JUMI applications when they are developing facilities overseas and to encourage their suppliers, customers, licensees and joint-venture partners to do so.

Finally, the formation of informal partnerships (or 'collaboratory') could be helpful by bringing together multinationals in water-using industries, companies offering water treatment technology and services, the financial sector and municipal representatives to identify and share best practice for JUMI projects. Such a collaboratory could move JUMI into the sustainable enterprise mainstream by documenting JUMI processes, measuring the cost savings obtained, examining reputational or community-relations benefits and determining locational and technical factors associated with successful use of JUMI approaches.

References

ACB (Alliance for the Chesapeake Bay) (1999) 'Shenandoah Area Switches to Innovative Waste-water Treatment', *Bay Journal* 8.10 (www.bayjournal.com/newsite/article.cfm?article= 1028).

Baron, C., L. Equihua, and J. Mestre (2000) 'BOO Case: Water Management Project for the Use of Reclaimed Waste-water and Desalted Seawater for the "Antonio Dovali Jaime" Refinery, Salina Cruz, Oaxaca, Mexico', *Water Science and Technology* 42: 29–36.

Biswas, A., and C. Tortajada (2001) 'Environmental Management of Water Resources in Mexico', *Water International* 25.1.

HDC Consulting (2001) *Water in Mexico: Government Objectives and Opportunities for Private Investment* (HDC Consulting, Seminar Summary, Prepared for the Institute of the Americas, August 2001).

International Trade Administration (ITA) (1996) 'Finance Issues in the Environmental Sector', web.ita.doc.gov/ete/eteinfo.nsf, accessed February 2003.

Nestlé (2000) 'Nestlé Environment Progress Report', www.ir.nestle.com/NR/rdonlyres/43946C7B-327E-451C-BD8C-7C576BBCB998/0/2000_EnvironmentProgressReport.pdf, accessed February 2003.

Smith-Vargo, L. (1990) 'Difficult Waste-waters', *Water Engineering and Management*.

Sondy, E., and N. Shah, (1999) 'Development of the Mexican Water Sector', *Journal of Structured Finance* 1.9.

Suarez, P. 'Current Projects for Reducing Water Consumption in the Refinery of Petroleum', presentation to the Institute of the Americas Water Conference, Session on Projects in Latin America for Improved Water Management, 24 April 2002, San Diego, CA.

WEEA (World Energy Efficiency Association) (1992) 'Business Focus Series: Mexico's Environmental Markets', www.weea.org/USAID%20Reports/Documents/Mexican%20Market.pdf, accessed February 2003.

Winpenny, J. (2003) *Financing Water For All: Report of the World Panel on Financing Water Infrastructure* (the Camdessus Report; Geneva: World Water Council).

Part 3
Technology

10

Autonomous water supply of a remote island community
THE CASE OF GEOTHERMAL WATER DESALINATION ON MILOS, GREECE

Thomas Nowak

Heinrich-Heine-University Düsseldorf, Germany

10.1 Water as key factor for regional sustainable development

Only 0.7% of the total amount of water covering the Earth is accessible and potable sweet water. Uneven geographic distribution leads to scarcity in many regions of the world, but even with sufficient amounts of water available the quality does not always meet minimum hygienic standards. Both insufficient quantity as well as insufficient quality severely limits the development potential of the affected regions. Extreme water shortage even puts a health risk on its population (WHO/UNICEF 2001: 4). Victims of water scarcity deal less flexibly with environmental change and are limited in their overall economic development. The World Water Assessment Programme (WWAP 2003: 4) comes to the conclusion that owing to the mismanagement of water resources and insufficient application of water saving technologies 'the world is facing a serious water crisis'. In 1995 458 million people were suffering from either water scarcity or water stress, a number expected to reach 2.8 billion by 2025 (Hinrichsen *et al.* 1997; WWAP 2003).

Consequently, a sufficient water supply is necessary to deal with this issue. This is important for development in general and for sustainable development in particular, as has been recognised, with water being one of the main themes of the Johannesburg Summit. Remarkably, it was one of the few areas where agreement for a necessary change was widespread. The Summit's final declaration states the goal of reducing the number of people without access to clean water by 50% by the year 2015 (United Nations 2002). This goal was originally set in the Millennium Declaration (United Nations 2000) and was re-emphasised in Johannesburg.

Small islands are particularly vulnerable to water scarcity because of their easily depleted aquifers. Consequently, a stable external yet costly water supply is necessary, posing a threat to the islands' sustainable development (Falkland 1991). Milos is a small Greek island located in the Cyclades region. It covers an area of 161 km² and has approximately 6,570 permanent inhabitants as well as approximately 760,000 tourist overnight visitors. With a total annual precipitation of 400 mm and an available stable natural supply base of 80,000 m³ (Fyticas 1977; SPEED 1997), it suffers from water scarcity.[1] Neither the demand of the local inhabitants nor that of an ever-increasing number of tourists (currently a total of approximately 580,000 m³ per year) can be covered from the existing supply base. The overuse of this small groundwater reservoir and an ageing and inefficiently managed distribution infrastructure led to leakage and decreasing water quality. Demand by inhabitants, population and industry can be covered only by direct (liquids) and indirect (products) water imports, which are costly and cannot be maintained indefinitely. To paraphrase the original report of the World Commission on Environment and Development (WCED 1987), water supply on Milos does not meet the needs of the present generation because of inadequate water quality and, at the same time, the needs of future generations are at risk. In short, it is not sustainable.

Sustainable development has been described as a society-wide search-and-learn process (Busch-Lüty 1995). Widely agreed on but rather broad criteria of this process demand human activity to:

> strive to conserve finite resources, respect ecological limits, harvest renewable resources sustainably, protect biodiversity, lower environmental emissions, reduce ecological degradation and take preventive action to avoid potentially irreversible environmental change (Jackson 2000: 199; based on, among others, Daly 1980; Pearce and Turner 1990).

To measure the contribution of current activities towards sustainability, these criteria need to be more specific. Such guidelines have to be specified as part of a societal development process. They will be the result of communication, co-operation and compromise by relevant players within this process and will eventually enable the change of current production and consumption patterns. The complexity of this process, because of the differing opinions of players and their motivations, makes it especially complex, demanding more innovative institutions (i.e. networks) for its successful completion.

10.2 Networks as options for sustainable development

Networks are characterised as social systems consisting of at least two organisations that are (1) co-ordinated through the means of social relations, (2) provide

---

1   Falkenmark developed a rather broad indicator for water-related problems from a supply-side perspective. The method distinguishes between water stress (a supply of less than 1,700 m³ per capita per year) and water scarcity (a supply of less than 1,000 m³ per capita per year). A supply of less than 500 m³ per capita per year is considered life-threatening (see Falkenmark and Widstrand 1992; see also DSW 2001). From a demand-side perspective, a minimum water supply of 50 litres per capita per day (18–36 m³ per capita per year) has been recommended by Gleick (1996: 88).

a shared common identity and reflexively co-ordinate the conditions of system reproduction, (3) maintain an exit option for the partners and (4) use shared resources to achieve the goal of the network. Networks use price, fiat and trust as co-ordination mechanisms to achieve efficient results (Sydow 1992; Williamson 1991). Their flexibility is based on the resolution of conflicts over the appropriate use of common resources, on the balancing of power and trust and on the integration of the co-operative as well as the competitive tendencies of their participants. When this balance can be successfully maintained they are suitable for accomplishing the complex and innovative tasks involved in the process of striving for sustainable development. (A vast body of literature on the efficiency of networks in different industries exists. For a general overview, see Håkansson and Jan 1993; Miles and Snow 1986; Sydow 1992.)

A strategic network, as a special type of network, is managed by a single 'focal' corporation that creates, co-ordinates and controls the network. These activities include the identification of a suitable network goal (i.e. a certain project), the definition of tasks necessary to achieve this goal, the recruitment and management of partners capable of fulfilling these tasks, the control of results and the distribution of costs and benefits. The focal corporation is also responsible for the creation of a meaningful communications infrastructure within the network, setting up documentation requirements and establishing technical interfaces. When successfully executed, this leads to a commonly shared construct of reality among the network participants and provides a background for the development of trust and the possibility of asymmetric action.

A sustainable society requires far-reaching and comprehensive innovation processes that include learning by the different players. Governing values and theories-in-use have to be re-evaluated and are subject to change (Argyris and Schön 1978, 1999). Organisational learning (for a comprehensive overview on organisational learning and knowledge management, see Dierkes *et al.* 2001) has been described as 'routine-based, history-dependent and target-orientated' (Levitt and March 1988: 319). A strategic network of players is the ideal institution within which to co-ordinate the development of such routines and to create a common history of action towards a shared target, thus facilitating the necessary learning processes.

Sustainable development requires not only innovation (Weaver *et al.* 2000: 6) but also 'sustainable innovation'—innovation that goes beyond simple improvements of existing products, services and institutions. It requires the integration of its guiding principles in all steps of the innovation process (WBCSD *et al.* 2002). Learning and 'unlearning' (Hedberg 1981) by the participating actors is inevitable. Innovative technologies enable efficiency gains called for by 'Factor X' concepts (among others, see von Weizsäcker *et al.* 1997) while social and institutional inventions and innovation reflect individual needs and are required for sufficiency-oriented lifestyle changes (Matten 1998). Minsch *et al.* (1996: 65-87) provide a framework for sustainable innovation on different levels of society, encompassing efficiency and sufficiency innovations. Although originally geared towards individual corporations, its implications are far-reaching. It integrates the idea of sustainability networks—the co-operation of different players within a specific field of need or value chain—to reach a common goal according to sustainability criteria. Four different areas of innovation were identified. Within the corporation, **process innovations** lead to ecologically optimised production processes. Beyond corporate boundaries, an ecological optimisation of each product's life-cycle is proposed. This so called **product innovation** concentrates on the optimisation of the single product throughout its life-cycle without changing its nature or the relation of the players to each other. This results in a closed life-cycle with reduced negative side-effects. **Function-related innovations** focus on optimising the network of players who are co-operatively supplying the consumer with products and services Questions about the legitimacy of a consumer need for such products and services are finally addressed by the **need-oriented innovation**. This recommendation is far-reaching and requires a reflection on current and future lifestyles, resource supply levels and quality of life in general.

Projects related to the field of sustainable development and water should integrate innovations on different levels to contribute to long-term economic, environmental and social well-being. Preferably, they should be functional innovations acceptable by multiple stakeholders. They should be economically, ecologically and socially affordable, replicable and durable as well as monitored and well documented. Water-related projects, in particular, should meet a basic need for water, increase the efficiency of its use, equally distribute costs and benefits of consumption and increase water quality (Owens-Viani *et al.* 1999: 17).

Such innovations need communication strategies beyond corporate boundaries that utilise learning of the participating players. Strategic networks are institutions that could support this process. They enable initial reflection on the direction of sustainable development as well as on its implementation process. On Milos a strategic network was created to manage the reorganisation of the water supply system accordingly.

10.3 Water supply on Milos

The main sources of water on the island are rain and groundwater. This basic but insufficient supply is supplemented by water shipped to Milos in tankers and bottled on freight ships.

The end-consumer stores water in a cistern for further use. This 'backup' storage is filled from three sources:

- **Rainwater.** This is collected on roofs and concrete sealed areas.

- **Water from the main supply network.** This network supplies 2,300 consumers and is itself fed from public drillings and from two main tanks in the harbour that store water delivered by tanker. Owing to its age, inadequate maintenance and an increasing demand, the network's daily delivery capacity is insufficient to supply the total demand. Water can be supplied only to individual segments of the network at any given time.

- **Water from water trucks.** Seven licences for the transport of water exist on the island itself. The owners take water either from the storage tanks in the

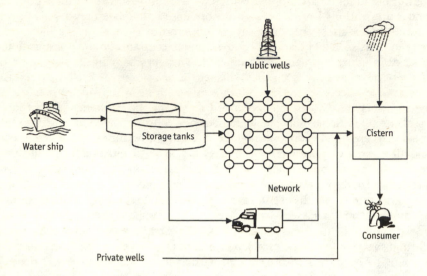

FIGURE 10.1 Water supply on Milos

harbour or from private drillings and deliver it to homes and hotels. It is also possible for individuals to buy water from the storage tanks for their own use.

Owing to the different water qualities produced, the multitude of players involved in the distribution process and the variety of transport media employed it is impossible to maintain consistency in water quality. A system to control water quality does not exist.

Transportation of water to the island is not only an expensive form of supply but transportation relying on fossil fuels also pollutes the air and water. In addition, empty bottles are usually not properly disposed of and further pollute the countryside. Even when collected, their disposal in open landfills or their incineration leads to additional pollution of the air and soil.

Using water from wells—public or private—lowers the water table of the island's water reservoir and consequently leads to a salt intake, reducing water quality. Overuse increases the salt content of the produced water over the summer months. Water high in salt content when used for irrigation harms the soil and has rendered several areas on Milos unusable for agriculture. This increases the dependence on food imports and further reduces employment opportunities on the island.

Water-related appliances are damaged from high salt concentrations and their average life-expectancy is considerably reduced. Dishwashers and washing machines, for example, are only about 50% utilised before they expire. Consequently, maintenance and replacement costs for these appliances are higher than necessary. Water of better quality would prevent these problems but is available only at a considerably higher price.

Production costs for local water sources consist of costs for electricity and maintenance, which are comparatively low. Water delivered to Milos is paid for by the national government. The water price is low and reflects neither the total cost of production nor the external cost of water supply. Although two water-pricing schemes with slightly different price ranges exist for different parts of the island, only one offers an incentive to use water efficiently. It does so by using a price per m³ measure that rises exponentially in tandem with the amount of water consumed. Owing to the low price turnover from water sales, this pricing method continues to be ineffective because it does not reflect the maintenance and repair costs of the infrastructure. This results in decay of infrastructure and increased leakage of water from that infrastructure. While there have been repairs and upgrades on the major supply pipes of the network, its overall reliability is still declining. Traditionally, additional demand for water has been covered by additional supply (supply-side management). To date, a demand-side management strategy designed to encourage more efficient use of water is missing.

Today's water production and distribution scheme results in poor quality of water and creates above-average direct and indirect costs for water. Increasing demand for water and a decreasing natural supply base aggravate this situation and demand a change in system design that is sustainable in the long term.

10.4 Geothermal energy: an option for sustainable island development

Sustainability of the island system depends on the sustainable production of its key development factors: water, food and energy. Water is used ubiquitously; its availability sustains ecosystems and it is a prerequisite to human survival (for drinking, irrigation and recreation). Sustainable production of water thus dramatically impacts tourism, agriculture and industry, thus justifying an examination of its value chain. Although the efficiency of water supply benefits from process and product innovations, a reorganisation towards long-term development requires functional innovation.

In the case of Milos, the requirements of a sustainable water supply are obvious. First, and primarily, the natural supply base must not be overused. The amount of water to be drilled from the groundwater reservoir has to be limited to its regeneration capacity, thus implying a need for stricter controls to prevent overuse. Second, additional supply should be achieved through use of renewable energy sources. Although transportation of bulk and bottled water to the island as well as fossil-fuel-based desalination are technical options, they do not meet this criterion.

The existing geothermal potential (estimated at a minimum of 120 MW electricity) provides an emission-free, renewable ('sustainable') form of energy for the production of sufficient amounts of water to meet current and future demand on Milos. Geothermal energy can be used for different purposes, depending on the temperature of the fluids produced. Those in the low-enthalpy range (with a temperature of less than 150°C) are used mainly as an energy source for direct application (for heating, cooling, water desalination and drying). Fluids in the high-enthalpy range (with a temperature in the range 150–450°C) can be used for electricity production and even to provide excessive waste heat available for secondary use. The exploitation rights of the geothermal potential in Greece are granted by different agencies, depending on the temperature of fluids used (see Table 10.1).

Temperature of fluids used	Agency granting licence
Below 90°C	Regional government (licence unexploited)
90–100°C	Ministry of development (licence unexploited)
Above 100°C	Ministry of development (licence granted to Public Power Corporation)

TABLE 10.1 Agencies granting the licence to use geothermal energy

Source: unpublished documentation of the Milos Project, Gerling Sustainable Development Project GmbH, Athens, 22 September 2002.

On Milos geothermal energy is currently unused. A 2 MW electrical power test installation for electricity production was established by the Public Power Corporation of Greece in 1984 but was abandoned in 1989 after the drill hole was destroyed by a blow-out. Subsequent emissions of stinking, hot fluids negatively influenced the public perception of geothermal energy use in general.

A solution to the island's current water problems based on geothermal energy thus requires intensive communication efforts to convince the population of the benefits. Aside from this social aspect of project implementation, technical, legal, environmental and economic issues have to be dealt with. Players providing their respective knowledge co-operate via new and improved relations within a reorganised value chain. Partly, this will involve an exchange of current actors or at least a change in their attitudes, an intensification of their communication patterns. A strategic network is a suitable organisational form to support this process because of its capacity to integrate participants from different backgrounds and to enable their meaningful, goal-oriented communication.

10.5 Water desalination based on geothermal energy

Commercial exploitation of the low-enthalpy geothermal potential for water desalination was suggested by the Gerling Sustainable Development Project GmbH (GSDP), a project development company founded and owned by the German Gerling Insurance Group. GSDP proposed the installation of a 400 MW desalination facility with a net capacity of 1,600 m³ per day (584,000 m³ per year), an amount sufficient to cover the island's annual demand for high-quality water. The modular design of the plant will enable inexpensive extensions to capacity, and the innovative technology employed generates the total energy demand of the desalination process from geothermal energy. It combines an organic ranking cycle (ORC) turbo generator, a multi-effect desalination unit and an absorption chiller. This technology has successfully been proven by a smaller experimental unit.

The project is to start with the production of high-quality water usable for human consumption and industrial use. The use of 'waste heat' for the production of warm water, heating and cooling services would be possible and would further improve the efficiency of the installation. There is the potential to expand the application of this project to other regions where similar characteristics exist, and other projects would benefit from the experience and contacts made on Milos.

A continuous supply of water to the island requires not only the completion of the plant but also the renovation of key parts of the supply network. GSDP has successfully assisted the municipality in finding private funding and government subsidies for this task.

The long-term economic stability of the project is dependent on a stable revenue stream that can be used for the refinancing of the initial investment as well as for the future maintenance of the production and supply infrastructure. A new pricing scheme for water is necessary to achieve this goal. Water pricing should start at a low price for small consumption quantities, increasing exponentially with growing consumption, thus providing affordable water to the inhabitants (the social aspect), encouraging an efficient use of water (demand-side management) and creating an awareness of its value. The improved water quality will allow customers to stop purchasing expensive water from trucks and to replace costly bottled water with water from the network. Improved water quality should also lead to the increased durability of appliances and should free finances previously used for maintenance and reinvestment. It is hoped that use of innovative, water-saving devices will be encouraged as a result of the larger savings potential. The total cost of water should decline.

The need to assess technical risks, engage technology and scientific partners, obtain a licence for exploitation and to raise funds for the project required preliminary discussions with potential partners from the fields of engineering, law, geography, business and sociology. As a result, a project network that co-ordinated the aforementioned players as well as stakeholders from the island was created (see Fig. 10.2). This network was used for the presentation of the project and supported communication between and among the different players.

The network was especially useful, as the project initially met strong opposition because of previously unsuccessful attempts to use geothermal energy for electricity production (see Section 10.4). It was feared that water desalination would only be used as an excuse by GSDP eventually to produce electricity again. Mistrust of the use of geothermal energy for this purpose has been widespread. In addition, several incumbents of important positions in the existing power structure of the water business feared a loss of power and influence (for the opinions, positions and interests of the various actors, see Table 10.2).

It became obvious that the island's inhabitants had to be convinced of the project's benefits before the project could be successfully embarked on. An intensive information exchange between project stakeholders and the project corporation was initiated to provide information about the project, its benefits and the

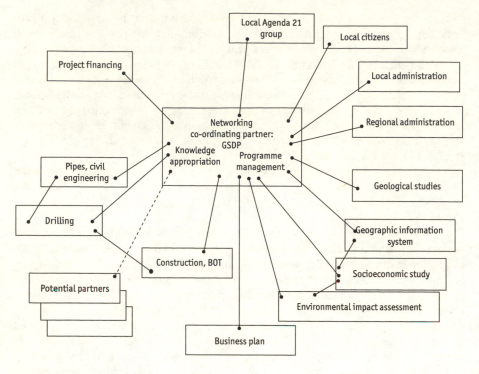

BOT = build–operate–transfer

GSDP = Gerling Sustainable Development Project GmbH

FIGURE 10.2 The Milos project network of actors

technology employed. This exchange was also used to identify and record the concerns of the local population. Network participants from several backgrounds were able successfully to address a variety of concerns raised through this process. This resulted in finally convincing the local population of the project's beneficial character.

Several means of communication were used:

- The project manager visited the island on a monthly basis to meet decision-makers and to discuss project progress.

- A development company was founded. Its local office was established as a communications link between residents and GSDP.

- Advertisements and reports in the local newspapers were used to create awareness of the project and of the company. Economic, ecologic and social benefits were stressed.

Player	Opinion, position or interest
Regional government (Prefecture of Cyclades)	Grants licence for the direct use of low-enthalpy geothermal energy
Local administration	Eligible to apply for licence
	Operates the existing network and is responsible for billing and collection of fees
	Its image benefits from successful project implementation
Opinion leaders	Influence local administration
	Promote approval by population
	Opposing leaders see their own influence at risk; supporting leaders see the project as an opportunity
Public Power Corporation	Licensee for high-enthalpy geothermal usage
	Successful project proves the possibility of geothermal energy use for electricity production and is a risk to its monopoly
Water truck drivers	Some perceive a threat to their monopoly and a loss of power but their services will be needed in the future for the supply of remote settlements
Hotel and B&B owners	Advantage from clean water but shy away from extra cost or investment
	Fear increased price for water
Individual consumers	Advantage from clean water
	Fear increased water price
	No perception of investment or benefit relation
Agriculture	Today, agriculture is rarely economically feasible
	Use of high-quality water provides advantages (irrigation is possible without ruining soils; it provides a new revenue stream from current [increased yields] and new crops; it decreases the island's dependence on imports; it provides employment)
	Fear of high cost
Competitors for water production	Aim at producing energy on Milos
	No real ambition for water supply
	Perceive project as a risk to their own benefits
	Try to reach preferred treatment by local authorities

B&B = bed and breakfast

TABLE 10.2 Players influenced by and influencing the desalination project

- Two major conferences were organised within the scientific community to discuss different aspects of the use of geothermal energy in the Mediterranean. The local population was invited to attend and to voice its opinion.

- Two socioeconomic studies were conducted. The interviews were not only used to collect data but also to inform the interviewees about the project.

Finally, the project was approved by several stakeholders on the island. Almost simultaneously, the exploitation licence was obtained. GSDP was eventually considered a responsible and trustworthy business partner. This proved especially useful when a competitor's attempt to realise a similar project on the island was foiled as a result of the well-maintained relationships with local and regional authorities.

10.6 Conclusions and update on progress

A strategic network was successfully created to reorganise the existing water value chain. Communication within this network helped overcome initial resistance against the project. Today, geothermal energy is perceived as a viable energy source, and widespread support for the project prevails. Its activities continued after the resolution of technical and legal obstacles (after successful test drillings and the obtaining of a production licence). However, several decision-makers have not yet been convinced of the advantages of a water desalination based on geothermal energy. As a consequence, the plant has not yet been built and the situation described in Section 10.4 still obtains. The reorganised water value chain could provide a functional innovation to the island that provides sufficient quantities of an improved product based on emission-free renewable energy to the island. Once realised, it will create economic development opportunities and may reduce the dependence of the island on imported water resources. The improved water quality and the new pricing structure will eventually result in more evenly distributed costs of water production and lead to a decrease in total water-related cost. The expected revenue stream from water sales enables refinancing of investments and the maintenance of future infrastructure The project is economically, environmentally and socially self-sufficient and is accepted by the stakeholders. Once realised, it can be considered sustainable.

As a consequence of this project, several choices on future development trajectories, however, remain a major challenge. In terms of the choice between mass tourism and eco-tourism, effects on the island and the needs and wants of its inhabitants have yet to be discussed. This discussion creates a unique opportunity to pursue a sustainable island development plan and enables the development of needs-oriented innovations as future steps towards a sustainable island society.

Apart from these achievements, the project's at least partial success proves the validity of the theoretical concepts presented in Section 10.2 and their value for implementing sustainable development programmes.

References

Argyris, C., and D. Schön (1978) *Organisational Learning: A Theory of Action Perspective* (Reading, MA: Addison-Wesley).

—— and —— (1999) *Die lernende Organisation* (Stuttgart: Klett-Cotta).

Busch-Lüty, C. (1995) 'Welche politische Kultur braucht nachhaltiges Wirtschaften?', in H. Dürr and F. Gottwald (eds.), *Umweltverträgliches Wirtschaften* (Munich: Agenda): 177-200.

Daly, H.E. (1980) *Economics, Ecology, Ethics: Essays toward a Steady-state Economy* (San Francisco: Freemann).

Dierkes, M., A. Bertoin Antal, J. Child and I. Nonaka (eds.) (2001) *Handbook of Organisational Learning and Knowledge* (Oxford, UK: Oxford University Press).

DSW (Deutschen Stiftung Weltbevölkerung) (2001) *Weltbevölkerungsbericht 2001: Bevölkerung und Umwelt* (Hannover: DSW).

Falkenmark, M., and C. Widstrand (1992) *Population and Water Resources: A Delicate Balance* (Population Bulletin, Number 3; Washington, DC: Population Reference Bureau).

Falkland, A. (ed.) (1991) *Hydrology and Water Resources of Small Islands* (Paris: United Nations Educational, Scientific and Cultural Organisation [UNESCO]).

Fyticas, M.D. (1977) *Geological and Geothermal Study of Milos Island* (Athens: Institute of Geological and Mining Research).

Gleick, P. (1996) 'Basic Water Requirements for Human Activities', *Water International* 2: 83-92.

Håkansson, H., and J. Jan (1993) 'The Network as a Governance Structure: Interfirm Co-operation beyond Markets and Hierarchies', in G. Grabher (ed.), *The Embedded Firm: On the Socioeconomics of Industrial Networks* (London: Routledge): 3-25.

Hedberg, B. (1981) 'How Organisations Learn and Unlearn', in P. Nystrom and W. Starbuck (eds.), *Handbook of Organisational Design* (Oxford, UK: Oxford University Press): 8-27.

Hinrichsen, D., B. Robey and U. Upadhyay (1997) *Solutions for a Water Short World* (Population Report, Series M, Number 14; Baltimore, MD: Population Information Program, Johns Hopkins School of Public Health).

Jackson, T. (2000) 'The Unfinished Symphony', *International Journal of Sustainable Development* 3: 199-220.

Levitt, B., and J.G. March (1988) 'Organisational Learning', *Annual Review of Sociology* 14: 319-40.

Matten, D. (1998) 'Sustainable Development als betriebswirtschaftliches Leitbild', *ZfB-Ergänzungsheft* 1: 1-23.

Miles, R.E., and C.C. Snow (1986) 'Organisations: New Concepts for New Forms', *California Management Review* 3: 62-73.

Minsch, J., A. Eberle, B. Meier and U. Schneidewind (1996) *Mut zum ökologischen Umbau: Innovationsstrategien für Unternehmen, Politik und Akteurnetze* (Basel: Birkhäuser).

Owens-Viani, L., A. Wong and P. Gleick (eds.) (1999) *Sustainable Use of Water* (Oakland, CA: Pacific Institute for Studies in Development, Environment, and Security).

Pearce, D.W., and R.K. Turner (1990) *Economics of Natural Resources and the Environment* (Baltimore, MD: Johns Hopkins University Press).

SPEED Ltd (ed.) (1997) *Survey on Current Water Usage Patterns and Future Development of Demand in the Cycladic Island Region* (Athens: SPEED Ltd).

Sydow, J. (1992) *Strategische Netzwerke* (Wiesbaden, Germany: Gabler).

United Nations (2000) *Milleniums-Erklärung der Vereinten Nationen. Verabschiedet zum Abschluss des Milleniums Gipfels* (6–8 September 2000; New York: United Nations, www.runiceurope.org/german/sg/millennium/millenniumerklaerung.pdf, accessed 30 June 2001).

—— (2002) *The Johannesburg Declaration on Sustainable Development* (Johannesburg: United Nations, www.johannesburgsummit.org/html/documents/summit_docs/0409_l6rev2_pol_decl.pdf, accessed 12 October 2002).

Von Weizsäcker, E.U., A.B. Lovins and L.H. Lovins (1997) *Faktor Vier: Doppelter Wohlstand: halbierter Naturverbrauch* (Munich: Droemer Knaur).

WBCSD (World Business Council for Sustainable Development), J. Dormann and C. Holliday (2002) *Innovation, Technology, Sustainability and Society* (Geneva: WBCSD).

WCED (World Commission on Environment and Development) (1987) *Our Common Future* (Oxford, UK: Oxford University Press).

Weaver, P., L. Jansen, G. van Grootveld, E. van Spiegel and P. Vergragt (2000) *Sustainable Technology Development* (Sheffield, UK: Greenleaf Publishing).

WHO/UNICEF (World Health Organisation/United Nations Children's Fund) (2001) *Global Water Supply and Sanitation Assessment 2000 Report* (Geneva: WHO/UNICEF).

Williamson, O.E. (1991) 'Comparative Economic Organisation', *Administrative Science Quarterly* 36: 269-96.

WWAP (World Water Assessment Programme) (ed.) (2003) *Water For People, Water For Life: The United Nations World Water Development Report* (New York: United Nations).

11

Ecological sanitation
REACHING FOR THE MDGs

Mayling Simpson-Hebert
Catholic Relief Services, Regional Office, Kenya

Arno Rosemarin
Stockholm Environment Institute, Sweden

Uno Winblad
Kyoto University, Japan

11.1 The challenge

One of the key messages from the 2002 World Summit on Sustainable Development
in Johannesburg was that the world is in a sanitation crisis. At least 2.6 billion
people in the world today, mostly in Asia and Africa, are without any form of
'improved' sanitation (defined by the World Health Organisation [WHO] as connection to a public sewer, connection to a septic system, a pour–flush latrine, a simple
pit latrine or a ventilated improved pit [VIP] latrine). A key commitment from the
Summit is now one of the Millennium Development Goals (MDGs) to 'halve the
proportion of people without basic sanitation by the year 2015'. This call to arms is
not just for the next ten years but also for several decades to come given expected
increases in human population, especially in developing countries. To reach
universal coverage by 2025, more than 4 billion extra people will need sanitation
(WHO/UNICEF 2001).

Businesses wanting to make a difference in the world by creating more ecologically sound environments might consider the option of contributing to the
development and provision of ecological sanitation (ecosan) options. Most lower-
cost ecosan toilets can be constructed by builders with minimal training (Clark 2002;
Esrey *et al*. 2001), but higher-cost systems, such as those being developed in Europe,
require new kinds of hardware and services. A business opportunity exists for
innovative companies that could produce simple hardware in plastic, fibreglass or
porcelain for an emerging market in less-expensive ecological toilets, as well as
hardware and services for more upscale systems.

Global monitoring of water supply and sanitation by WHO and UNICEF (WHO/UNICEF 2001, 2004) indicates where efforts should go: 80% (2 billion) of those without 'improved' sanitation live in rural areas and 1.3 billion of them live in China or India. Most of the remaining 0.9 billion live in rural Africa, Latin America or the Caribbean. Some 20% of the unserved, or 480 million people, live in urban areas of these countries and continents. The urban proportion unserved by sanitation is expected to increase in the coming decades (UN Millennium Project 2005).

Between 2002 and 2015, more than 25 million households per year (averaging 5 persons per household) will need new sanitation facilities if the Summit goal is to be achieved. The actual number will be much larger because of the need to replace ageing sanitation systems, rural-to-urban migration and the short life (5–10 years) of pit toilets (which are at present the basis of the sanitation system of the majority of rural inhabitants). Rural families are generally cash-poor and less likely to have sufficient water for flush systems, so most of these new systems will need to be waterless (i.e. not flush toilets) as well as being easy and inexpensive to build. The reality is that in rural areas of China, India and South-East Asia, Africa and Latin America, where most efforts will need to be focused, integrated sewerage systems, septic tanks and even simpler pour–flush technologies are not feasible for the majority of the unserved population.

11.2 The need for nutrient recycling

The Food and Agriculture Organisation (FAO) warns that the planet is losing 25 billion tons of topsoil per year (Engelman and LeRoy 1995). Artificial fertilisers cannot replace valuable humus, a product that is composed of decayed plants and animals and animal excreta. The global population currently stands at about 6 billion, and since, on average, human beings each produce 1,150 g of urine and 200 g of faeces per day (Gotaas 1956; Wagner 1958), a global total of 6,900 million kilos of human urine and 1,200 million kilos of human faeces are generated each day. Urine is rich in phosphorus, potassium and nitrogen (PKN), nutrients needed by plants. Urine diluted with water can be an excellent fertiliser. Faeces are rich in carbon, and also contain PKN. They can be dried or composted into a safe soil conditioner and used to replace, in part, lost topsoil (Morgan 1999, 2001). This is something that current sanitation technologies, for the most part, fail to do.

11.3 A lack of water for flushing

To meet the WHO/UNICEF definition of 'improved sanitation', human excreta either can be flushed with water into a sewer system, a septic system or a pour–flush toilet or excreta can be disposed of in a pit toilet. Water, however, is a serious limiting factor in the rural areas of many developing countries. Even those with adequate water supplies usually do not have the funds to install the large piped systems required for flush toilets and indeed cannot afford to use scarce water resources for flushing toilets.

Although flush systems may be viable for newer, more wealthy, urban communities with abundant water supplies, the great majority of those without sanitation (i.e. mostly rural poor in developing countries) will require dry systems.

Dry options currently acceptable to the development community for promotion are limited to two types of pit toilets—simple and ventilated. The simple ordinary pit toilet often deteriorates into a health risk, becoming smelly, fly-ridden and unpleasant. The ventilated improved pit toilet is a good design that solves the common problems of ordinary pit toilets but it is more costly. Neither of these options is designed to allow the recycling of nutrients in human excreta.

11.4 The economic problems of sewer systems

For many reasons, conventional sewerage treatment is not an ideal method for managing human excreta. It is expensive and wasteful of water, bringing large amounts of clean water to the home (an average of 15,000 litres per toilet user per year). It pollutes this clean water with human excreta and other substances and then transports it via an expensive pipe network to a treatment plant (if such exists) where the water passes through primary, secondary and tertiary treatment processes to clean it before discharging it to the environment. This not only wastes valuable water, energy and monetary resources for communities but it also fails to address the most basic ecological imperative of the planet—the need to recycle the nutrients in human excreta back to the soil.

Sewerage is expensive even for rich communities. Ten years after the adoption of the EU Directive on Urban Waste-water Treatment 91/271, which requires primary, secondary and advanced or tertiary treatment of urban sewage,[1] EU countries are still not able to fulfil their obligations: 37 large cities still discharge untreated waste-water (Brussels had no treatment at all until 1998 and presently treats only 30% of its waste-water; Milan still has no sewage treatment). Only 79 of 542 cities have advanced sewage treatment, and 44% have no treatment or have incomplete primary or secondary treatment (European Union 2001). Figure 11.1 tells the story.

11.5 The pollution problems of sewer systems

Sewerage systems and other flush toilet options were developed when the world had far fewer people, a billion or less, and when only a tiny fraction of them were served with sewerage. With the exception of a few sites, the environment had the capacity to handle the relatively low level of discharge from sewer systems into large bodies of water. The number and kinds of pollutants in the sewerage was also

---

1   Primary treatment consists only of settling of solids from waste-water before discharge to a watercourse. Secondary treatment adds biological treatment and secondary settling of solids. Tertiary or advanced treatment adds additional removal of specific pollutants such as phosphorus, nitrogen, heavy metals or other chemical contaminants as well.

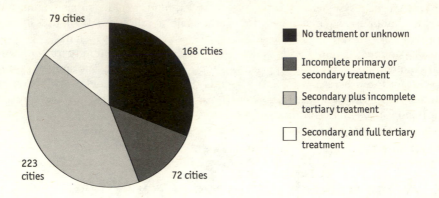

FIGURE 11.1 Sewage treatment in major EU cities

Source: information from the Second Forum on Implementation and Enforcement of Community Enviironmental Law, 'Intensifying our Efforts to Clean Urban Waste-water', Brussels, 2001

smaller, with few toxic chemicals or heavy metals. As cities grew and expanded during the 1800s and 1900s, so did the popularity of sewage systems, but they were not without their problems. Outbreaks of typhoid fever and cholera in downstream communities required those communities to institute chlorine treatment for drinking water taken from rivers and lakes, and they began to demand that up-stream cities treat their sewage before discharge (for further information on the history of sewerage, see Rockefeller 1997).

Today only about one billion of the six billion people in the world are served by sewerage systems (Matsui 2002), and much of this sewage is discharged with little or no treatment. The main pollutants are nitrogen and phosphorus, which result in eutrophication, together with heavy metals, pathogens and endocrine-disrupting chemicals. Even a high level of treatment does not remove all of these pollutants but often produces a residual polluted sludge that cannot be recycled in agriculture and instead requires deep burial (Rockefeller 1997). Tertiary treatment also fails to deal adequately with endocrine-disrupting chemicals (Matsui *et al.* 2001). When one includes these inadequate sewerage systems that disperse pollution into the wider environment, then estimates of the number of people in the world with ecologically sound sanitation shrink from the WHO/UNICEF estimate of 3.6 billion to about 300 million (Matsui 2002). Human excreta from the remaining 5.7 billion is discharged in one way or another directly into the environment, either into bodies of water, directly on soil through open defecation or by pollution of groundwater through pit toilets.

11.6 Ecological sanitation: an alternative

During the past ten years an interesting and very promising area of research and development around the world has focused on largely waterless sanitation options: 'ecological toilets'. Ecological sanitation, or ecosan, is more of an approach than a set of technologies. To qualify as ecosan, the system must prevent spread of disease, prevent groundwater pollution, recycle nutrients and, importantly for many parts of the world, save water. The toilets are of various designs, from very simple pit types to the upscale systems found in middle-class European apartment blocks and townhouse communities. They also work under different biological principles, but the key common principle is that they turn human excreta, a normally dangerous, pathogen-rich product, into a relatively hygienic and fertile soil (Esrey *et al.* 1998; Winblad and Simpson-Hebert 2004).

Pilot projects in ecosan from around the world are demonstrating the effectiveness of the approach. Projects are under way in China, India, Mexico, El Salvador, Mozambique, Zimbabwe, South Africa, Ethiopia, Uganda, Palestine, Sweden and Germany. The projects involve a wide economic range of users, many varieties of designs and are based in rural and urban settings. Three designs suitable for helping to meet the Johannesburg Summit goal on sanitation (primarily for rural inhabitants of developing countries) will be explained here: the ArborLoo, the Alterna Fossa and the double-vault urine-diverting toilet (see the resources listed at the end of this chapter for further information about systems being tested for European cities as an alternative to sewerage.)

11.6.1. The ArborLoo

The ArborLoo (or 'tree toilet') is a soil–composting toilet that does not require high temperatures. It is designed to recycle nutrients directly to food-producing plants without having to handle the humus produced from the human excreta. This protects farmers from possible contamination from pathogens. A pit of about one metre deep by half a metre wide is dug, reinforced at the top and covered with a concrete latrine slab into which two handles have been cast for the later easy removal of the slab. A moveable superstructure surrounds the pit. The pit is half-filled with straw before first use. Each time a person uses the toilet, she or he puts a cup of a soil or wood ash mixture on top. This prevents odour and insect breeding by keeping the pit dry and raising the pH, making it unfavourable for insects and pathogens. Once the pit is two-thirds full of human excreta, the slab is removed and the pit is topped up with garden compost, kitchen waste and soil. The contents are then lightly watered down and a young tree is planted there. While the young tree is growing, the contents of the pit are slowly being converted to soil by the surrounding soil bacteria, and the young tree's roots are gradually reaching deeper into the nutrient-rich pit. Beside this first pit, a second pit can be dug at a proper distance to allow the first tree, and later a second tree, to grow. In this way, over time, an orchard of fruit or nut trees can be established. Since there is no excavation of the contents, this is perhaps the easiest and safest of all ecosan options but, for obvious reasons its urban application will be limited.

The ArborLoo is being promoted among rural farmers in Zimbabwe and Mozambique with some success. It is often selected over other options, including ordinary pit toilets, VIP toilets and the next ecological toilet to be described, the Fossa Alterna, because farmers have seen its obvious benefits in rapid growth of trees and increased agricultural production.

11.6.2 The Fossa Alterna

The Fossa Alterna is also a soil–composting toilet that works on the principle of two alternating shallow pits. It is designed to be a permanent toilet for a rural household. Two pits of about 1.2 metres in depth and 0.9 metres width are dug beside each other. Like the ArborLoo, the pits are reinforced at the top and are covered with a concrete slab having handles for easy removal. The entire structure may be within one superstructure, or some families use a movable superstructure that switches from pit to pit. One pit is used for one year then topped up with soil and covered for a full year while the other pit is used. Like the ArborLoo, each time the toilet is used, the user covers the contents with a cup of soil or wood ash mixture to prevent smells and insect breeding and to kill pathogens.

After one year of composting, the first pit is dug out and the humus, rich in nutrients, is used to grow vegetables. Experience has shown that vegetables grown in this soil–composted humus produce more by weight than do vegetables grown in ordinary soil on the same area (Morgan 1999, 2001). Some pathogen testing has been done on the humus from the Fossa Alterna, showing that the soil is antagonistic.

About 2,500 soil–composting toilets have been built so far in Mozambique in collaboration with the non-governmental organisation (NGO) WaterAid. WaterAid always offers communities a range of toilet options and carries out community participation and education activities to empower households in making their choices. What households like about the Alterna Fossa is that it is a permanent toilet, unlike pit latrines that need replacing every five to ten years.

11.6.3 Double-vault urine-diverting toilets

Double-vault urine-diverting toilets are sometimes called Vietnamese composting toilets, as they were first field-tested in Vietnam. Rather than composting, they actually operate on the principle of urine diversion away from a raised vault and dehydration of the faeces. The toilet involves building two raised vaults that are used alternately every 6–12 months. The size of each vault is about 0.9 by 0.9 metres across by about 0.7–0.9 metres high for a family of five to six persons. The opening at the top is fitted with a urine-diverting squat pan or a raised toilet seat, depending on the local culture. Each vault has a small door or opening closed with concrete or bricks that can be opened from the outside. The urine is diverted to a container inside or outside the house, where it is collected, diluted with water and used directly to water crops. As with the soil–composting toilets, after defecation into the vault the user puts a cup of wood ash or an ash–soil mixture to cover the faeces. This prevents smells and insect breeding and makes the contents very unfavourable for the survival of pathogens because of the dryness and a high pH of about 9.5. A pH of 9.5 or greater will eliminate most pathogens and parasites present, which is a higher standard of sanitisation than even that of the most advanced sewage treatments plants (Stenström 2002). After six months of drying in a closed vault, the contents can be removed and the humus used to grow crops. The toilet seat or squat plate is often commercially produced, but it can be made locally from concrete. Toilets of this type can be built inside or outside the home.

Double-vault urine-diverting toilets are very popular in China, Vietnam, Mexico and El Salvador. In the Guangxi Region of China over 30,000 had been built in middle-income and low-income rural homes by 2001 (Wei 2002). This increased to 685,000 installed by 2003 in 17 provinces (NPHCC 2004). In the past, families had ordinary pit toilets and public pit toilets, the contents of which they periodically dug out and used as fertiliser. These generally unhygienic practices have been replaced with a system that reduces the possibility of pathogen survival. The new toilets are built inside or adjacent to houses. Drainage and ecological treatment systems for grey water from kitchen and baths, such as evapotranspiration beds (small, constructed wetlands), are also installed. These toilets have proved popular, requiring little maintenance. They have advantages in dry and wet areas. During the monsoon season in southern China, sewerage systems and common pit toilets often fill with water and are made inoperable. The dry toilets survive periodic flooding, since they are built above ground level: they retain their contents and can be used immediately once the water subsides. In the water-scarce areas of the north and west of China, they provide excellent service, saving water for other hygiene purposes. The urine and faecal material can also be used as feedstock in biogas digesters, a common practice in rural China (Tang *et al.* 2001).

Current conventional practices based on pit toilets, cesspits, septic tanks, which overflow, and the use of untreated sewage in agriculture have created major environmental and human health problems in China that will be mitigated through the introduction of ecosan systems. The potential and capacity for expansion in China is great, with nearly 800 million people unserved (WHO/UNICEF 2001). The current target group for the urine-diverting dry toilets is around 500 million people, or about 100–150 million installations.

Mexico stands in the middle of a South–South technology exchange process that began with the transfer and adaptation of the Vietnamese dry toilet model to Guatemala, El Salvador and Mexico about 20 years ago. There has been no accurate recent count of ecological toilets in Mexico, but they are estimated to be in the tens of thousands. Mexican NGOs have been leaders in the development of rural dry sanitation. The main motivations for Mexicans to adopt ecological toilets are limited water availability and non-functional or non-existent sewage treatment. In addition, there has been extensive experience in the use of human excreta in organic agriculture (Guadarrama *et al.* 2002).

NGOs in Mexico have been working at the grass-roots level with villages and rural families, educating them about ecological toilet options and giving them choices. The social aspects of developing alternative solutions are just as important as the scientific and technical components. One NGO, ESAC (Espaccio de Salud AC), promotes the development of cottage industries by providing self-financing mecha-

FIGURE 11.2 The double-vault urine-diverting toilet as used in Mexico

nisms and training (Añorve 2002; Clark 2002). The Mexican moulds to manu-
facture fibreglass and concrete pedestal toilets have been exported to South Africa,
Uganda and Zimbabwe, where they are now mass-produced with only small modifications. Figure 11.2 shows the design of the double-vault urine-diverting toilet
used in Mexico. This design is essentially the same in China and elsewhere.

Systems for densely populated areas are currently being developed in China and
Mexico. The total ecosan system, including urban collection services for urine and
humus, 'ecostations' (community collection points for secondary treatment) and
grey-water treatment are being tested in full-scale urban pilot projects.

11.6.4 A variety of other options: systems in Sweden and Germany

Sweden and Germany have been leaders in developing knowledge and experience
in ecosan. Several successful pilot projects have been carried out in middle-class
neighbourhoods and multi-storey apartment buildings, including urine-diverting
low-flush and dry toilets as well as composting toilets. Extensive studies have been
carried out on community projects that have adopted these alternative approaches,
including recycling of urine and faecal material (Jönsson 2002).

Sweden has a well-developed manufacturing and technology development sector in this field, producing modern dry and low-flush urine-diverting as well as composting toilets for various needs. Several pilot projects have been carried out in large modern housing complexes consisting of 50–100 households. These involve large-scale storage of urine, which is periodically collected for recycling to farms. They have also included collection and recycling of conventional septic tank contents to wheat fields in order to develop large-scale methods. Full-scale constructed wetlands have been built in several small cities to handle the effluent from traditional sewage treatment plants. Ecosan has become a mainstream option in Sweden for rural and recreational housing.

11.7 Concerns and cautions about ecological sanitation

Some practitioners are concerned that crops grown with the aid of urine fertilisers will not be acceptable to consumers. Pilot projects to date have shown that rural households usually have no problem accepting crops grown from their own urine (Morgan 2001), but whether consumers buying crops in the market will reject them remains to be discovered. The pathogen risk in urine is very low (Vinnerås 2002) so it usually needs no further treatment before use on crops. Another possible concern is whether urine applied to fields will contaminate groundwater. So far this has not proved to be a problem, but as a precaution it is best to apply it to surface soils where there is some plant growth (grass or trees) to trap the nitrate before it reaches the groundwater.

Concerns also exist over the pathogen kill-off rates in dried or soil–composted faeces and whether the process of removal of the humus product from vaults could contaminate handlers. Although it has to be accepted that no sanitation system is completely pathogen-free, assessments have been made of the efficacy of pathogen destruction in dry toilets (Stenström 2002). In addition to the use of lime and wood ash to increase pH in order to sanitise faecal material, experiments have been carried out using warm composting methods and also adding urea, which transforms to ammonia, which is lethal to microbes (Vinnerås 2002). The conditions for pathogen survival in ecological toilets are extremely unfavourable: long periods of drying and/or composting and the addition of ash or lime to raise the pH above 9.5. In one toilet design, the ArborLoo, there is no excavation or handling of humus at all. In cases where families using the double-vault designs are known to be infected by enteric pathogens or parasites, toilet contents can be treated using lime, hot ashes or incineration.

Some sceptics refuse to believe that ecological toilets do not smell. Odour in pit latrines is caused primarily by moisture and, in particular, the mixture of urine and faeces. That same moisture is responsible for fly breeding. When these toilets are kept dry or mixed with biologically active soil, even when the urine and faeces are mixed, as in the Fossa Alterna or the ArborLoo, they do not smell. In response to this frequent comment, ecosan expert Paul Calvert wrote a widely circulated paper, 'Seeing (but not Smelling) is Believing: Kerala's Compost Toilet' (Calvert 1997).

Some practitioners are concerned that the humus or dehydrated faeces may not be disposed of properly. All of the systems described in this chapter are designed to allow the faecal product to be used in agriculture to enrich soils. Such arrangements for use need to be in place before the toilets are built and to be carefully monitored for follow-through. Experience shows that rural farmers usually do realise the benefits of re-using human excreta in agriculture after only a few trial households have demonstrated them.

The challenge of ecosan is that users will not use the toilets carefully. The urine-diverting toilets for example require that urine and faeces be kept separate in order to facilitate drying and to prevent smell and fly breeding. If this rule is not followed and people urinate in the dry vault the system could fail. Another potential risk is that if dried or composted faeces are removed before the six-month to eight-month resting period is completed they may contain harmful pathogens. The products also have to be used with care: in particular, users need to know how to apply urine to crops in a way that does not kill the plants. Each of these aspects demands a good education campaign and user follow-up to accompany any programme. In contrast to 'flushsan', where users can usually 'flush and forget', users of ecosan must understand how the system works and demand compliance from others.

11.8 The cost of ecological sanitation

Ecological sanitation is a potential solution for all societies and all economic levels. In Sweden and Germany, the systems that are being developed are sophisticated, many using in-house ceramic ware and pipes that can be as costly as those required for conventional systems. Nearly all of the cost is at the front end of construction, and the savings arise from not having to connect to a sewerage system or septic tank. Ecosan systems can be low-cost or high-cost, depending on consumer desires and resources. The current average cost of an ecological toilet in a developing country is US$50.

Even this sum is beyond many families and governments in poor parts of the world, and to make the Johannesburg Summit (MDG) goal reachable a global fund for sanitation will be required. The education and communications effort alone will cost millions, if not billions, of dollars, even if we assume (unrealistically) that households will pay for their own toilet installations. Consider the cost of subsidising 250 million ecological toilets—the number that would approximately meet the goal in 2015. At US$50 per toilet, the total would be US$12.5 billion. Add to that an administrative cost of about 15%, or $1.9 billion, and the total is US$14.4 billion, or about US$1 billion per year over 14 years. The added economic value of the nitrogen and phosphorus recycled from these systems is, however, significant, running at about $5 billion per year if the MDGs were to be met using ecosan (SEI 2005). These figures provide an idea of the scale of the endeavour. Subsidising household installations of toilets is probably not the best way to achieve the goal. Experience shows that the most important part of achieving successful and sustainable sanitation is through communication, education, outreach and follow-up support, and although these activities may not cost much less they are likely to result in greater sustainable social change.

According to estimates made by WHO and UNICEF:

> to achieve the international development target of halving the proportion of people without access to improved sanitation . . . by 2015 . . . about 2.2 billion will require access to sanitation facilities . . . To achieve these goals will require immense effort and investment. If the change over the 1990s is used as a guide to future progress . . . then least progress might be expected in the area of rural sanitation (WHO/UNICEF 2001: 29).

Ecosan offers an immediate potential solution mostly for the currently 80% of rural inhabitants of the world who have no adequate sanitation system and who would benefit from the recycling of nutrients to improve food security. Nevertheless, we should acknowledge that the need to change from flush systems to dry systems in the developed, urban, world may be just as urgent as meeting the needs of the 2.6 billion mainly rural inhabitants with no sanitation. Unfortunately, research into ecological systems suitable for densely populated cities is only now being promulgated, and investment continues to favour large-scale water-borne systems, so the likelihood of such changes remains very remote at the moment.

Information sources

Networks

Centre Régional pour l'Eau Potable et l'Assainissement a faible coût (CREPA), www.oieau.fr/crepa
EcoSanRes, www.ecosanres.org
GTZ-EcoSan, www2.gtz.de/ecosan/english
Redseco, www.laneta.apc.org/redseco
Sanitation Connection, www.sanicon.net

Conferences

CSIR (2005) 'Third International Ecological Sanitation Conference', Durban, South Africa, May 2005, www.conference2005.ecosan.org.

EcoSanRes (1997) 'Ecological Alternatives in Sanitation', in *Proceedings of the Sida Sanitation Workshop, Balingsholm*, www.ecosanres.org/ecological_alternatives_in_sanit.htm.

EcoSanRes (2001) 'First International Conference on Ecological Sanitation', Nanning, China, November 2001, www.ecosanres.org/Nanning%20Conf%20Proceedings.htm.

GTZ (2000) 'Ecosan: Closing the Loop in Waste-water Management and Sanitation', First International Symposium, Bonn, Germany, October 2000, www2.gtz.de/ecosan/english/symposium1.htm.

GTZ (2003) 'Ecosan: Closing the Loop', Second International Symposium on Ecological Sanitation, Lubeck, Germany, March 2003, www2.gtz.de/ecosan/ english/symposium2.htm.

References

Añorve, C. (2002) 'Dry Toilet Workshops in Mexico: An Example of Local Autonomous Actions', in *Proceedings of the First International Conference on Ecological Sanitation, Nanning, China, November 2001*, available from www.ecosanres.org/Nanning%20Conf%20Proceedings.htm.

Calvert P. (1997) 'Seeing (but not Smelling) Is Believing: Kerala's Compost Toilet', *Waterlines* 15.3: 30-32.

—— (2002) 'Ecological Sanitation in India and Sri Lanka', in *Proceedings of the First International Conference on Ecological Sanitation, Nanning, China, November 2001*, available from www.ecosanres.org/Nanning%20Conf%20Proceedings.htm.

Clark, G. (2002) 'Ecological Sanitation in Mexico: Strategies for Sustainable Replication', in *Proceedings of the First International Conference on Ecological Sanitation, Nanning, China, November 2001*, available from www.ecosanres.org/Nanning%20Conf%20Proceedings.htm.

Engelman, R., and P. LeRoy (1995) *Conserving Land: Population and Sustainable Food Production* (Washington, DC: Population Action International).

Esrey, S., I. Andersson, A. Hillers and R. Sawyer (eds.) (2001) *Closing the Loop: Ecological Sanitation for Food Security* (Stockholm: United Nations Development Programme [UNDP] and Sida).

Esrey, S., J. Gough, D. Rapaport, R. Sawyer, M. Simpson-Hebert, J. Vargas and U. Winblad (1998) *Ecological Sanitation* (Stockholm: Sida).

European Union (2001) 'Intensifying Our Efforts to Clean Urban Waste-water', paper presented at the *Second Forum on Implementation and Enforcement of Community Environmental Law*, Brussels, 19 March 2003.

Gotaas, H.B. (1956) *Composting: Sanitary Disposal and Reclamation of Organic Wastes* (Monograph Series, Number 31; Geneva: World Health Organisation).

Guadarrama, R., N. Pichardo and E. Morales-Oliver (2002) 'Urine and Compost Efficiency Applied to Lettuce Cultivation under Greenhouse Conditions, Intemixco, Morelos, Mexico', in *Proceedings of the First International Conference on Ecological Sanitation, Nanning, China, November 2001*, available from www.ecosanres.org/Nanning%20Conf%20Proceedings.htm.

Jönsson, H (2002) 'Source Separation of Human Urine: Separation Efficiency and Effects on Water Emissions, Crop Yield, Energy Usage and Reliability', in *Proceedings of the First International Conference on Ecological Sanitation, Nanning, China, November 2001*, available from www.ecosanres.org/Nanning%20Conf%20Proceedings.htm.

Matsui, S (2002) 'The Potential of Ecological Sanitation', *Japan Review of International Affairs*, Winter 2002: 303-14.

——, M. Henze, G. Ho and R. Otterpohl (2001) 'Emerging Paradigms in Water Supply and Sanitation', in C. Maksimovic and J. Tejada-Guibert (eds.), *Frontiers in Urban Water Management* (London: IWA Publishing): 229-63.

Morgan, P. (1999) *Ecological Sanitation in Zimbabwe: A Compilation of Manuals and Experiences* (Harare, Zimbabwe: Aquamor Pvt. Ltd).

—— (2001) *Ecological Sanitation in Zimbabwe: A Compilation of Manuals and Experiences. Volume II* (Harare, Zimbabwe: Aquamor Pvt. Ltd).

NPHCC (2004) *NPHCC News Bulletin* 3 (9 June 2004), Beijing (in Chinese).

Rockefeller, A. (1997) 'Civilisation and Sludge: Notes on the History of the Management of Human Excreta', *Current World Leaders* 39.6: 99-113.

SEI (Stockholm Environment Institute) (2005) *Sustainmable Pathways to Attain the Millennium Development Goals* (Stockholm: SEI).

Stenström, T. (2002) 'Reduction Efficiency of Index Pathogens in Dry Sanitation Compared with Traditional and Alternative Waste-water Treatment Systems', in *Proceedings of the First International Conference on Ecological Sanitation, Nanning, China, November 2001*, available from www.ecosanres.org/Nanning%20Conf%20Proceedings.htm.

Tang J., X. Chen and Z. Wang (2001) 'An Integrated Cropping–Livestock–Biogas–Dwelling Eco–Agro–Engineering (ILBDE) Model and its Functions for Ecological Sanitation Improvement in

Rural China', in *Proceedings of the First International Conference on Ecological Sanitation, Nanning, China, November 2001,* available from www.ecosanres.org/Nanning%20Conf%20 Proceedings.htm.

UN Millennium Project (2005) *Health, Dignity, and Development: What Will It Take?* (Task Force on Water and Sanitation; London: Earthscan Publications).

Vinnerås, B (2002) *Possibilities for Sustainable Nutrient Recycling by Faecal Separation Combined with Urine Diversion* (doctoral dissertation; Uppsala: Department of Agricultural Engineering, Swedish University of Agricultural Sciences).

Wagner, G.R. (1958) *Excreta Disposal for Rural Areas and Small Communities* (Monograph Series, Number 39; Geneva, World Health Organisation).

Wei, B. (2002) 'Rural Sanitation, Ecosystem and China Western Region Development Strategy', in *Proceedings of the First International Conference on Ecological Sanitation, Nanning, China, November 2001,* available from www.ecosanres.org/Nanning%20Conf%20Proceedings.htm.

WHO/UNICEF (World Health Organisation/United Nations Children's Fund) (2001) *Global Water Supply and Sanitation Assessment 2000 Report* (2000) (Geneva: WHO/UNICEF).

—— (2004) *Meeting the MDG Drinking Water and Sanitation Target: A Mid-term Assessment of Progress* (Joint Monitoring Programme for Water Supply and Sanitation; Geneva: WHO/UNICEF).

Winblad, U., and M. Simpson-Hebert (eds.) (2004) *Ecological Sanitation* (Stockholm: Stockholm Environment Institute, rev. enlarged edn).

12

A measured step toward sustainability for rural water supply
ONE METERING STRATEGY THAT WORKS

*Eric Johnson**

Aquasanitas, USA

12.1 Why rural metering does not work

In the challenge of building sustainability into improved water supply for rural communities in the developing world there is no shortage of closely interconnected problems. Poorly targeted subsidies, egregious waste of water, unrealistic expectations for service levels, a lack of distinction between water itself and the service of delivery, gross under-capitalisation, increasing scarcity of water and cost of delivery, a lack of positive private-sector participation, inequitable distribution and manifestly inadequate mechanisms for creating local revenue streams all combine to make truly sustainable rural water supply an extremely hard-to-reach goal.

The problems seem so inevitable and incurable that it sometimes appears as though development workers and others have become complacent, accepting them as an operating reality rather working on the conviction that something can be done to change the situation.

Yet, for all the complaints listed, the mundane residential water meter provides an answer or at least a step in the right direction:

- It hugely reduces waste.

- It brings transparency and impartiality to all questions of consumption.

- It is strongly linked to equitable distribution, providing the basis for fees that vary according to what a wide range of families can afford and to what they consume (as opposed to flat-fee tariffs).

* The author gratefully acknowledges the contributions of Jonathan Claros and Rodolfo Pacheco to the development of this chapter.

- Through differentiated block pricing, it provides one of the few good options for directing water subsidies to those most in need.

- It is an immensely useful tool for improving revenue flow and cost recovery.

In short, it is a pillar in making a water system work well.

Given that meters are beneficial in so many ways it is no surprise that they are considered as being essential in the creation of rational urban water-distribution schemes in cases where water is scarce. In many places, one would no more expect unmetered water than one would expect unmetered petrol. But, somehow, even with all the benefits it brings to a water system, the perception of metering is at best that of a necessary evil, and almost all poor rural areas appear to have been exempted from its beneficial discipline in a dubious act of charity.

If one looks at the situation more closely, there is a big problem with the metering of water in rural areas. Despite its benefits and acceptance as necessary in an urban setting, for rural areas it is often regarded with hostility by engineers, development workers and project beneficiaries alike, and it is rejected both on philosophical and on technical grounds. For those opposed to, or ambivalent about, the idea of payment for the delivery of water in principle, the water meter is a symbol of injustice. On the technical side, previous traditions of extremely low (read: unsustainable) prices for water delivery and difficulties in collecting the small fees make the metering of water appear impractical. Unfamiliarity with water meters by end-users and by the builders of rural water projects also goes against their acceptance. The end result is that guiding examples of successful rural metering are rare, and this essential tool of sustainability is unavailable to many of those working to improve rural access to water.

Countering the belief that rural metering is not viable, however, is a promising experience in El Salvador that has shown that rural metering can work if applied *differently* from what is assumed to be the correct methodology based on the urban application of metering. In this chapter I provide a description of the alternative CARE El Salvador approach, with specific information for implementation.

12.2 How rural metering can work

CARE El Salvador is the local representation of the international non-govermental organisation (NGO) of the same name. In El Salvador it has operated a health programme with a community potable water supply component for some nine years, funded by the US Agency for International Development (USAID). The work has been directed both at relatively dispersed rural communities and at small towns. Implementation has been independent of the national water agency (though not inconsistent with national norms or policy). The CARE El Salvador office appears also to enjoy a high degree of autonomy from its headquarter organisation. Between 1993 and 1997, CARE El Salvador completed 24 water supply systems that relied on electromechanical pumping as the delivery technology, 12 of them complemented with residential meters to improve revenue flow in order to pay electricity bills and fund capital equipment replacement. In 1998, when the organisation moved to a broader focus on sustainability in its water system work, residential metering was established as a standard for all systems, without regard to whether they were based on electric pumping or gravity flow or served communities of an urban or a rural nature.

It should be noted that the techniques carried out by CARE staff are not in themselves unique to the CARE organisation or to the circumstances of El Salvador. World Bank (2003) data places El Salvador in a lower–middle-income classification, with a per capita income of about US$2,000 per year (ranked 101 of the 208 nations listed). The work carried out by CARE generally has focused on poorer beneficiaries with incomes far below the national per capita average. The experience described in this chapter is well suited for application in other poorer-country settings. The system described below includes both mundane and subtle techniques, but all have been found to make a critical difference to how metering is first perceived, then accepted and finally implemented. Some points are of the commonsense variety, others are highly counterintuitive; together they represent the distillation of five years of trial and error on a conscious path toward a policy of including meters as a cornerstone element in every potable system constructed, urban or rural. The result has proved to be an unusually powerful strategy that cuts through the prejudices and hostility to metering, permitting it to be seen as a tool for fair and efficient operation of community water systems.

The startling feature of the combination of techniques identified here is that it makes rural metering seem positively normal and rational. A stark contrast can be found between CARE-developed rural community water systems in southern El Salvador, and those a short distance away on the other side of the Honduras frontier. In the metered systems, a random walk through the community will lead to poor and elderly women emerging from their houses to defend the meters as a protection and saving grace of the system! Across the border in Honduras, meters in rural systems are virtually unknown and discussion on the topic reveals little understanding of their function or value.

There are two common characteristics to the techniques described: they are pragmatic and they are politically astute. Metering here is not about new technology or social philosophy; it is simply about making community water systems work better. The techniques advocated by CARE El Salvador are described in the following sections.

12.2.1 The promotion of metering

Water meters are *not* promoted among communities. In communities that already have a water system, it is only in cases where a problem appears and where CARE's help is solicited that meters are mentioned. In the development of a new water supply system metering is now part of the integrated project, but the subject of metering is broached only in the form of the techniques listed in the following sections. Furthermore, this is done only after establishing clearly with the community the limitations of the water source, the necessity of a functional tariff system and the management and operation responsibility that will rest with the community once the system is constructed. In short, there is *no* talk of meters *unless* a community is confronting a shortage or allocation problem that is already recognised as such or, in the case of a new system, the community is fully aware of the shortage, allocation and management challenges that lie ahead.

12.2.2 The presentation of options, not imperatives

For proposed new water systems and for existing water systems, discussion of meters occurs *only* in the context of three options. Initially, CARE staff attend a meeting of the community or water board where a water shortage or water allocation concern is brought up (the word 'allocation' here often refers to problems where there is insufficient pressure in the water lines to consistently reach houses at higher elevations in the system). No response or solution is presented at this first meeting. Instead, the staff ask to record the relevant data (the number of users, details of water supply, estimated shortfall and so on) and for permission to respond at the next meeting. At this later time three possible options generally are presented:

*   First, the option to raise the water fee paid by each family is presented. This would bring in the capital necessary to develop an additional water source or to modify the distribution lines in order to solve the problem at hand. Usually, to meet the anticipated cost of drilling a new well and/or extensive distribution line changes, a considerable increase will be necessary. The CARE staff provides estimates of what the realistic burden will be for each family by dividing the predicted cost of the work and new equipment required by the number of families in the community.

*   The option of some form of water rationing is discussed. For shortage and allocation problems, one solution is to rotate the water delivery among the various community home clusters, giving each a few hours of service each day. This usually requires a complex arrangement of daily valve openings and closures to ensure that each cluster receives some water at an adequate pressure. The CARE staff acknowledge that under this option no new water is going to be available; instead, there will be a redistribution of the limited supply, giving more water to some, but taking from others.

*   Water meters are also proposed as a possible solution. As their use dramatically reduces waste from leaky taps or taps left open, and as this simultaneously helps to improve water pressure in distribution lines, they can be discussed as a direct solution both to a serious shortfall in water resources and to a serious problem with water pressure and allocation. Their cost is objectively compared with the drilling of a new well or digging in a new distribution system.

Once the information on the options has been presented the CARE staff request that no decisions be considered at that time, but rather that the community members discuss the options among themselves so that the pros and cons of each can be assessed at a further meeting.

For that subsequent meeting the CARE staff are prepared with objective answers to the most common questions and doubts regarding meters. The presentation of the three options identified usually opens an intense but necessary debate among community members about what is really in the best interest of all. Through the examination of the true cost of adding an expensive new source of water or the redesign of the distribution system, and agonising over how to redistribute through rationing a resource that most community members feel to be in short supply, metering begins to emerge as an attractive alternative. Questions from community members regarding metering are routine: How do they work? What do they cost? How long do they last? Do they reduce pressure to the house tap? How accurate are they? Who will own the meters? How much will each family have to pay under a metered system? For the answer to the last question CARE staff propose actions outlined in Sections 12.2.3–12.2.5.

For new systems the inclusion of meters is examined carefully during the technical feasibility stage, particularly as part of the discussion of tariffs versus level of desired service. The range of options is the same: additional capital investment, which the community will have to absorb, rationing to reduce natural tendencies toward waste, or metering.

12.2.3 The use of meters for information only

To counter the understandable doubts and suspicions about water meters, CARE staff will, when appropriate, suggest placing the meters for a trial period, *but with the readings being used for information only*. That is, the water will be metered but readings will not be the basis of any charges, and the current household tariff will remain unchanged until a final decision is taken by a vote of the community. This tactic of *not* initially charging on the basis of the readings makes the meters a lower-risk proposition to wary community members. In addition, the informational metering is linked to strategic measures outlined in Sections 12.2.4 and 12.2.5.

12.2.4 Transparency

The meters are offered on an informational basis, but *on the condition* that the results each month are shared publicly on a chalkboard at a community meeting. This small but crucial measure encourages impartiality and transparency and clearly establishes who the big users of water are. It also provides a powerful incentive for *all* families to fix the leaky taps and stop letting water run unnecessarily without resorting to charging one centavo on the basis of the readings! Interestingly, the CARE experience is that water demand begins to fall as soon as the meters are installed, and this in turn brings an immediate improvement in system performance, including both availability and line pressure. This change is noted by all and sets the stage for what comes next in the process.

12.2.5 Fireworks and democracy

The small water system with water-shortage or allocation problems typically serves a community where a few wealthy users dominate the consumption (often for productive purposes), along with a number of poor but prolific wasters of water.

The wealthy big users of water can be expected to defend ruthlessly their privilege, but the transparency technique of public sharing of consumption data tends to isolate them and empower democratic forces to seek equitable solutions. The goal is not to create conflict along class lines but rather to loosen the hold that a few big users often have over water systems. Though most big users usually oppose metering initially, some will recognise that metering is a way to legitimise their consumption (at an admittedly higher but fair price). This angle is actively pursed to engage them and encourage their co-operation.

The other high-consumption group, the poor but prolific wasters, are effectively constrained by community pressure not to abuse what is a limited resource and by the possibility that they may soon have to pay according to their use.

The most powerful technique in this phase is the use of the figures on household consumption within the community to engage a calculated majority for action. The public consumption data for a typical community after the meters have been in place for two or three months reveals that the majority of families will have reduced their water consumption to 15 m³ or less per month. The 'wasters' will consume up to perhaps 40 m³ per month, and a few big users (owning livestock, orchards and so on) will use as much as 100 m³ per month. Once the pattern of use becomes clear the CARE staff design a proposed block rate chart for the water, carefully selecting a 'basic family water block' that is guaranteed to cover at least 51% of the families, say 16 m³ per month. A popular price is proposed for the basic block, with consumption up to 16 m³ set at one low tariff, usually close to the current flat rate. Fees for consumption beyond the 16 m³ are calculated on a per-cubic-metre basis, with blocks of increasing rates (usually for every subsequent 5 m³ or 10 m³). The majority of the community suddenly sees that it has to pay little or nothing more for water than the current fee, ensuring a broad base of political support for the scheme. The wasters and the big users find themselves divided and in a difficult-to-defend position. CARE experience is that at this point some of the big users join the majority, publicly embracing the metering scheme. Perceiving that their block fee is still a reasonable price, considering the productive value they extract from use of the water, they acknowledge that it is only fair to pay more for their higher consumption. They also are not blind to the manifest evidence of the improved system performance that the metering provides in terms of a more reliable supply, thus better protecting their water-dependent investments.

12.2.6 Subsidy allocation

For initial work the cost of the meters may need to be subsidised for the community, but because their use reduces waste so effectively this cost is largely offset by savings in other components of the water system. As the meters have become more accepted in El Salvador and their value recognised, CARE has been more insistent that communities pay fully the cost of the meters. In the past five years, most CARE project communities have purchased their own meters outright, typically for around US$20 per meter, a figure equivalent to a few months of the typical individual family water bill.

A further benefit of the use of meters is that they permit a much better focus for any consumer subsidies applied in the rural water systems. Most commonly, CARE has used the meters to direct available subsidies towards a basic block of low-priced water, similar to 'lifeline-tariff' strategies used elsewhere, with subsequent blocks charged at increasing prices per unit.

12.2.7 Addressing the weak spots frankly

There are a small number of technical issues with meters that, if unaddressed, can become the focus of highly emotional complaints at the community level and derail an otherwise successful metering project. CARE has found that the best policy is to have a generous plan available to 'calm the waters' and to defuse such reactions and to be ready for these concerns. Such concerns may include the following.

- **Inaccurate readings.** Many people initially complain that their meters 'read high'. Rather than be drawn into a debate over whether that is really the case, CARE has found it politically prudent to advise community water associations simply to accept the replacement of a number of meters early on and regard this as a cost of gaining confidence.

- **Metering air.** Community members will complain bitterly about 'paying for air' if the system is not pressurised continuously, as is the case with many small systems. The tactic to counter this is to set the basic block rate slightly above the desired price level and then provide a universally applied discount for potential air that might flow when checking the tap for water.

- **Meter breakdowns.** Because small residential meters used in the CARE systems are cheap (costing only US$20 compared with US$60 for top-quality residential meters) and are prone to failure CARE encourages community water associations to have a number of spare meters on hand for quick replacement when failure occurs. (When a meter does break down, the monthly rate paid typically will be the same as the amount paid in the month preceding the breakdown or a monthly average taken over the previous three months.)

12.2.8 Investing in social marketing

The CARE approach clearly requires that well-trained, competent and articulate staff dedicate adequate time to the social development aspects of the community water system. The typical community metering project in an existing water system can easily take up to a year. Getting communities to accept metering is not easy work, and this level of effort is probably a necessary condition for the success of the metering initiative.

12.2.9 Meter ownership

In CARE's work, all of the meters are community-owned and the metering process is community-managed. On numerous occasions during community visits it was mentioned that, had the meters been seen as property of the government water agency or even of CARE, the project would have failed. Obviously, work had been done to foster a sense that the meters were truly a community asset used to defend the interests of all citizens.

12.2.10 Simplified metering

The metering arrangements for the more rural communities are intentionally rather primitive but *always* include a paid staff member employed by the community water association for readings and billings. Rates are divided into blocks for easy calculation of bills. The improved revenue that metering is likely to bring increases the prospect of having proper staffing for reading, billing and collection. For the smaller rural systems, the meter reading, billing and collection takes just a few days per month.

12.2.11 Using community water boards for replication

Once a few of the metered systems were in place CARE made use of board members of community water associations to speak to other communities about their experiences with metering. This has in more recent years substantially eased the burden of convincing communities to adopt metering.

12.2.12 Low connection fees

CARE recommends community water associations to keep residential connection fees low, especially for families that join after the water system is built. This reduces the incentive to make informal connections, which would undermine the metering effort. It is a sensitive issue, however, that must be addressed carefully with families who have contributed their labour to assist in the building of the water system. Some communities structure the connection fee to be payable over time, which enables levying a higher overall fee without driving new residents to informal connections. Also, system administrators are finding ways for new families to make labour contributions to an existing system: for example, by doing environmental protection work, such as planting trees around a well site, or health-related work such as home visits to check if latrines are being properly cared for.

12.3 Failure as a measure of success

In looking at the level of organisation and flow of resources in the communities that have meters it is possible to see that what has evolved are really community-owned water enterprises with a social mandate. The meters are key to the success of these enterprises, not just by promoting fair and equitable distribution but also by making the whole water-delivery process more efficient, businesslike and profitable. The community water associations are well aware that the meters are an administrator's tool, reducing non-payment problems, social conflicts and environmental and resource issues. CARE has encouraged this sort of thinking with regard to the meters, helping small associations run in a businesslike and profitable way while pursuing a social purpose.

Few solutions can resolve a problem without creating a new one, however, and metering is no exception. One rather unfortunate but significant indicator of the success that metering brings to rural communities was a peculiar issue said to be not uncommon in the CARE rural systems and seen in two of the eight communities visited for the review that forms the basis of this chapter. In these communities, the boards struggle with the consequences of new and highly effective revenue streams enabled by metering. The substantial bank accounts generated by successful schemes, with a healthy surplus of income over operation and maintenance expenses, are ideally directed to a capital replacement fund. Unfortunately, they can create a real temptation for some board members unaccustomed to handling the relatively large sums of money entrusted to them to engage in some form of theft. They also serve as an excuse for others with planning horizons shorter than the design life of the water system to clamour for rate reductions or other populist measures.

Theft from a well-funded association treasury, or lack of political will to save surpluses for capital replacements, are unquestionably serious problems, but they are also the almost inevitable by-products of the first stages of successful democratic association. In a world where the shortfall of investment for basic water supplies runs in the tens of billions of dollars annually, the smaller headaches of how to manage the better revenue flows as a result of rural metering offer a welcome relief from the endlessly demoralising problems of too little water and too little money.

References

CARE, www.careusa.org/careswork/projects/SLV035.asp
World Bank (2003) 'World Development Indicators', www.worldbank.org/data/databytopic/
    GNIPC.pdf.

13

Sustainable water supply for a remote rural community in Mozambique

OXFAM AUSTRALIA AND THE CHICOMO RURAL DEVELOPMENT PROJECT

Elizabeth Mann

Oxfam Australia*

In 2000 it was estimated that 43% of the rural population in Mozambique had access to improved water sources (World Bank 2001: 143): a rapid rise from 6% in 1980 (DNA 1995). While the figures demonstrate a substantial investment in infrastructure, primarily in the form of boreholes fitted with hand pumps, they do not address the Mozambique government's concern that 'in rural areas where hand-pumps are installed it is still difficult to keep them operational' (DNA 1995). This concern is substantiated by the estimation that, of the approximately 250,000 hand pumps in Africa, less than half are operational (SKAT 2000). This chapter reflects on the difficulties associated with providing sustainable water supplies to communities living in the rural area of Chicomo in Southern Mozambique where groundwater is up to 93 metres below the surface. Pump selection and technical modifications for deep-well hand pumps, as well as community ownership, training and resourcing are discussed. While many of the lessons learned by Oxfam Australia are specific to the context, the broader issues of appropriate technology and capacity building of community structures will be relevant to service providers working in a variety of sectors.

Oxfam Australia has worked in Inhambane Province, Mozambique, since the early 1980s and in the Chicomo locality of Massinga District since 1992, the year that marked the end of the civil war. During the war 80% of the population of Chicomo fled, seeking refuge in safer areas closer to the coast. As people returned they found

---

* Oxfam Australia is an independent, secular and not-for-profit organisation dedicated to building a fairer world in which people control their own lives, their basic rights are achieved and the environment is sustained.

their homes and the majority of their water sources destroyed. Oxfam Australia's initial work in the locality was an emergency project that distributed clothing, food and shelter materials. This was followed by a project providing seeds and tools and rehabilitating two boreholes.

A study conducted by Bagnol (Projecto Chicomo 1994) as part of the project design phase of the Chicomo Rural Development Project found that, during the war, 11 boreholes had been destroyed and in 1994 a population of 10,000 survived from four boreholes. With a distance of 99 km between two of the boreholes, women walked up to 50 km, a 2 day journey, including a wait of up to 7 hours in the queue, to collect 20 litres of water. When these pumps broke down, the women walked to the hand-dug wells closer to the coast, several days' journey, or lived off the sap of roots and tree trunks.

While access to water was the main priority of the women and men of Chicomo, they had other needs that included health, education and agriculture. The Chicomo Rural Development Project attempted to address all of these priorities to varying degrees. The project had five components: health, education, agriculture, community development and water. In this paper the other non-water components will only be discussed where they intersect with the project's purpose of improving the availability of water to households.

Between 1997 and 2000 the Chicomo project drilled 23 boreholes and rehabilitated another four, ensuring water coverage to approximately 12,500 people. Water supply coverage by boreholes rose from approximately 30% in 1994 to 88% in 2000, with improved reliability. Unlike some other parts of Southern Africa, households in rural areas of Inhambane Province are dispersed rather than clustered in small villages. People identify as belonging to a specific community but may be kilometres from their nearest neighbour. While actual distance between the pumps varies from 1 to 23 km, the average distance between pumps has been reduced to 11.4 km. Communities mostly live within a radius of 10–90 minutes' walking distance to collect water from a given pump.

13.1 Community involvement in site selection

In the absence of a village centre in which to locate a well, decisions on where to locate the boreholes were, in the majority of cases, reached by consensus. Representatives from a range of communities agreed on the areas most in need of a borehole, basing the decision on population numbers and distance to the nearest water source. On three occasions traditional leaders or government-appointed local councillors chose the location. Each community proposed two sites and cleared the land around them so that a geophysical survey could be carried out using vertical electrical soundings to verify the presence and quality of water likely to be encountered. Boreholes were drilled at the more appropriate of the two sites, sometimes with traditional ceremonies held to bless the site prior to the start of the drilling. Community involvement in the selection of the site promoted a sense of ownership of the process, increasing the chance of sustainability and participation both in training and in financially contributing to the cost of repairing and maintaining the pump.

As well as selecting the site and clearing the land, each community was asked to form a group which would collect monetary contributions to the repair and maintenance fund for the new hand pump. Prior to 1995 and the establishment of a user-pays system, the government water department was responsible for financing rural water supplies. In 1995, the National Water Policy established that rural communities are totally responsible for the operation and maintenance of their water supplies (DNA 1995). The Chicomo project made it a prerequisite for each community to collect the equivalent of US$50 prior to the installation of the pump. Funds were difficult to raise from communities that believed that the responsibility for rural water supply should remain with the government. The change of the role of the government from implementer to facilitator, combined with the change in Oxfam Australia's approach from emergency response where goods were distributed without cost, to requiring community contributions for water, was difficult to grasp for very poor rural communities struggling to rebuild their lives. In retrospect it appears that in a hierarchical society such as Mozambique the communities might have been more accepting of these changes if government officials and the Oxfam Australia Field Representative had personally explained and justified the changes.

In line with the National Water Policy objectives of community-managed water sources, management, maintenance and repair groups (MMRGs) were formed. These groups were composed of three men and three women, selected by their communities. The project employed two water technicians and a water component team leader who together had the responsibility for all technical aspects of the water component, including training each community to maintain and repair their pumps. While the MMRGs received additional attention during training it was important for each community to have a large number of members with a sound understanding and the skills to repair the hand pump. In Figure 13.1 the community of Ndimande are pictured with their Afridev hand pump, which they have learned to dismantle and reassemble. Initially, male members of the MMRGs carried out the maintenance and repair of the pumps, with the female members responsible for maintaining the cleanliness of the pump site and advising people on hygienic use of the pump and its surrounds. Gender training conducted with all staff members aided the technicians in their work with communities; women were encouraged to dismantle and reassemble the pump, to the initial amusement of the men, but the women gained their respect as they demonstrated their skills. Chicomo is a very patriarchal society and the project's successes in empowering women were limited to a handful of communities and individuals. Again, in hindsight it was felt that additional training for both the management of the project and the staff on gender issues might have improved the final outcomes.

Complete sets of all the tools required to dismantle, reassemble and repair the pump were issued to each MMRG. The distribution of these toolkits did not occur at the time of the first training, and in some cases it was years before a complete toolkit was provided. This disadvantaged those communities without a complete toolkit as they were not able to put into practice the skills they had learned and were dependent on the water technician's tools for some or all repair work.

FIGURE 13.1 The community of Ndimande with their Afridev hand pump

An additional measure taken to strengthen the technical capacity within the locality was the identification of local mechanics. Chicomo locality is divided into four sections, known as circles. Within each circle two community members with either particular aptitude or technical expertise were identified and trained to play the role of local mechanic. The concept was that if a MMRG was unable to repair the pump it would call on the local mechanic for assistance. The project provided each local mechanic with a bicycle to facilitate transport. Such a backup system should be factored into any project, particularly in areas where HIV/AIDS rates are rising and/or a culture of migration to other areas in search of paid employment exists. Relying on the skills and knowledge of a small number of individuals makes the sustainability of a borehole and the community that relies on that water source vulnerable to the loss of trained people.

13.2 Technical aspects of the programme and modifications implemented

The project installed hand pumps in all 27 boreholes. Three different types of hand pump, ten Afridevs, ten Volantas and seven Nationals were installed, consistent with the dynamic water levels, the deepest of which was 93.5 metres. The Government of Mozambique's National Directorate of Water authorises the use of two hand pumps, the Afridev for depths up to 60 metres, despite the manufacturer's recommended limit of 45 metres, and the Volanta for boreholes deeper than 60 metres. The high cost of the Volanta hand pump (three times the cost of the Afridev), its lack of spare parts in the country (the pump is manufactured in the Netherlands) and the manufacturer's recommended installation depth limit of 80 metres encouraged the project to carry out a trial with the National pump from South Africa on the seven deepest boreholes. The community had experience with this pump prior to the commencement of the project, and their confidence in the pump contributed to its adoption as a technical solution for boreholes with greater than 80 metre depths. Of the three pumps the National is the only hand pump that is not of a village-level operation and maintenance design (VLOM) and its construction is predominantly steel.

Three staff with technical skills in water were employed but none of the following had a technical background: the project manager in Massinga; Oxfam Australia's field representatives; or the programme co-ordinator in Melbourne, Australia. It was not until 1999 that Paul Tyndale-Biscoe, Oxfam Australia's water engineer, conducted a study of the performance of the three pumps to evaluate the appropriateness of the National pump. Based on this study, Tyndale-Biscoe made two main recommendations. The first was for improvements to the National pump, which were followed up with the manufacturer. The second was for the bottom support system (BSS), explained below, to be installed in the two deepest boreholes fitted with Afridev pumps. This would reduce the stress on the most vulnerable parts as both pumps were installed at depths nearing 60 metres, well beyond the manufacturer's recommended depth limit of 45 metres (Tyndale-Biscoe 2000).

These recommendations were implemented but, even with anti-corrosion treatment of some parts of the National pump and other changes that had caused ineffective operation, it was concluded during 2000 that the National pump was not a sustainable proposition due to its oil leaks, heavy fly wheel and low water yield in relation to high energy inputs for turning the heavy wheel and the need for a pulley and rope system to lift the rising main.

This finding left the project with no option other than to replace the seven National pumps; and, with no government-authorised alternative, seven Volantas were installed with the BSS as a means of reducing breakdowns due to failure of the rising main. Oxfam Australia staff member Paul Tyndale-Biscoe, in collaboration with David McMurdie, designed the BSS during 1998 while supporting a water project in Ethiopia. The system was modified further with input from the international standards body SKAT (Swiss Centre for Appropriate Technology). Tyndale-Biscoe described the system in his pump performance report as follows:

> Rather than suspending the rising main column from the top as with most hand pump installations, the rising main sits on the bottom of the borehole on a specially designed bottom support pipe. The connection between the pipe and the pumphead at the top is modified to provide a watertight seal, but to allow vertical movement in case of settlement, and to ensure that none of the weight of the column is carried by the pumphead.
>
> The advantages of such a system relate to both loading and efficiency. PVC is strong in compression but relatively weak in tension. In a top hung

system, the PVC pipe not only carries its own weight, but the weight of the water as well. As the installation depth, and so the length of the rising main column increases, so the tensile load in the column (particularly near the top) increases. Loading on all joints also increases, and any weaknesses in the column or stress concentrations become likely places where failure will occur.

When the column is sitting on the bottom of a borehole, the entire column is placed in compression rather than tension. The effect of any tensile stress concentrations such as bent boreholes is minimised as the tensile and compressive loading tends to cancel one another out. In addition the weight of the water is not carried by the rising main column, but rather is transferred through the footvalve to the bottom support pipe, which is made of heavier PVC pipe.

PVC pipe is elastic and when suspended from the top and filled with water, it can stretch significantly. It has been estimated that an 80 metre length of Afridev riser column full of water will stretch around 100 mm.

Given the arrangement of plunger/footvalve type pumps, there is a transfer of load from the footvalve to the plunger valve and back again with every stroke. When water is being lifted, the weight of the water is carried by the plunger rods, however on the down-stroke (when the handle is lifted), the weight of the column of water is transferred to the footvalve. When the column is top hung, this causes the entire column to stretch and retract with every stroke, which has the effect of reducing the effective stroke of the pump by the amount of the stretch (Tyndale-Biscoe 2000).

BSS was installed into two Afridev pumps in Chicomo during August 2000 and in all pumps working beyond their design specifications by July 2001. The reduction in breakdowns due to rising main-related problems has been significant. During mid-2002 BSS was installed in all pumps irrespective of their depths after demands from those communities without the technology to have it installed.

13.3 Maintaining and repairing the pumps

While appropriate technology and technical skills within a community are essential, they are not the only factors for a sustainable water supply project. Even with BSS, which has reduced the number of breakdowns due to failure of the rising main, pumps still require spare parts, whether that involves replacement of seals and other wearing parts or the replacement of broken rods (now the most common breakdown). This raises issues of both payment for the parts and access to them. The Government of Mozambique's National Water Policy is clear on the issue of payment. It is each community's responsibility to fund the costs involved in sustaining the water source. In Chicomo an average contribution of US$30 per year per pump is collected, the amount recorded and banked by a local structure known as the Unity Group, formed in an earlier phase of the project to supervise and manage a credit scheme. With no other structure present in the area, the project supported the registration of the Unity Group which contained within its statutes the objective of sustaining the water sources in place. Even without any formal employment opportunities within the area, none of the communities told the evaluators of the project that this contribution was too high (Thompson and Milagre 2000).

Access to spare parts proved beyond the capacity of the project to resolve. For communities in Chicomo the nearest town is Massinga, which is a growing trading centre 60 km from the closest pump and 160 km from the most remote. Massinga does not have a reliable stock of parts for any of the pumps. Maxixe, another 70 km south of Massinga, has a reasonable supply of Afridev parts but no parts for the Volanta. The sole supplier of Volanta parts in the country is based in the capital, Maputo, 530 km south of Massinga. Even if the nine-hour bus journey from Massinga to Maputo was made, there would be no guarantee that the parts required would be in stock as the supplier only keeps a small supply of spares and, periodically, when new pumps are ordered, replenishes the spare parts stock. Staff of the project negotiated with traders, suppliers and the government in an attempt to resolve supply chain problems with limited success. Supply chains do form part of the current World Bank-funded studies on the water sector in Inhambane Province. During the life of the project spare parts for all pump types were kept in a warehouse managed by the project staff. As individual communities required spare parts, their balance in the Unity Group records was checked and the cost of the part deducted from their contributions. The complete management of spare parts was handed over to the Unity Group only at the end of 2000, leaving no time for project staff with appropriate experience to mentor those responsible for sustaining the system.

Oxfam Australia, wherever possible, programmes in partnership with existing local non-government organisations and in so doing strengthens the capacity of these organisations. As there were no organisations operating in the Chicomo area, water technicians, agricultural technicians and management staff were recruited and companies contracted to drill the boreholes. This staff team worked on the project until December 2000. To finalise a number of activities, solidify the training and support the communities the two water technicians returned to Chicomo for seven months during 2001. Follow-up occurred twice during 2002 to monitor the pumps and install BSS modifications into the remaining boreholes. This continued contact with the communities at less and less regular intervals was very important in ensuring the sustainability of the water sources as the communities gained confidence in their own ability to manage the hand pumps.

13.4 Lessons learned from the project

The key lessons that we would recommend any organisation involved in rural water supply to take into account are:

- Use the most appropriate technology available and seek more information from Oxfam Australia or SKAT about BSS if installing pumps beyond the manufacturer's design specifications.

- Involve highly skilled technical staff to support the work in the field from the outset of the project.

- Provide lengthy and comprehensive hands-on training to a wide range of community members, especially women, at regular intervals, which build on previous training courses.

- Strengthen community capacity in all areas of the project—technical, financial and management—from the outset. Give the communities control over all resources and assets as soon as practical with staff playing a mentoring and support role.

- Further strengthen the support to individual communities by developing and resourcing local expertise with responsibility for a number of hand pumps.

- Do not leave supply chain constraints until the end of the project; join with others with the same problems in the area to lobby government or negotiate a deal with the private sector.

The lessons learned from this project were incorporated into the design of Oxfam Australia's current Food Security Project in the neighbouring Funhalouro district of Inhambane Province. To promote sustainability within this project Oxfam Australia works with União Nacional de Camponeses (UNAC), a local organisation that has placed a technically skilled co-ordinator within the project site and developed strong links with the district agricultural department. Oxen rather than mechanised alternatives were reintroduced into the area to assist with ploughing and transportation. Training in technical and management matters for equal numbers of men and women from the community occurred early in the project cycle. Initial findings from the evaluation report demonstrate that a community-led and -managed approach has enhanced the likelihood of sustainability.

13.5 Conclusion

Drilling a borehole and installing a hand pump in a rural community is an event for celebration, especially for women. A hand pump provides water closer to home, saving both time and energy. The drilling and installation are in themselves not sufficient to sustain the water supply. Maintaining a functioning hand pump and creating a sense of ownership of the water source are essential and require more than a single training session and a formal handover of the hand pump and borehole to the community. Oxfam Australia found that sustainability is strengthened by community involvement in all aspects of the process. This includes site selection, agreement on the amount and mechanism for collecting contributions to pay for spare parts, and periodic training of a large number of both men and women in the maintenance and repair of the hand pumps over a number of years. Additional support to community structures in the form of advanced technical support from persons with technical expertise created a safety net for communities faced with more complex repairs. While technical modifications such as BSS can reduce the number of breakdowns in hand pumps, the sustainability of any technology is dependent on the skills and confidence of community members to maintain and repair the equipment in addition to a commitment to financially contribute to the cost of spare parts.

References

Bagnol, B. (1994) *Projecto Chicomo* (unpublished)

DNA (Direcção Nacional de Águas) (1995) 'National Water Policy', www.dna.mz/natwpol.htm.

Oxfam Community Aid Abroad (2001) *Chicomo Rural Development Project, Project Completion Report* (unpublished).

SKAT (Swiss Centre for Appropriate Technology) (2000) 'HTN (Network for Cost Effective Technologies in Water Supply and Sanitation) for Africa', www.skat.ch/htn/About/focusafrica.htm.

Thompson, G., and D. Milagre (2000) *Chicomo Rural Development Project: Final Evaluation Review* (unpublished).

Tyndale-Biscoe, P. (2000) *Chicomo Rural Development Project, Handpump Performance Report* (Oxfam Community Aid Abroad, unpublished).

World Bank (2001) '2001 World Development Indicators', www.worldbank.org/data/wdi2001/index.htm.

Part 4
Regionally focused case studies: rural environments

14

Indigenous people, women and water

THE IMPORTANCE OF LOCAL KNOWLEDGE FOR PROJECT PLANNING IN AN AFRICAN CONTEXT

Fenda A. Akiwumi

Texas State University, USA

> The present practice of the friends of africa is to frame laws according to their own notions for the government and improvement of this people, whereas God has already enacted the laws governing in these affairs, which laws should be carefully ascertained, interpreted, and applied; for until they are found out and conformed to, all labour will be ineffective and resultless . . . in this direction, and this direction only, lies the hope of Africa's future (Edward W. Blyden, 1888).

Sustainable water reform in developing countries calls for the participation of indigenous people, particularly women, as major partners. While the need for input from those persons most affected by developments has been acknowledged at the international level, in practice it rarely occurs (United Nations 1993; El-Ashry 1993; Wolfensohn 1997; Second World Water Forum 2000). Despite the fact that indigenous value systems and methodologies have been declared worthy of emulation, the only means of involvement to date have been incorporation and co-optation into Western-style models. A comprehensive list of actions that could rectify these discrepancies has emerged from numerous deliberations, but implementation of actions in developing countries such as Sierra Leone remains a challenge. This chapter addresses the discrepancy between the theoretically ideal level of participation by indigenous people and what is actually practised, with a focus on water projects in Sierra Leone.

14.1 Uses of water resources in Sierra Leone

This West African country has abundant water resources; rainfall averages 3,000 mm per annum with an annual per capita run-off of 38,000 m³ (Gleick 1993: 130).

Nine main river basins ranging in size from 14,145 to 2,979 km² and associated swamps traverse its 71,740 km² surface area. Over much of the country the weathered zone and alluvial deposits form secondary aquifers, locally tapped for groundwater.

Traditional water-based livelihoods include recessional cultivation or floodwater farming, fishing and palm oil production. Water has major spiritual and social dimensions also, and the river is often a sacred site. Modern Western development approaches, on the other hand, view water as an economic good, promoting income-generating hydroelectric power, potable water supply, swamp drainage, and alluvial and dredge mining schemes.

Imposition of the policy along these lines by the national government often results in unequal access and control over the resource, disruption of traditional lifestyles, and hence conflict. Such inequity is often countered with overt non-compliance or other subtle forms of protest by indigenous people in ways which can undermine capital-intensive projects. In spite of over 200 years of efforts at Western-style water development, major challenges still remain for implementation of sustainable ventures in Sierra Leone (Akiwumi 1982). Material incentives, easier access to water, the prospect of multiple crop yields, educational and motivational campaigns and 'capacity building' strategies have not improved the extent of community co-operation. The problem lies in the inability to balance the indigenous people's views on water with methodologies based on modern development techniques. To redress this, a cross-cultural and interdisciplinary approach to water resources planning needs to be employed in order to ensure a better understanding of the indigenous perspective.

14.2 Differing Western and African viewpoints on management and organisation

The problem of poor community participation in projects can be viewed in the context of organisation and management models. As Wren (1972: 36) notes, 'the development of a body of knowledge about how to manage has evolved within a framework of the economic, social and political facets of various cultures. Management thought is both a process in and product of its cultural environment.'

In a Western context, organisations exist primarily to carry out production and work towards economic goals efficiently and effectively. The scientific management method devised to facilitate this approach sees human beings as 'cogs in machines', being both rational and primarily motivated by economic incentives. This legal-rational approach to management was formally introduced to the African continent during colonisation, the process facilitated by co-optation of native leaders into the administration (Selznick 1949). The charismatic authority of indigenous institutions, where family or group loyalties supersede notions of merit, is in marked contrast (Heady 1995). Furthermore, the limited view of cause and effect in Western thinking differs from the transcendental level of interpretation in African indigenous epistemology on organisation goals and behaviour (Wariboko 1999). To illustrate this, this chapter will examine organisation among the Mende, the largest ethnic group in Sierra Leone.

Political, economic and cultural aspects of life among the Mende are developed and governed by religio-legal institutions known as *Hale* (Abraham 1978). The paramount chief is overall political and spiritual leader. Sub-organisations under *Hale*, called *Poro* and *Sande*, govern the affairs of men and women, respectively. Law and order are maintained by the imposition of sanctions. Knowledge crucial to the community's development and survival, considered a divine gift, is possessed by leaders who pass it on to persons accredited by the community. As such, these organisations are often referred to as 'secret societies'.

The balance between 'aggressive individualism' and the 'aggressive welfare consciousness' characteristic of African communal societies is maintained by 'levelling mechanisms' that operate in the traditional system (Abraham 1994; Wariboko 1999). These include kinship obligations and sanctions against the wealthy. Reciprocity and consultation in social relations are fundamental to compliance and co-operation in activities that sustain communities (Boone 1986; Hardin 1993; Ferme 2001). As regards land rights, a patrilineal land tenure system prevails. A tribal authority of elders determines land allotment and use within the traditional administrative unit, the chiefdom. Water-based activities such as rice farming, fishing, collection of construction material from riparian and swamp forests, and rites of passage occur within a well-ordered timetable. Within each of these activities the gender roles are clearly defined.

14.3 A suggested interdisciplinary approach to planning

Adoption of an interdisciplinary approach to planning reflecting the social characteristics of a people accustomed to a hierarchical, socially sensitive, gender-differentiated framework, true of some 70% of the population of Sierra Leone, can facilitate the implementation of modern projects at grass-roots level. Project evaluators from technical backgrounds have often puzzled that, despite a variety of inducements and availability of modern technology, water project success rates have not improved. Anthropologists and sociologists may be more able to identify the root cause of failure, but unfortunately interdisciplinary teams are rarely employed in project planning (Akiwumi 1994, 1998). Rather, the focus has been on scientific assessment by scientists who rarely recognise the importance or relevance of data outside their expertise. The limitations of this approach were perceived by Debenham many years ago in a colonial report on some British East African Territories and Protectorates:

> the water professional must have a wider view than his original training would of itself give him, since he is concerned not only with the existence of water but its potential uses. He therefore finds himself called upon to estimate social, economic and even political values in his work, and these judgements may often be of greater actual importance than his purely

scientific training in finding or measuring water (Debenham, cited in Waldock *et al.* 1951: 99).

Debenham's theory is particularly relevant to the African-born, Western-educated scientist. He or she is implicitly expected to be a sociocultural synergiser and guide to the local environment. However, most lack the expertise to operate within an indigenous framework and are more comfortable serving on poorly conceived 'modern' projects, where many develop 'a mentality which discriminates against indigenous systems, products and ideals while glorifying anything foreign' (Ihonbvere 1992: 169). Case studies in this paper reveal the conflict between different 'ways of knowing the world of water' and consequences for sustainable development in Sierra Leone.

14.4 Taking the river: the paradox of female empowerment through water projects

Giving women leadership roles on water projects is considered a means of female empowerment. Women have been identified as logical choices to manage village-based extended family producer co-operatives to support diamond mining because they play important roles in other forms of production and consumption (USAID 2000). In Sierra Leone, as noted above, women are intimately involved with water through *Sande*, a traditional organisation described by Boone (1986) as 'the ruling, governing institution in a female's life . . . an extraordinary instance of female power in traditional African government'. Almost all rural women belong to the organisation. The *Sowei* (leader) has great social significance as role model, teacher, judge and healer of women. Through the society, girls learn life skills in herbal medicine and agricultural techniques, leadership and fine arts, and positive personality traits including responsibility, stamina, persistence, truthfulness, straightforwardness and courage are emphasised. Water as 'mystical space' is symbolic in the rituals and belief systems and the river is regarded as a sacred site where 'spirits enjoy a divine existence of beauty and peace' (Boone 1986: 50). The sacred initiation grove or *kpanguima* is located near water, and religious paraphernalia buried in the river depths are brought up by a diver, a senior member of the organisation, for special ceremonies. Daily beauty and cleansing rituals are likewise carried out here, as are productive activities such as shallow-water fishing, typically women's work.

14.4.1 Dredge mining, women and fishing

Many projects have inadvertently eroded the traditional female power base that arises from this association with water. In south-west Sierra Leone the damming of rivers has created artificial lakes (dredge-ponds) for mining. Legislation gives the operating company exclusive rights to water in the lease area, allowing the operating company to 'dig, widen and deepen channels in rivers streams and water courses as necessary . . . to use water from any natural course . . . to divert streams, to build temporary dams and to impound water to secure the supply of water needed for mining operations' (FAO/UN 1979: 173). Although wells have been dug in some villages to serve as alternative water sources, local populations continue to use contaminated surface supplies. During an environmental impact assessment study a group of women complained about the effects of mining on their shallow-water fishing activities (Lamin *et al*. 1991). They explained how in March the peak dry-season water levels naturally recede to a level at which women can wade with the mouth of small scoop nets up against the banks of streams or water pools where fish can be easily caught. Following dam construction, seepage beneath the new structure raised water levels in the downstream channel to the point where this could no longer be done. Under an Environmental and Community Development Programme (ECDP) Bamba-Belebu pond was subsequently stocked with fish to provide an alternative resource, despite the poor results of a water quality analysis by fishery consultants. Recommendations called for ponds to be flooded to maximum holding capacity in order to develop the non-aquacultural local fishing industries (Steffen Robertson & Kirston [BC] Inc. 1990; Cremer & Warner Ltd 1991). In the pilot phase of the project, information on local fishing practices and needs and the social and nutritional impact of the venture was collected. The only complaint documented in this pilot study was villager dissatisfaction over the variety of fish selected by the company, although Kamara (1997: 27) records that 'the feasibility of fish management in mined-out ponds is completely at odds with the experience of local peoples'.

From a traditional perspective, water and fishing are central to both *Sande* initiation and childbirth. Seasonal fishing is one of the few production activities under community guidelines that can be carried out independently. Although it is a communal activity carried out with much camaraderie, any fish catch is for individual consumption. Unlike the larger fishing and hunting nets employed by men, the scoop nets are individually owned. They are often personalised with creative designs or coloured beads and secret esoteric substances applied to surfaces to ensure good catches. Weaving scoop nets requires a higher level of technical expertise than that required for producing large nets. Women, therefore, take great pride in their craftsmanship and the art is one of 'two practices that rural Mende women consider[ed] central to their everyday worlds' (Ferme 2001: 69). None of the reports prior to the project addressed these three important aspects: the change in water depth which prohibited the use of traditional fishing methods; the way in which seasonal changes fitted the timetable of community activities; and the implications for gender–social power relationships.

14.4.2 Groundwater versus surface sources

In Sierra Leone underground water is primarily used in the dry season when surface sources shrink. From a Western scientific perspective, exploitation of groundwater is often seen as a cost-effective method of providing clean water in developing countries. Water well projects, therefore, are widely promoted. An evaluation by the organisation, WaterAid, of rural water supply and sanitation schemes in the

Eastern Province of the country (Abitbol 1989) revealed the difficulty of adequately assessing the effectiveness of projects in the absence of a holistic approach. He noted that the beneficiaries' 'quality of life has undoubtedly greatly been improved' (1989: 3-4) and 'Villagers were emphatic in their appreciation of the quality of the piped water' (1989: 6). At the same time, however, he questioned the continued use of polluted surface sources and suggested that a further study should explore the reasons for this. Other problems raised in Abitbol's study included the difficulties experienced in collecting the stipulated financial contributions to the scheme from communities and the anomaly of including a vigorous education and motivation campaign designed to 'stimulate the self-help ethic' (1989: 7) among Mende people whom he notes are historically known for their 'strong social cohesion' (1989: 11). The difficulty of defining appropriate roles for women was also noted; some assignments were rejected on the basis that they constituted 'men's work'. Recommendations in the WaterAid report emphasised the need to gather information on customary water use patterns and to involve secret societies in decision-making prior to project commencement.

In this case, as in many others, preliminary sociocultural studies would have revealed that a river or stream in close proximity to a village is central to life in many different ways. The 'walk' to the stream and communal activities like bathing, laundering and fishing in designated female areas are important aspects of social interaction. Women find space for free expression and children can be supervised as gender-defined chores or water-based livelihoods such as palm oil production are carried out. Final cleansing rituals following rites of passage through *Poro* and *Sande*, and the walk from the waterside back to the village afterwards as an accredited member of the society are highly significant. Indeed the social and spiritual aspects of interacting with others during such communal water use are usually seen as much more important than intangible parameters such as water quality, and the idea of using wells purely from a water-quality perspective is sometimes viewed with scepticism (Akiwumi 1987). Nevertheless, traditional environmental concerns such as water contamination from the ruptured gall bladder of a dead crocodile or anthropogenic pollution that affects livelihoods are taken seriously (Wohlwend 1978).

14.5 The problem of artificial water control for swamp rice cultivation in Sierra Leone

Swamp rice cultivation using artificial water control was introduced in 1921. Forced labour to clear swamps for rice cultivation began in 1924 and during the Second World War every male in rural areas had to produce 2 bushels of rice a year for sale. Expansion of swamp projects continued after the war with the Inland Swamp Clearance Scheme which significantly modified the land tenure system. Land was allotted at the discretion of the agricultural officer who also decided which varieties of crops should be planted and when. A rent system was established, and farmers could be punished for failing to satisfy the stipulated requirements (Saylors 1967).

Various FAO and World Bank agricultural projects in the last 15–20 years have continued to promote these schemes. Incentives include provision of funds to cover farming implements, seeds and storage facilities, and access to agricultural extension officers to impart technical knowledge. The overall success rate has been poor in spite of these inducements.

Indigenous swamp rice cultivation has been the norm for centuries in coastal and tidal areas. Upland rice farming by shifting cultivation remains the preferred method in the greater part of the country. Local expertise in rice cultivation was documented in 1922 by an Indian irrigation adviser, A.C. Pillai, brought to Sierra Leone in 1921 by the colonial administration. He described a highly efficient, non-labour-intensive method that worked with the natural conditions of fertility and water flow in coastal swamp environments. Pillai wrote:

> If it is made known to the rice growing public of other countries that the Africans are getting up to 4,000 lb in an acre of swamp without tilth, without manure, without weeding, and without artificial irrigation and lastly by continued cropping for over thirty years, some will doubt the truth of the statement. But I submit as I myself did the work and saw the crop from planting to harvest (Government of Sierra Leone 1922: Appendix A).

Nevertheless, Pillai cautioned against the 'social and political codes' imposed on communities which killed individual incentive to pursue agriculture as a profitable business venture. These codes conform to the aforementioned 'levelling mechanisms' in the traditional system. Western-style projects introduce new opportunities for creation of wealth and status which are exploited by unscrupulous patrons who show favouritism in the disbursement of agricultural loans. As a result the goal of fostering community participation by involving local authority sometimes backfires in the face of cultural norms (Richards 1986). This very important aspect of Pillai's 1922 report was ignored in later development work, and the Department of Agriculture forcefully imposed its swamp policy with the prime aim of increasing yields. The Annual Report of the Agricultural Department for 1927 confidently stated: 'there is little doubt that people will grow increasing amounts of swamp rice without much encouragement from us' (Government of Sierra Leone 1927: 1-2).

Little consideration was given to the importance of rice production in Sierra Leonean life. Rice is a staple, key item of sacrifice to the ancestors and dictates the division of farming family labour. Farming fits into a well-ordered timetable of events, and its farming operations have inspired the movement of a traditional dance. This introduction of year-round utilisation of swamps, made possible by water control structures, causes major disruption in lifestyles, and the labour requirement for swamp cultivation using artificial water control greatly exceeds that for both indigenous swamp methods and upland cultivation (Richards 1986). Environmental problems have been created in the form of clogged drainage systems and high iron toxicity in swamps. Farmers typically explain their reluctance to participate in swamp schemes by citing poor physical conditions in swamps, the risk of disease and a preference for the taste of upland rice.

Animosity and distrust created by the long-standing disregard for local opinion and the forceful imposition of policy including taxation and fines are more significant factors (Kamara 1997; Segkoma 1986). Subtle forms of protest are revealed in the refusal to repay agricultural loans, or impart more than 'simple knowledge' to researchers' questions. Any kind of government aid is considered a right and compensation for past injustices. Generally, water professionals working at grass-roots level are ignorant of the historical causes of the current non-compliance. This was graphically illustrated in an educational and motivation campaign slogan in the 1980s.[1] A zealous Peace Corps volunteer's T-shirt read, in the lingua franca, Krio, 'Baafa Bums! None potor potor nor too wor wor' ('Farm hut bums! There is no such thing as a bad swamp!'). The implication was that farmers were merely being lazy, using physical conditions in swamps as an excuse not to farm but rather to lie in a hammock under a farm hut (*baafa*).

14.6 Conclusions

Indigenous peoples' perspective on water use and management in Sierra Leone contrasts with modern Western approaches adopted by the national government. Conflict between the two styles of management limits community participation and hence effective development of the resource. Many of the problems arise because projects do not adopt a cross-cultural and interdisciplinary approach in planning. Although the preparation stage for many water projects acknowledges the importance of including women in leadership roles in ways that are intended to empower them, the traditional female power base centred around water and the river is often diminished by developments.

Project implementation without adequate consultation and consensus accounts for continuing suspicion and distrust of outsiders and perhaps even more of Africans seen as representing 'outside interests'. This, in addition to cultural constraints on knowledge sharing, influences how easily information is divulged by indigenous people and innovative ideas received. Hence, the quality of data collected at the grass-roots level may be compromised.

To prevent such problems, water scientists must broaden their knowledge base to encompass a variety of relevant disciplines such as history, sociology and anthropology. Multidisciplinary data in the annals of colonial and recent reports must be analysed to access the depth of the problem. The centuries-old oral tradition of Africa, somewhat like shifting sand, must be thoroughly documented because increased knowledge about achievements, beliefs and values, and what sustained peoples of Africa in the past, form the foundation on which to build for the future.

African nationals, acting as counterparts to foreign experts on international aid projects or water-based mining ventures, must act as advisers and guides to the local environment. The exercise of political will by government, and of corporate responsibility by mining companies should be effected by acknowledging past mistakes, taking responsibility and showing genuine respect for and sensitivity to indigenous systems. These simplistic but realistic approaches are fundamental to 'paving the road' to sustainable development.

1   Personal communication with A.S. Lamin, Ministry of Agriculture, Freetown, 1983.

Bibliography

Abitbol, E. (1989) 'Interim Evaluation of Water Supply and Sanitation Schemes in the Eastern Province, Sierra Leone', Global Applied Research Network, www.lboro.ac.uk/departments/cv/wedc/garnet/allcasewateraid2.html.

Abraham, A. (1978) *Mende Government and Politics under Colonial Rule, 1890–1937* (Freetown, Sierra Leone: Sierra Leone University Press).

—— (1994) *Development Issues in Sierra Leone: Selected Essays* (Freetown, Sierra Leone: Institute of African Studies, University of Sierra Leone and Civic Development Education Centre).

Akiwumi, F.A. (1982) 'Water Resources Development in Sierra Leone: A Summary of Proposals and Developments in the Field of Water Resources Planning', paper presented at the *Seminar on Land Use Planning for Rural Development with Special Attention to Environmental Management*, Freetown, Sierra Leone, November 1982.

—— (1987) *Report to Sierra Rutile Ltd on the Appraisal of Water Supply for the New Locations for Pejebu, Vaama and Mondoko* (Freetown, Sierra Leone: Sierra Rutile Ltd).

—— (1994) 'Some Humanistic Perspectives on Sustainable Water Resources Development in an African Nation', *Proceedings International UNESCO Symposium on Water Resources Planning in a Changing World*, Karlsruhe, Germany, 28–30 June 1994: I-21–I-31.

—— (1998) 'Water Use in an African Setting: History, Culture and Perception as a Barrier to Sustainability', paper presented at *International Workshop on Barriers to Sustainable Management of Water Quantity and Quality*, Wuhan, China, 12–15 May 1998 (www.up.ac.za/academic/libarts/polsci/awiru/papers.html).

Blyden, E.W. (1888) *Christianity, Islam and the Negro Race* (Edinburgh: Edinburgh University Press, repr. 1968).

Boone, S.A. (1986) *Radiance from the Waters: Ideals of Feminine Beauty in Mende Art* (New Haven, CT: Yale University Press).

Cremer & Warner Inc. (1991) *Draft Report on Environmental and Community Development Plan for the Sierra Rutile Mining Region* (L4263, D91124; Freetown, Sierra Leone: Sierra Rutile Ltd).

El-Ashry, M.T. (1993) 'The World Bank's Post-Rio Strategy', *EPA Journal* 19.2 (April–June 1993).

FAO/UN (1979) 'Sierra Leone', in D.A. Caponera (ed.), *Water Law in Selected African Countries (Benin, Burundi, Ethiopia, Gabon, Kenya, Mauritius, Sierra Leone, Swaziland, Upper Volta, Zambia)* (Legislative Study No. 17; Rome: Food and Agricultural Organisation of the United Nations): 162-205.

Ferme, M.C. (2001) *The Underneath of Things: Violence, History, and the Everyday in Sierra Leone* (Berkeley, CA: University of California Press).

Gleick, P.H. (ed.) (1993) *Water in Crisis: A Guide to the World's Freshwater Resources* (Pacific Institute for Studies in Development, Environment and Security; Oxford, UK: Oxford University Press).

Hardin, K.L. (1993) *The Aesthetics of Action: Continuity and Change in a West African Town* (Washington, DC: Smithsonian Institution Press).

Heady, F. (1995) *Public Administration: A Comparative Perspective* (New York: Marcel Dekker, 5th edn).

Ihonbvere, J. (1992) 'Obstacles in the Development of Science and Technology in Contemporary Nigeria', in B. Thomas-Emeagwali (ed.), *Science and Technology in African History with Case Studies from Nigeria, Sierra Leone, Zimbabwe and Zambia* (Lewiston, NY: The Edwin Mellen Press): 165-82.

Kamara, S. (1997) 'Mined Out: The Environmental and Social Implications of Development Finance to Rutile Mining in Sierra Leone', Friends of the Earth Trust, www.foe.co.uk/pubsinfo/briefings/html/19971215144610.html, April 1997.

Lamin, A.S., F. Akiwumi, M.A.R. Conteh and W.B. Sannoh (1991) *Water Balance of the Sierra Rutile Mining Area; Water Year May 1990 to April 1991* (Freetown, Sierra Leone: Sierra Rutile Ltd).

Richards, P. (1986) *Coping with Hunger: Experiment and Hazard in an African Farming System* (London: Allen & Unwin).

Saylors, R.G. (1967) *The Economic System of Sierra Leone* (Durham, NC: Duke University Press).

Second World Water Forum (2000) 'Water and Indigenous People', www.worldwaterforum.net/ Dossiers/indigenous_water.html.

Segkoma, G.A. (1986) *The History of Mining and Agriculture in Sierra Leone: A Study of the Impact of Some Aspects of Colonial and Post Colonial Government's Economic Policies, 1929–1982* (PhD thesis, Dalhousie University, Canada).

Selznick, P. (1949) 'The Co-optative Mechanism', in J.M. Shafritz and A.C. Hyde (eds.), *Classics of Public Administration* (Fort Worth, TX: Harcourt Brace & Co., 4th edn, 1997): 147-53.

Sierra Leone, Government of (1922) *Annual Report of the Agricultural Department for the Year 1922* (Freetown, Sierra Leone: Government Printer).

—— (1927) *Annual Report of the Agricultural Department for the Year 1927* (Freetown, Sierra Leone: Government Printer).

Steffen Robertson & Kirston (BC) Inc. (1990) *Draft Report on Resources Development and Reclamation Planning for the Environmental and Community Development Plan* (Freetown, Sierra Leone: Sierra Rutile Ltd).

United Nations (1993) *The Global Partnership for Environment and Development: A Guide to Agenda 21* (Post-Rio edition; New York: United Nations).

USAID (US Agency for International Development) (2000) 'Diamonds and Armed Conflict in Sierra Leone: Proposals for Implementation of a New Diamond Policy and Operations', Office of Transition Initiatives Working Paper 05-08-00, www.usaid.gov/hum_response/oti/country/ sleone/diamonds.html.

Waldock, E.A., E.S. Capstick and A.J. Browning (1951) *Soil Conservation and Land Use in Sierra Leone* (Sessional Paper No. 1 of 1951; Freetown, Sierra Leone: Government Printer).

Wariboko, N. (1999) 'The African World View and the Structure and Strategy of Traditional Business Enterprises: The Case of Kalabari of Southern Nigeria', *Nordic Journal of African Studies* 8.2: 18-51.

Wohlwend, B. (1978) *Water Legislation in Sierra Leone* (Rome: Food and Agricultural Organisation of the United Nations).

Wolfensohn, J.D. (1997) 'We Must Have Sustainable Prosperity: The Challenge of Inclusion', *Vital Speeches of the Day* 64.1 (15 October 1997): 5-9.

Wren, D.A. (1972) *The Evolution of Management Thought* (New York: Ronald Press).

15

The commitment of the chlorine industry to sustainable societies
A PARTNERSHIP CASE STUDY IN GUATEMALA

C.T. 'Kip' Howlett Jr

Chlorine Chemistry Council, USA

According to the World Health Organisation (WHO) and the United Nation's Children Fund (UNICEF), '.2 million people in developing countries, most of them children, die every year from diseases associated with a lack of safe drinking water, inadequate sanitation and poor hygiene' (WHO/UNICEF 2001: v). The main health benefits of water supply and sanitation interventions lie in the reduction of diarrhoea. The average child under the age of five in developing countries suffers 2.6 episodes of diarrhoea per year. On average, infants suffer five episodes per year (Bern *et al.* 1992).

The chlorine industry plays a key role in providing safe drinking water and sanitation to communities in need. The use of chlorine in water treatment has been one of the most significant public-health advances ever, permitting the control of pathogens that can cause water-borne disease. In 1997, *Life* magazine wrote that 'the filtration of drinking water, plus the use of chlorine, is probably the most significant public health advance of the millennium' (*Life* 1997: 80).

The fact that so much of the world's population continues to lack safe drinking water and adequate sanitation indicates that chlorine is still urgently needed around the world. The chemical will inevitably play a significant role in meeting the targets set at the World Summit on Sustainable Development (WSSD) in Johannesburg, when the global community committed to halving by 2015 the proportion of people without access to safe drinking water and basic sanitation (United Nations 2002: 11).

15.1 The benefits of chlorine use in the provision of a water supply

Chlorine is added to drinking water to destroy pathogenic (disease-causing) organisms. On adding chlorine to water, two chemical species, known together as 'free available chlorine', are formed. These species—hypochlorous acid (HOCl, which is electrically neutral) and hypochlorite ion (OCl^-, electrically negative)—penetrate first the slime coatings and then the cell walls of bacteria, either upsetting the natural bacterial life-cycle or altering cell enzymes. Water is made bacteriologically safe as organisms either die or are rendered incapable of reproducing.

The primary forms of chlorine used in water treatment are chlorine gas, sodium hypochlorite (liquid) and calcium hypochlorite (solid, in tablet form). Although chlorine gas is by far the most commonly used disinfectant, systems may use either of the other two forms, other chlorine-based disinfectants (chloramines, chlorine dioxide) or non-chlorine alternatives (ozone, ultraviolet radiation). There are many factors to consider when deciding on a disinfection method, including: efficacy against pathogens; ease of use and reliability; the safe and easy shipping, storage and handling of disinfectants; potential hazards to people and the environment; and financial affordability.

Chlorine is highly effective against most pathogens, is relatively easy to use and is more affordable than the alternatives—an important factor when considering water disinfection in developing countries—but perhaps the most distinguishing benefit that chlorine-based disinfectants have is that chlorine is the only disinfecting agent that provides residual disinfectant action, continuing to protect the water during storage or distribution through pipes, valves and taps. In the USA, regardless of the method used for primary disinfection, the US. Environmental Protection Agency (EPA) requires a 'residual' level of disinfection to be maintained in water systems to protect treated water from being re-contaminated as it travels from the treatment plant to the consumer's tap (US EPA 1989). Only chlorine-based disinfectants provide this residual protection.

Although all chemical disinfectants form by-products, the by-products of chlorine disinfection have been the most thoroughly studied. The main concern about the use of chlorine in drinking water is the formation of disinfection by-products (DBPs)—chemical compounds such as trihalomethanes that form 'unintentionally' when chlorine reacts with natural organic matter in the water. The US EPA set the first US regulatory limits for DBPs in 1979. Since then, a wealth of research has improved the understanding of how DBPs are formed, their potential health risks and how they can be controlled. Recent US EPA regulations (the Stage I DBP Rule; see US EPA 1998) have further limited the presence of DBPs in drinking water. Most water systems in the USA now meet these new standards by controlling the amount of natural organic material in the water prior to disinfection.

The International Programme on Chemical Safety (IPCS), a joint venture of the United Nations Environment Programme (UNEP), the International Labour Organisation (ILO) and the WHO strongly cautions

> The health risks from these by-products at the levels at which they occur in drinking water are extremely small in comparison with the risks

associated with inadequate disinfection. Thus, it is important that disinfection not be compromised in attempting to control such byproducts (IPCS 2000: 13).

Indeed, a 1991 epidemic of cholera that started in Peru and spread to 19 Latin American countries was caused by inadequate chlorination as a result, at least in part, of the concern Peruvian water officials had about chlorination by-products. (Otterstetter and Craun 1997: 8-10). The bottom line is that DBPs should be limited when feasible but never at the cost of compromised protection from microbial water-borne disease.

The non-chlorine alternatives, ozone and ultraviolet (UV) radiation, have limitations that make them a poor choice for use in a rural community of a developing nation. Ozone is an unstable gas that is generated on-site at water-treatment facilities by passing oxygen or dry air through a system of high-voltage electrodes. It is far more complicated than a chlorine or UV system; it generally has a higher financial cost and consumes more energy than chlorine-based disinfection; it requires special handling; and it does not provide residual protection. Special lamps generate UV radiation. Although UV radiation has the advantage of requiring no chemical generation, storage or handling, it also provides no residual protection, is less effective in turbid water, provides no control over taste and odour and is generally more expensive and consumes more energy than chlorine-based systems.

15.2 A partnership to meet basic needs

In 1996, the Chlorine Chemistry Council (CCC), a US trade association representing manufacturers and users of chlorine and chlorine-related products, launched the Water Relief Network (WRN) and created a unique partnership with the American Red Cross (ARC). The WRN was born out of a need to equip impoverished communities with knowledge and resources to protect against water-borne disease in the wake of floods or other natural disasters. Today, the programme has expanded to include other members of the World Chlorine Council, including industry associations in Canada, Europe and South America. In addition, the scope of the WRN has shifted to place an increasing emphasis on helping to build the long-term, sustainable infrastructure that provides safe drinking water and basic sanitation to communities in less-developed countries.

The WRN is a partnership true to the WSSD Johannesburg Declaration on Sustainable Development that 'in pursuit of their legitimate activities, the private sector, both large and small companies, has a duty to contribute to the evolution of equitable and sustainable communities and societies' (United Nations 2002: 3). It heeds the WSSD Plan of Implementation in that it utilises a partnership between a non-governmental organisation and industry.

The WRN is funded by the voluntary contributions of approximately 60 companies (manufacturers of chlorine and chlorine-related products) and chlorine industry associations around the world. These participating companies provide the ARC with financial resources (administered by the CCC) earmarked for specific water projects in developing countries. Most of this money is used to purchase water-disinfection chemicals, surface disinfectants such as chlorine bleach, plastic water containers to help residents carry water home from temporary distribution sites, plastic sheeting to temporarily cover and protect homes damaged by high winds, and polyvinyl chloride (PVC) pipes and fittings to create or repair permanent water distribution systems. These are all products produced with use of chlorine or its derivatives. In 2002 the WRN received a total of US$92,000 in funding. The Guatemalan project described in this chapter represented US$45,000 of this total.

The CCC is the driver of the WRN and serves as the WRN Secretariat from its headquarters in Arlington, Virginia, USA. As the Secretariat, the CCC retains final authority over all projects. The CCC evaluates all funding proposals that are brought to the WRN by the ARC.

The ARC's role, through its International Services Division, is to identify communities in need, bring specific project proposals to the CCC (e.g. see ARCGD 2002), ensure all logistics concerning the delivery and receipt of chlorine-industry resources and actively implement the projects.

During its initial years, the WRN provided assistance in Cuba, Haiti, Antigua, Tajikistan, Moldova, Madagascar, Mexico and the USA. In 2001 the WRN provided disaster assistance in Malawi and India and funded a long-term sustainable project in the Dominican Republic that brings safe drinking water to several communities in need. The project described in this chapter, of rural communities in Guatemala, began in 2002.

15.3 Products of impact: chlorine disinfectants and polyvinyl chloride pipe

The two chlorine products that have had the greatest impact on the communities described are chlorine-based disinfectants and PVC piping. When used together to purify and transport water these products are welcomed by community residents for the public health improvements they facilitate.

Chlorine-based disinfectants help ensure that drinking water is safe—a fundamental building block for healthy people and communities. Safe water is an essential step in establishing sustainable, long-term development.

Untreated or inadequately treated drinking water contains microorganisms that can cause outbreaks of cholera, hepatitis and typhoid A. The scourge of diarrhoeal diseases in the developing world reinforces the importance of disinfection of public water (AAM 1996). In 1993, the WHO stated in its *Guidelines for Drinking Water Quality* that 'disinfection is unquestionably the most important step in the treatment of water for public supply . . . efficient disinfection must never be compromised' (WHO 1993: Vol. 1, §3.6.4). Chlorination is, by far, the most common way to disinfect drinking water.

In addition to making water safe to drink, products of the chlorine industry also help deliver water to those in need. More than a third of all chlorine-based PVC produced is made into pipe, including pipes for municipal water delivery and waste-water removal, culverts and industrial piping systems. Strong, flexible and durable, PVC pipes last up to 100 years or more and require virtually no main-tenance. They are also lighter than other materials and easy to install. All of these factors make PVC pipes extremely cost-effective. According to a report commis-sioned by the American Water Works Association Research Foundation, the expanded use of PVC pipe in the USA, and the phasing-out of other materials (con-crete and metal), has the potential to cut maintenance and repair costs by 93% or more (Moser and Kellogg 1994).

Most importantly, PVC pipes help to keep disinfected drinking water safe. Compared with metal and concrete alternatives, PVC is much more resistant to the formation of microbial and bacterial activity, which can be present in almost every water-distribution system. PVC does not serve as a nutrient to bacterial growth as some other pipeline materials do. PVC pipes are immune to corrosion; they do not rust, scale, pit or react chemically with the water they convey. They also resist the formation of biofilm better than do metal or concrete pipes, a property that helps PVC pipes to provide water of a consistent quality.

15.4 Water Relief Network case study: Guatemala

In Guatemala, infant, child and female mortality rates are among the highest in Latin America. Diarrhoea is a serious health problem in Guatemala. The general mortality rate for children under the age of five yeaers in Guatemala is estimated to be between 60 and 70 per 1,000 (WHO/UNICEF 2001). Some 25% of these deaths are attributable to diarrhoea. Intestinal infections, related to inadequate sanitation and hygiene, is the leading cause of death among females and the leading cause of illness among both sexes.

Less than half of the rural population in Guatemala has access to improved (piped) water supply systems, and only 50% have access to disposal facilities (latrines). Less than 50% of rural Guatemalans have access to running water, and only 25% have electricity.

The ARC and Guatemalan Red Cross have been active in a Guatemalan water and sanitation programme since May 1999. In a rehabilitation programme that came to an end in December 2001, 30 projects serving 25,512 people were completed. In January 2002 the ARC began a Developmental Water and Sanitation Programme with the Guatemalan Red Cross that concentrated on four departments: Quiche, Jalapa, San Marcos, and Alta Verapaz. The ARC approached the CCC and the WRN for water supply and sanitation assistance in two of the poorest communities in Alta Verapaz.

15.4.1 The communities: Sacoyou and Cha Ki Rocja Sataña

General water and sanitation interventions have been shown to decrease diar-rhoeal rates by approximately 25% (Billig *et al.* 1999), and the addition of appro-priate education programmes results in an even greater decrease. With these positive results in mind, the WRN began a long-term initiative in April 2002 to bring safe drinking water and sanitation to two rural communities in Guatemala: Sacoyou and Cha Ki Rocja Sataña. These communities are located in one of the poorest regions in Guatemala, are heavily indigenous and were already involved in ongoing ARC projects.

Sacoyou and Cha Ki Rocja Sataña are situated some 65 km from the regional capital of Alta Verapaz; generally, the geographic centre of the country. Some 81 families, or approximately 486 individuals, of the Que'q'chi Mayan ethnic group form these two communities. Prior to the WRN project, the residents relied on contaminated well-water and river-water sources situated some distance from their houses.

The goals of the project are to increase appropriate hygiene behaviour in beneficiary households, improve access to and hygienic use of latrines in beneficiary communities; increase access to and use of an improved, sustainable water supply; and to increase the local ARC chapter's capacity to successfully assess water and sanitation needs, train communities in water supply management and implement sanitation and community education interventions.

In keeping with ARC water and sanitation programme methodology, the project is to be accomplished in five phases: a baseline evaluation, community participation, water supply, a latrine programme and final evaluation.

15.4.2 Phases 1–2, April 2002 to June 2002: baseline evaluation and community participation

An ARC evaluation team visited Sacoyou and Cha Ki Rocja Sataña in November 2001, meeting with community leaders and conducting legal research on land-ownership in the communities. According to the ARC, one of the greatest challenges with rural water projects is the legal work that needs to be completed prior to pipeline excavation and installation. Often the owners of the land where the pipeline must pass are not easily located in order to provide permission to work on their land. This was not a problem in Sacoyou and Cha Ki Rocja Sataña.

The evaluation team returned to the two communities in April 2002 (the dry season) to conduct a feasibility study and to have further discussions with each community about the communties' needs and recommendations. ARC staff conducted in-depth interviews with key residents, performed a baseline evaluation and collected water samples for comprehensive testing. A total of 13 samples were taken in Sacoyou and Cha Ki Rocja Sataña and were analysed with use of a portable laboratory. Some 9 of the 13 samples were deemed unfit for human consumption.

Part of the ARC initial feasibility study was an evaluation of the community's willingness and ability to contribute to project success and sustainability through labour, local materials and a monthly fee. The vast majority of ARC water interventions involve low-technology solutions; the community's ability to pay is considered and the solution is designed accordingly. For example, with pump systems, public communal tap stands can be used instead of household taps. Meters are used so that families can monitor their water use and, if necessary, ration it to lower their water bill. If one or two families in a community cannot afford to pay the ARC encourages them to provide in-kind payment of labour to the local water committee. This can mean standing guard at the pump station at night, taking care of children or preparing lunches at the local school and so on.

ARC staff received signed agreements from the Sacoyou and Cha Ki Rocja Sataña communities and facilitated community decisions on a small monthly tariff that all families would pay to cover the maintenance and operational costs of the water system. Beneficiary families in both communities on average will pay 3 quetzales per month, which is equivalent to US$0.38. ARC officials estimate that connection charges and ongoing charges are approximately 3–5% of the monthly family income. The residents also agreed on the hours that all participants would work on the construction phase of the project. The ARC has begun teaching residents the training modules aimed at reorganising and strengthening the water committees in each community.

ARC experts determined that a spring-fed gravity system was a feasible solution. These systems are safe, cost-effective and easy to maintain. No new water sources can be tapped for these communities. Rather, the existing contaminated spring water must be pumped through the chlorine disinfection process of the low-technology gravity water system. Owing to the sandy nature of the soil, composting latrines were to be constructed in each location to avoid pollution of the groundwater.

A cornerstone of the intervention is the community participation phase, typically conducted two to three months prior to implementing the water system. An ARC educator has been situated in the communities to assist residents in completing five training modules, covering: community organisation and leadership; the strengthening of social organisation and the community board; the administration of water systems; the operation and maintenance of community water systems; and the operation and maintenance of latrines.

15.4.3 Phase 3, August 2002 to December 2002: water supply

The goal of the water supply side of the project is to ensure that enough water is available for washing hands, for use in food preparation and for environmental hygiene. The spring-fed gravity system utilises the chlorine, chlorine-related products and other hardware purchased with WRN funding. PVC piping, simple O-ring attachments, chlorinators, chlorine disinfectant, pumps and a supply tank are all used in a system that pumps the contaminated spring water through the chlorine disinfection process and on to the distribution tank and connections at each household.

In Sacoyou, the completed water system now consists of:

- A spring catchment
- A 10 m^3 distribution tank
- A Pelton turbine pump
- A chlorination system
- 51 households with an outside standpipe
- 4,242 m of PVC pipes of various diameters

The cost per connection was US$437.50, and the total water supply cost will be US$27,625.

In Cha Ki Rocja Sataña, the completed water system now consists of:

- A spring catchment
- A 5 m³ distribution tank
- A chlorination system
- 31 households with an outside standpipe
- 2,773 m of PVC pipes of various diameters

The cost per connection is US$500, and the total water supply cost will be US$17,375.

15.4.4 Phases 4–5, January 2003 to March 2003: latrines, to completion

The Sacoyou and Cha Ki Rocja Sataña communities are continuing the community participation phase and the latrine phase. To date, two model composting latrines have been built in each community in order to demonstrate their construction, operation and maintenance. Eventually, 31 latrines will be constructed in Cha Ki Rocja Sataña, and 50 in Sacoyou. Each latrine costs US$250 and serves the needs of a family of six. Cha Ki Rocja Sataña's latrines will cost US$7,750, and Sacoyou's will cost US$12,500.

In his most recent status report on the WRN project in Guatemala, Corey Michaud, Regional Associate–Americas, ARC, stated:

> With properly constructed water systems and with proper hygienic practices, we are confident that we can greatly improve water quantity and quality in the communities, thus improving health status for the 81 families . . . The communities are very enthusiastic to complete the projects on time and conform to technical specifications. They are very appreciative of the assistance given to them by ARC, the Chlorine Chemistry Council and the World Chlorine Council (Michaud 2002: 5).

The project was scheduled to be completed in May 2003, and a final report and full evaluation will follow.

Future WRN projects are tentatively being considered for El Salvador and Nicaragua.

15.5 Conclusions

The WRN project in Guatemala is on track to substantially improve water quality and increase access to potable water via the establishment of safe, cost-effective water systems in the two targeted communities. What will surely follow is a significant decrease in sickness and death from water-borne disease—particularly diarrhoea.

The project was modelled after the WRN projects that came before it in Cuba, Haiti, Antigua, Tajikistan, Moldova, Madagascar, Mexico, Malawi, India and the

Dominican Republic. The Guatemalan project continues to affirm some basic lessons learned:

- Chlorine-based disinfectants and PVC piping are effective solutions to providing safe drinking water. Their advantages (cost-effectiveness, ease of use and durability) can transfer to rural communities in developing countries.

- In poor rural areas, access to safe drinking water and proper sanitation is instrumental in improving community health and reducing infant mortality.

- To be effective, water and sanitation programmes must involve NGOs to oversee implementation.

- Partnerships between the public and private sector allow the leveraging of resources (both financial and time) to support change.

Access to safe drinking water and sanitation remains an international crisis. Only through global co-operation and partnerships such as the WRN will significant resources be brought to bear on this challenge. The WRN alliance demonstrates that NGO–industry partnerships can make important progress in building water infrastructure that helps those communities in developing countries that are in need.

According to the World Business Council for Sustainable Development (WBCSD),

> a coherent corporate social responsibility strategy, based on integrity, sound values and a long-term approach can offer clear business benefits . . . [such as] better alignment of corporate goals with those of society; maintaining the company's reputation; securing its continued license to operate; and reducing its exposure to liabilities, risks and associated costs (WBCSD 2002: .2).

Through participation in the WRN initiative, chlorine-industry companies have a ready vehicle that helps them demonstrate their commitment to corporate social responsibility. This is key because in the USA in recent years there has been a sharp increase in American's expectations regarding companies' social role (Cone 2001). In fact, more Americans than ever are reported to be making investment, purchasing and employment decisions to reward companies that support community needs. In 2002, 89% of Americans said that, in light of the Enron and WorldCom financial situations, it is more important than ever for companies to be socially responsible (Cone 2002). More significantly, it has been found that Americans are willing to use their power as investors, consumers and employees to punish companies that do not support community values by switching to another company's products, by speaking out against that company, by refusing to invest in that company's stock, by refusing to work at that company and by boycotting that company's products or services (Cone 2002).

The chlorine industry recognises the potential business growth that can come from global efforts to improve access to water. For decades, particularly in the developed world, chlorinated products have been meeting water and sanitation needs while advancing industry's economic vitality. The participating companies of the WRN view their humanitarian support in countries such as Guatemala as part of their social responsibility; but building water infrastructure and providing access to safe water is also a long-term investment for the chlorine industry. The industry is seeking out opportunities to be a valuable global citizen, and its experiences in this area serve as an example that corporate social responsibility is an integral part of doing business.

Industry can be a powerful force for positive change. As the chlorine industry lends a hand in alleviating water crises in the developing world, charitable and business relationships form and generate a better universal understanding of how products can be used to improve quality of life.

References

AAM (American Academy of Microbiology) (1996) *A Global Decline in Microbiological Safety Water: A Call for Action* (Washington, DC: AAM).

ARCGD (American Red Cross Guatemala Delegation) (2002) *Water and Sanitation Project Proposal, April 2002 (Washington*, DC: ARCGD).

Bern, C., J. Martines, I. de Zoysa and R. Glass (1992) 'The Magnitude of the Global Problem of Diarrhoeal Disease: A Ten-Year Update', *Bulletin of the World Health Organisation*, January 1992: 705-14.

Billig, P., D. Bendahmane and A. Swindale (1999) *Water and Sanitation Indicators Measurement Guide* (Washington, DC: Food and Nutrition Technical Assistance Project, Academy for Educational Development).

CCC (Chlorine Chemistry Council) (2002) *The Chlorination of Drinking Water* (Arlington, VA: CCC).

Cone Inc. (2001) *The 2001 Cone/Roper Corporate Citizenship Study* (Boston, MA: Cone Inc.).

—— (2002) The 2002 Cone Corporate Citizenship Study (Boston, MA: Cone Inc.).

Howlett, C.T. (2002a) 'Combating Disaster and Building Communities: Working the Waterways in the Dominican Republic', *Water Conditioning and Purification*, October 2002: 74-76.

—— (2002b) 'Delivering Safe Water to the World: The Chlorine Industry's Commitment', *Sustainable Business Investor: Worldwide* 2: 70-72.

IPCS (International Programme on Chemical Safety) (2000) 'Disinfectants and Disinfectant By-products', *Environmental Health Criteria* 216: 13.

Life (1997) 'The Millennium', *Life* 20.10: 80.

Michaud, C. (2002) *American Red Cross Water and Sanitation Interventions in Guatemala: Report to Chlorine Chemical Council, December 2002* (Washington, DC: American Red Cross).

Moser, A.P., and K. Kellogg (1994) *Evaluation of Polyvinyl Chloride (PVC) Pipe Performance* (Denver, CO: American Water Works Association Research Foundation).

Otterstetter, H., and C. Craun (1997) 'Disinfection in the Americas: A Necessity', *Journal of the American Water Works Association*, September 1997: 8-10.

United Nations (2002) *Report of the World Summit on Sustainable Development* (New York: United Nations).

US EPA (US Environmental Protection Agency) (1989) 'Surface Water Treatment Rule 54', Federal Register 27486, 29 June 1989.

—— (1998) *Stage 1 DBP Rule* (Washington, DC: US EPA).

WBCSD (World Business Council for Sustainable Development) (2002) *Corporate Social Responsibility: The WBCSD's Journey* (pamphlet; Geneva: WBCSD).

WHO (World Health Organisation) (1993) *Guidelines for Drinking Water Quality. I. Recommendations* (Geneva: WHO, 2nd edn).

——/UNICEF (United Nations Children's Fund) (2001) *Global Water Supply and Sanitation Assessment 2000 Report* (Geneva: WHO/UNICEF).

16

Water-pricing policies and the Water Framework Directive 2000/60/EC
A FIRST APPROACH CONCERNING THE AGRICULTURAL SECTOR IN THE AXIOS RIVER BASIN

Konstantinos Sarantakos and Elias Dimitriou
Hellenic Centre for Marine Research, Greece

Areti Kontogianni and Michalis Skourtos
University of the Aegean, Greece

As the Water Framework Directive 2000/60/EC states in its introduction, 'water is not a commercial product like any other but, rather, a heritage which must be protected, defended and treated as such' (EP/CEU 2000: 1). Without adequate access to fresh water, sustainable development cannot be achieved. Indisputably, the management of such a fundamental good should not be viewed solely from a commercial perspective. The demand-management system, however, tends to devaluate this exceptional dimension of water, since it confronts it as if it were provided for free to the utilities, to the users or to the state.

The adoption of an integrated approach to water resource management emerges as the most promising option. Economic instruments such as consumption fees, abstraction fees, environmental taxes (i.e pollution taxes) and price incentives can contribute significantly to managerial efforts, and, adapted to local conditions, their implementation can provide additional efficiency in water management policies. Water resources in the Mediterranean countries of Europe suffer from significant pressures. The agricultural sector of these countries provides a considerable proportion of their gross national product (GNP) but, at the same time, irrigation constitutes the major water consumer. Local environmental (climatic) conditions exaggerate the problem of water scarcity. The cultivation season of the most important crops is in summer, when the weather usually becomes extremely hot and dry. During this period a peak in water demand is observed, caused primarily by irrigation and secondarily by household and tourist demand. These factors cause significant problems with seasonal water deficits that make it difficult to implement sustainable water management and that lead to serious environmental impacts. Given the recurrence of water famine, with a periodicity of approximately ten years (Margat and Vallee 1999), together with the uncertainty of climate change, the need for immediate action for improved qualitative and quantitative management of water resources is obvious.

The aim of this particular chapter, which focuses on the Axios River Basin in northern Greece, is to examine the strengths and weaknesses of the existing systems for water demand management and pricing in Greek agricultural areas. We also examine the environmental impacts of these systems and provide an analysis of the potential improvements that the Water Framework Directive 2000/60/EC may offer.

16.1 Management of water demand in Greece

16.1.1 Institutional context: property rights

According to Greek civil law, water constitutes a communal, non-commercial good. Overland flowing water, lakes and their shores, as well as riverbanks, are goods assigned to common use (Civil Law article 967, 1945). Groundwater is viewed rather differently. Civil law determines that the owner of the land acquires exclusive use right on the groundwater inside his or her property boundaries (Civil Law article 1001, 1945), though some scientists argue that groundwater should also be managed as a communal good (Karakostas 2000).

Since water is considered to be a communal good, and in order to protect public interest, a public law provides authority to the state to review any adjustments in the management of water in order to ensure the normal, unconditional and appropriate exercise of the use rights by all potential users. At the same time, a legal relationship between each individual and the state is established, as every person has the right to free access and to use the good, according to its availability (Karakostas 2000: 130).

Such laws pose problems analogous to those described in the 'Tragedy of the Commons' (Hardin 1968), and it is increasingly recognised that only the explicit determination and allocation of property and use rights among users of water and the enforcement of the administrative legislative context can guarantee a sustainable solution.

16.1.2 Market structure

In most cases the market is made up of two segments, the water service providers, and a number of competing users. All users seek, through consumption, to ensure the maximisation of their personal benefit; consequently, conflicts commonly occur if the management fails to control such behaviour. In such an environment, the distribution of the good among users would be considered efficient if the marginal profits gained for each user were equal. Theoretically, this equalisation of marginal profits could be promoted by the introduction of exchangeable or tradable property (or use) rights (Tietenberg 2000). In such a case, an individual would have the incentive to exploit water resources more efficiently both in order to satisfy his or her needs and to form a surplus in water volume that could be sold to another user, who would profit thereby. Thus, both would gain additional profit from this allocation, and equilibrium—at the market scale—would be achieved when the marginal profits of all users were equal. In the case of underground water, in particular, the institution of 'water-rights banking' (Winpenny 1994) would provide significant benefit, as an individual would have a motive to save an amount of water in the present in order to use it in the future. Moreover, he or she would be given the opportunity to schedule the timing of the consumption of that water.

The implementation of such managerial frameworks would previously have required the restructuring and modernisation of the institutional and/or legislative context. This fact would raise a significant difficulty. In particular, it would be very difficult to ensure the efficiency and credibility of the procedure for the initial distribution of the rights.

The operation of a water demand and supply system under the existing model is best represented by an analogy to the demand and supply curves of an environmental good (Fig. 16.1). The curve in Figure 16.1 shows that the average cost (AC) faced by the producer or provider of the good declines with increasing supply, implying an underlying increasing productivity rate. However, the demand curve lies at a lower level and does not cross the curve of average cost at any point. This means that the sale of the good is not accompanied by the gain of any profit and, of course, no enterprise would be willing to produce or provide a similar product under these particular circumstances.

Water constitutes a good with low price elasticity and with no close substitutes (i.e. it is a basic good). Given a standard price of water, the demand shows high seasonal fluctuations, with higher intensity in drier periods. Furthermore, the installation of the water supply infrastructure requires a substantial budget to cover the cost of the initial investment and the need for an extended distribution network. These parameters characterise the water supply environment as a natural monopoly. Given the indubitable strategic importance of the potential of water resources at a national scale, and the difficulty for an institution to be certain of making a profit, it may be argued that a 'public company' (the utility) is better suited to act as the provider. The public nature of the company, however, introduces contradictions in its operation. Its character can be neither merely governmental nor merely social or entrepreneurial, as several principles and criteria—free markets, social or combined criteria—influence its function (Babanasis and Gotsias 1998). Its social orientation aims at serving the public interest by providing the good at affordable prices and by ensuring equal access to all citizens. At the same time, it is argued that the utility should be allowed to gain some profit in order to form a surplus or to provide the state with significant revenues. It may also be expected to contribute to the stabili-

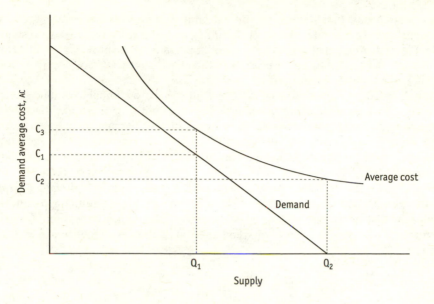

FIGURE 16.1 Demand and supply curves of an environmental good

sation of the economy and the realisation of anti-inflationary policy. It is sometimes claimed that such aims can be achieved only if the state has responsibility for the water utilities, allowing it to dictate policy according to government directives, but several sources of inefficiency in management systems derive from this practice.

16.1.3 Providers of water services in the agricultural sector: local and general organisations for land reclamation

In the Axios River Basin water supply for agricultural uses—primarily irrigation and cattle breeding—is provided by local organisations for land reclamation (LOLRs), operating under higher-level organisations for land reclamation (GOLRs) which are responsible for the co-ordination of actions of the groups under their supervision. Both levels of organisation are non-profit institutions; their purpose is to serve the public interest, interpreted as providing low-cost water for agricultural uses, without gaining any profit. Therefore it is expected that charges for water consumption will be set at a level that covers their operations and maintenance (O&M) costs only. Charges are in the form of fees related to the surface area farmed by consumers. The unit area is usually 1,000 m², but several different fees can be applied, including an adjustment for the crop type according to its irrigation demands. At the end of each year, the governing board of each LOLR develops a provisional budget for the following economic year and calculates new water consumption fees after having taken into account the relative area of each crop species and the potential maintenance costs of the infrastructure. This procedure ignores the components that determine the rational economic value of water (water scarcity, environmental services, opportunity cost and so on) and leads to such a complete devaluation of water that it is not important for the provider to collect any statistical data concerning its use. The outcome is that irrigation water is over-exploited and inefficiently used.

Such inefficient water-pricing practices also have an impact on land prices, which tend to vary according to the distance of a field from a given water source. One should discriminate between the incorporation of the marginal supply cost in the water price for each user (especially for the most remote users) serviced by a common supply network and the incorporation of this cost into the price of the land. In order to ensure social equity, this cost should have been incorporated in the price of the water and adequately allocated among all users. Providing low-priced water also aggravates the problem of land pricing by increasing the gap between irrigated and non-irrigated land (MNE 2001b). Furthermore, one should expect significant changes and disorder in the land market in case of an increase in water prices.

16.2 European legislative context and adaptation

16.2.1 Water Framework Directive 2000/60/EC

Today, the aim of managing water resources sustainably has been promoted as a priority in European policy-making procedure. The fundamental objective is to link the various existing policies that govern water quality and quantity into one integrated whole, providing EU member countries with a common platform for the assessment and monitoring of their water resources, as well as a guide to enable the sustainable management of those resources.

The intention to emphasise socioeconomic parameters is clear in the Directive, which highlights economic issues, public awareness and public participation as key factors for the success of managerial policy. Evaluation of policies should examine the rate at which they are adopted by society and the rate of functional integration within the existing legislative context. In accordance with the aim of the study that forms the basis of this chapter, the following issues, cited in Water Framework Directive (WFD) 2000/60/EC (EP/CEU 2000), should be highlighted:

- Determination of the study field at the level of the river basin area (Article 3)

- Demand for full cost recovery in the water service sector (Article 9)

- Public information and participation (Article 14)

Determination of the study area at the river basin scale reduces fragmentation effects, integrates the water management efforts and facilitates the environmental impact assessment of various management practices. Policy-makers need to take into account several scientific and socioeconomic factors, such as the geomorphology of the area, its geology and its hydrographic network, the rate of water abstraction, the number and condition of supply and drainage networks, the land uses of the area and the particular characteristics of the local population (age, occupation, income and so on). Evidently, the boundaries of each water management unit area are not always easy to determine since the administrative national boundaries as well as the geology of each area (especially the groundwater movement) do not always follow the basin formed by the overland hydrographic network.

Full cost recovery is accomplished when the price of water incorporates: (a) capital and O&M costs of supplying water services, (b) any cost of consequential environmental damage and (c) resource costs, arising when water is relatively scarce (Herrington 2001; Kindler 1999).

The implied need for an economic valuation of alternative water services in several categories of demand could be serviced by the guidance provided in WFD 2000/60/EC, outlined in Appendix III of the WFD and in relation to the 'polluter-pays' principle. For the performance of the economic valuation procedure, a series of alternative methodologies are available, depending on the corresponding sector of demand (Table 16.1).

Use of the full cost recovery principle would help the water service providers to afford their capital and operating costs arising from water supply and waste-water treatment and to gain a profit as well. As a result, the providers would have the incentive to invest in the maintenance and improvement of their infrastructure and to preserve the quality of their water resources. Otherwise, the need for the state to provide subsidies to the water providers will continue to exist, perpetuating the inefficient practice of today. Additionally, and in order to incorporate the

Type of demand	Technique for determining willingness to pay
Household demand	Analysis of market data
	Contingent valuation
Agricultural demand	Netback (or residual) analysis
	Stated preference
	Marginal productivity approach
Industrial demand	Marginal productivity approach
	Cost of internal recirculation
Hydropower	Marginal productivity approach
	Cost of alternative supplies
Navigation	Cost of alternative supplies
	Stated preference
Environmental services	Travel cost
	Hedonic pricing
	Stated preference

TABLE 16.1 Methodologies for determining the economic value of water

Source: Pearce 1999

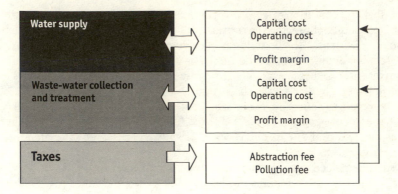

FIGURE 16.2 Proposed structure of a water billing system

Source: Courtecuisse 2001

environmental and resource costs, taxes, such as abstraction fees or pollution fees, could be applied. The collected revenues could be used for investment in the water supply sector or in waste-water treatment plants (Fig. 16.2).

Public information and participation should be promoted in order to provide feedback to policy-makers to guarantee the efficiency of the policy reform. They could help to avoid conflicts among stakeholders or between the stakeholders and the state. Local water management authorities, which have to be formed as a result of the WFD, can support this effort by setting as their primary target the design and implementation of water management plans that take into account the needs of the environment as well as the needs of citizens (Barth 2001).

16.2.2 Synoptic survey of the expected impacts of pricing policy reform

Among all categories of water users, households are characterised by the lowest price elasticity. Given their high dependence on the supply infrastructure, households are is the easiest target group to charge for water consumption, and this group usually contributes the most to the revenues of water utilities. It is nevertheless vitally important that policy-makers should recognise the exceptional social dimension of the nature of the good and ensure that even those in lower-income groups have access to at least the minimum necessary water quantity and quality for the fulfilment of individual needs.

The industry sector is relatively more price-elastic and therefore more flexible in responding to pricing policies. Allegations that increases in water pricing affects the competitiveness of enterprises, commonly expressed by representatives of this sector, should be considered with caution. Since water represents, in most cases, a fundamental inflow in the production procedure, an imposition of preferential charges would provoke significant distortion in the market and generate inequalities between enterprises, sectors of industrial production and so on. Enterprises need to internalise any additional costs incurred as a result of water price rises rather than passing them onto the end-users of the products. Water is not usually a major component of prices, and increasing costs can serve as a useful incentive for increased efficiency and productivity, in turn aiding the competitiveness of industry. When prices rise, internal recycling may prove to be a viable alternative source of water. Unfortunately, such incentives are lacking for industries where the fairly common practice of uncontrolled release of waste-water into freshwater bodies generates significant negative externalities.

Agriculture is both the most demanding and the most sensitive sector regarding water consumption. Farmers' incomes are usually low and dependent on unpredictable factors such as temperature, rain, frost, crop enemies (insects, fungi) and so on. The elasticity of water prices is difficult to estimate, since demand for irrigation water depends on a series of other factors, such as soil composition, weather conditions, the quality of the irrigation water, the reliability of the source of water, accessibility to the source and crop prices. Furthermore, the relative competitiveness of agricultural products is hard to estimate, since the market at the EU level is not homogenous and as the various products reach the market at different periods of the year (Strosser 2001).

In Greece, there is insufficient socioeconomic data available to form the basis of a thorough study of the particular sector, due to limited research efforts in the socioeconomic sector and due to the functional weaknesses of Greek agricultural research foundations and institutions. However, research shows that farmers are very sensitive to water prices, especially above a given level. In the event of price rises, the most predictable responses from competitive farm enterprises would be improvements to infrastructure and modernisation of irrigation techniques in the expectation that by increasing such investments they could achieve a more efficient rate of exploitation of the water. Undoubtedly, the possibility also exists of a reduction in irrigated area or of land abandonment in the case of small family-run enterprises or of increased dependence on crops protected by the Common Agricultural Policy (CAP) by which the EU provides subsidies to farmers for cultivating these particular crops (Arrojo 2001; Becker 2001; Garrido 2001). It is obvious that water pricing policy in the farm sector is strongly related to agricultural policy and in particular to the CAP supposedly accepted by all members of the EU.

The CAP reform that is now proposed is intended to dissociate crop yield from subsidies and to promote more responsible and environmentally friendly agricultural practices. As a result, more rational product prices could be expected—a change that would encourage farmers to fund and undertake improvements to infrastructure. Economic instruments such as abstraction and pollution fees could contribute additional revenues to the water industry, and these could be used to support investment either in the upgrading of irrigation networks or water treatment and sanitation plants. Cross-subsidisation could also be utilised to reduce farmers' expenses and to support their income if for some reason it were considered beneficial to foster farm production (e.g. to achieve socioeconomic benefits or to aid in environmental or landscape management). In this case, other, wider-based, social groups with higher and more secure income could be the target groups, and this particular confrontation would serve the public interest as it would ensure a reasonable allocation of the economic burden associated with the promotion of farm activity.

16.3 Axios River Basin area

The Axios River originates on the Sar mountain, close to the boundary between the former Yugoslavian Republic of Macedonia (FYROM) and Albania. It develops a broad hydrographic network within the FYROM and enters Greece through Kilkis Prefecture. The Axios River has a total length of 380 km, 76 km of which is within Greece. The river discharges into the Thermaikos sea gulf. The catchment area is approximately 23,747 km², 2,205 km² of which is within Greece (Fig. 16.3). The

FIGURE 16.3 The Axios River Basin

Source: Drakopoulou and Karageorgis 2002

mean annual rainfall in the wider study area (the Greek section) is 610 mm, the mean annual precipitation by volume is $1,220 \times 10^6$ m^3, and the mean annual discharge of the Axios River approaches $2,500 \times 10^6$ m^3. In this study, to ensure credible conclusions, we focus on the northern district of the Axios catchment (1,291 km^2), where the most representative land uses can be observed and for which detailed relevant data is available.

16.3.1 The structure of agricultural production

The Greek part of the river basin, which has a population of 209,339 people (2.04% of the Greek total; NSS 1991) is dominated by agricultural land (Fig. 16.4), and the area produces 70% of the country's rice harvest (Danos 2001). This fact, along with the crop types cultivated and the antiquated irrigation infrastructure and techniques, put the area's water resources, mostly derived from the Axios River, under great pressure in terms of both quantity and quality. Cotton growing occupies 38.9% of the cultivated land, with rice the second most extensive crop (35.54%). Both crops, but especially rice, are highly demanding regarding irrigation water.

The seven LOLRs in the study area, are responsible for the management of irrigation water. Most of the water supply networks consist of open pipelines, which results not only in significant losses to evaporation but also relatively low maintenance costs (Papazafeiriou 1999); only one LOLR (Mikro Monastirion) has installed an underground supply network.[1] At the end of each year all the LOLRs conduct a financial review and report the results to the administrative superior, which in this case is the General Organisation for Land Reclamation (GOLR) of Thessalonica.

Water pricing is based on the concept of surface fees, as described in Section 16.1.3, and, given the larger quantity of water required for growing rice, the surface fees charged for it are greater. Methods of rice cultivation are not compatible with modern, water-saving irrigation techniques, and significant quantities of pesticides are required, a fact that increases expenses and environmental damage. It should be stated that the highest proportion of the Greek rice yield is produced in the case-study area, which is the source of 70% of Greek rice production; much of this is surplus to the country's needs, creating problems in the storage and trade of the product (Danos 2001). A comparison of the cost of rice production, including the cost of water, with the income derived from it indicates that the growing of this crop is not always an economically beneficial option (Fig. 16.5). On average, rice has a lower profit margin than the other crops cultivated in the same region (Fig. 16.6), and the profit margin for rice would be even lower if other costs, such as expenses for pesticides or fertilisers, were also incorporated.

Rice has one important comparative advantage, as it can be cultivated in degraded fields with an elevated degree of salinity; but, given the aforementioned elements and negative consequences, policy-makers should reconsider the promotion of its cultivation on such a large scale.

---

1   L. Kartsiotis, Director of GOLR of Thessalonica, personal communication, 2001.

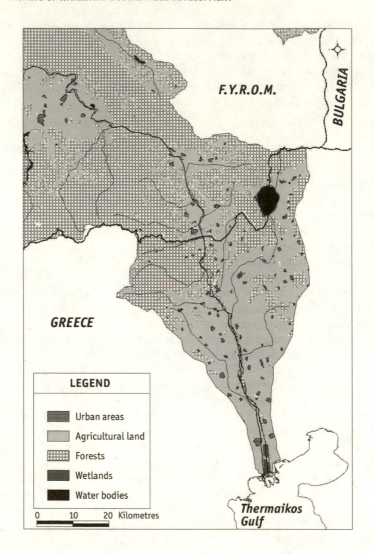

FIGURE 16.4 The Axios River Basin, Greece: land-use map of the wider study area

Source: Drakopoulou and Karageorgis 2002

A consequence of the way in which fees are calculated is that the equivalent fee charged for water consumption per volume per LOLR, relative to the total volume of water consumption, varies significantly across the various LOLRs in the case-study area (Fig. 16.7). The organisations that demonstrate higher O&M costs, or those that have less cultivated area under their authority, charge higher prices per volume of water. In the LOLR of Mikro Monastirion, even though an underground pipeline

(a)

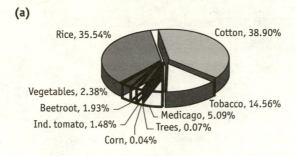

(b)

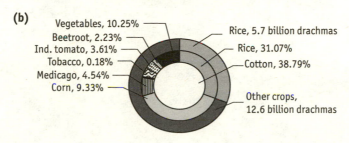

Note: € 1 = 340.75 drachmas

FIGURE 16.5 (a) Crop structure in Thessalonica's General Organisation for Land Reclamation (GOLR) district area and (b) the estimated percentage contribution of rice and other particular crops (inner ring) to agricultural income (outer ring [categorisation: rice; all other crops]) for 2001

Source: calculations based on data provided by Thessalonica GOLR and from MNE 2001a

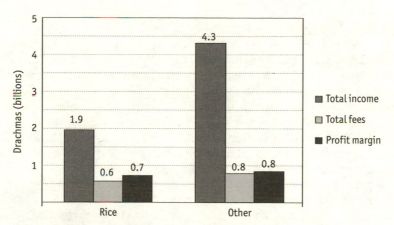

FIGURE 16.6 Total presumed income and total surface (water) fees for rice and the other crops in the Thessalonica General Organisation for Land Reclamation (GOLR) district

Source: calculations based on data provided by Thessalonica GOLR and from MNE 2001a

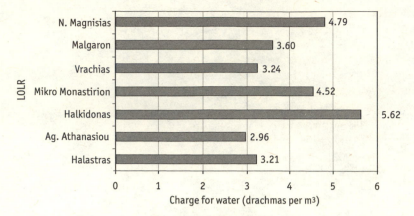

FIGURE 16.7 Equivalent charge for irrigation water in each local organisation for land reclamation (LOLR)

Source: calculations based on data provided by the Thessalonica General Organisation for Land Reclamation 2001

network has been installed, servicing a significant proportion of the area, inevitably leading to higher installation, depreciation and servicing costs, the charges are lower compared to other LOLRs with more depreciated supply networks (Fig. 16.7). This inconsistency illustrates the non-rationality of the pricing policies. The lack of a standard procedure for the development of an irrigation billing system also generates inefficiencies which obstruct the success of water management policies.

16.4 Conclusions

Restructuring of agricultural production is urgently needed, not only in the case-study area but also for Greece as a whole. As this case study indicates, rice cultivation in semi-arid regions is not a sustainable solution, as it incorporates high irrigation costs and significant environmental impacts yet provides relatively low gain to the farmers. Thus, reform to agricultural policy at the national and EU level should consider the viability of crop species under specific geographical and environmental (climatic) conditions and should introduce measures that promote the growing of the most efficient crop species for each climatic area.

The significant variation of irrigation water prices between LOLRs within the same catchment area introduces social inequity and environmental impacts. People living in the same area and exploiting the same water resource are assigned substantially different charges for irrigation water, mainly for administrative and organisational reasons. This results in the overexploitation of water and land resources on areas with lower-priced water, without consideration of aspects such as resource availability and quality, leading to serious ecological impacts.

Furthermore, the fragmented administrative system for the management of irrigation water in existence in the Axios River Basin, evident in the presence of many small LOLRs, has the effect of increasing O&M costs, as reflected in the water price. LOLRs should be merged to form water management authorities on a catchment scale. The larger authorities so formed could more effectively apply integrated and sustainable water management. Alternatively, the role of GOLRs could be modified to enable them to act in future as water agencies. Co-operation with the authorities of the FYROM should be promoted in order to approach an integrated system of water management in the Axios River Basin, in respect of WFD 2000/60/EC requirements.

Water pricing used correctly is an efficient economic instrument that can promote water saving and introduce incentives for more responsible behaviour from users, but its implementation has to be based on the economic valuation of all the associated alternative uses for the water. In doing this, protection must be given to the income of the 'weaker' social groups, such us low-income groups and farmers. Pricing policy can provide an appropriate option for this too, in the form of cross-subsidisation of consumption by other, higher-income groups or through use of state subsidies.

References

Arrojo, P. (2001) 'The Impact of Irrigation Water Pricing Policy in Spain', in proceedings of the conference *Pricing Water: Economics, Environment and Society*, Sintra, Portugal, 6–7 September 1999 (Luxembourg: European Communities): 177-84.

Babanasis, S., and A. Gotsias (1998) *Management of Utilities* (Athens: Papazisis).

Barth, F. (2001) 'The Common EC: Member Strategy for the Implementation of the Water Framework Directive (2000/60/EC)', presentation at the *Forum on the Water Framework Directive 2000/60 Concerning Water Policy*, Ministry of Interior, Public Administration and Decentralisation, Athens, Greece, 2–3 July 2001.

Becker N. (2001) 'Water Pricing: The Israeli Experience', in proceedings of the conference *Pricing Water: Economics, Environment and Society*, Sintra, Portugal, 6–7 September 1999 (Luxembourg: European Communities): 221-30.

Courtecuisse, A. (2001) 'Current Practice in Water Pricing in France: The Artois–Picardie Basin Case', presentation at the *Forum on the Water Framework Directive 2000/60 Concerning Water Policy*, Ministry of Interior, Public Administration and Decentralisation, Athens, Greece, 2–3 July 2001.

Danos, D. (2001) 'Seeking for Strategy Concerning Rice Production', *Ethiage* (journal of the National Agricultural Research Foundation [NAGRAF]) 3: 15.

Drakopoulou, P., and A. Karageorgis (2002) *AXCAT: Modeling of Axios River Basin* (EUROCAT Project).

EP/CEU (European Parliament/Council of the European Union) (2000) 'Water Framework Directive 2000/60/EC: Establishing a Framework for Community Action in the Field of Water Policy', *Official Journal of the European Communities* L: 327.

Garrido, A. (2001) 'Pricing for Water in the Agricultural Sector', in proceedings of the conference *Pricing Water: Economics, Environment and Society*, Sintra, Portugal, 6–7 September 1999 (Luxembourg: European Communities): 105-17.

GOLR (General Organisation for Land Reclamation) of Thessalonica (2001) Statistical Data, Thessalonica.

Greek Civil Law (1945) 'Law 777/1945', *Journal of Greek Government A* 327/31-12-1945 (Athens).

Hardin, G. (1968) 'The Tragedy of the Commons', *Science* 162: 1,243-48.

Herrington, P. (2001) 'Pricing and Efficiency in the Domestic Water Supply Sector', in proceedings of the conference *Pricing Water: Economics, Environment and Society*, Sintra, Portugal, 6–7 September 1999 (Luxembourg: European Communities): 203-11.

Karakostas, I. (2000) *Environment and Law* (Athens: Sakkoulas).

Kindler, J. (2001) *Managing Water Resources: Some Challenges*, in proceedings of the conference *Pricing Water: Economics, Environment and Society*, Sintra, Portugal, 6–7 September 1999 (Luxembourg: European Communities): 43-50.

Margat, J., and D. Vallee (1999) 'Mediterranean Vision on Water, Population and the Environment for the XXIst Century', MEDTAC, Blue Plan, Paris, available at www.worldwatercouncil.org/Vision/Documents/MediterraneanVision.PDF.

MNE (Ministry of National Economy) (2001a) *Tables for Land Income per 1000 m²* (Athens: MNE).

—— (2001b) *Rental Prices of Agricultural Land, per 1000 m²* (Athens: MNE).

NSS (National Statistical Service) (1991) *Population Census* (Athens: NSS, www.statistics. gr).

Papazafeiriou, Z. (1999) *Crop Water Demands* (Thessalonica, Greece: Ziti).

Pearce D. (2001) 'Water Pricing: Investigating Conceptual and Theoretical Issues', in proceedings of the conference *Pricing Water: Economics, Environment and Society*, Sintra, Portugal, 6–7 September 1999 (Luxembourg: European Communities): 55-66.

Strosser P. (2001) 'Influencing the Demand for Irrigation Water: At the Crossroads between Water Pricing and Agricultural Policy', presentation at the *Forum on the Water Framework Directive 2000/60 Concerning Water Policy*, Ministry of Interior Affairs, Public Administration and Decentralisation, Athens, Greece, 2–3 July 2001.

Tietenberg, T. (2000) *Environmental and Natural Resource Economics* (Athens: Gutenberg).

Winpenny, J. (1994) *Managing Water as an Economic Resource* (London: Routledge).

17

Reducing water and sanitation backlogs in rural areas
UMGENI WATER'S RESPONSE AS AN IMPLEMENTING AGENT WITHIN KWAZULU–NATAL, SOUTH AFRICA

*David A. Stephen**

Umgeni Water, South Africa

Umgeni Water is the largest catchment-based water utility in southern Africa, selling some 350 million m³ of water annually to almost 6 million people in the province of KwaZulu-Natal in South Africa (Umgeni Water 2002). Umgeni Water has been operating since 1974 and was established as a public utility in terms of the Water Services Act (No. 108 of 1997; DWAF 1997) (previously under the Water Act [No. 54 of 1956]). It is financially independent, receives no subsidies from government, reports directly via its board to the Minister of Water Affairs and Forestry, and is subject to, *inter alia*, the Public Finance Management Act (No. 1 of 1999; DOF 1999).

During 2002, Umgeni Water adopted a new strategic plan with a vision: 'To be the number one water utility in the developing world' and a mission: 'To provide water services for life'; a restructuring process is under way to enable the organisation to realise its long-term objectives and goals. Umgeni Water's intention is to be the preferred provider of a wide range of services in its chosen markets, and to positively influence the way in which water services are provided to consumers in

* The writer wishes to acknowledge the support given by Umgeni Water, the District Municipalities with whom Umgeni Water is working in partnership, and the Department of Water Affairs and Forestry and the Consolidated Municipal Infrastructure Programme as project funders, in striving towards the goal of providing access to appropriate water and sanitation infrastructure and ensuring ongoing provision of water services to the rural communities of KwaZulu-Natal. The positive contributions and efforts made by communities themselves are also appreciated and acknowledged.

urban, peri-urban and rural areas. Partnerships are being formed with both the public and the private sector in order to increase the rate of infrastructural delivery and to provide institutional and community-based capacity building and training, and skills development.

The Millennium Development Goals (MDGs) and the targets set at the World Summit on Sustainable Development (WSSD) in Johannesburg emphasised the urgent need to provide for the huge numbers of people who do not yet have access to basic water and sanitation services. This chapter describes Umgeni Water's response to this challenge with respect to reducing water and sanitation backlogs in rural areas within KwaZulu-Natal. It focuses primarily on the task of delivery of infrastructure, but also provides comment on interrelated aspects such as the sustainable provision of water services at the household level, integration of water, sanitation, health and hygiene awareness issues, and increasing the role of community management. It is written within the South African context, but it is hoped that the lessons learned will be of benefit to a wider international audience.

17.1 Umgeni Water's pre- and post-1996 response to rural communities' needs

When considering Umgeni Water's response to the needs of rural communities within KwaZulu-Natal over the past 14 years or so, it is imperative to recognise that this has been happening at a time of considerable changes in the constitutional, legislative, socioeconomic and sociopolitical landscape within South Africa. The extensive reforms within the water sector have impacted significantly on a number of organisations, some of which have only ever previously played a minor role in delivery of water and sanitation infrastructure or water services provision. There is an urgent need to align the water-sector legislation with the municipal legislation, to review the role of water boards, and to examine benefits that might be achieved through consolidation of the two water laws: namely, the Water Services Act (No. 108 of 1997; DWAF 1997) and the National Water Act (No. 36 of 1998; DWAF 1998). Intra-organisational review is also occurring within Umgeni Water, and this is likely to affect the ways in which it responds to the challenges of improving rural water and sanitation services both within KwaZulu-Natal and possibly further afield.

During the late 1980s (before the first democratic elections in South Africa in 1994), Umgeni Water undertook to provide basic water services to rural communities under its 'Rural Areas Water and Sanitation Plan' (RAWSP) as part of its social responsibility. This was done because no other agency (government or otherwise) was either required by law or felt morally obliged to undertake the work, which essentially fell within an 'institutional vacuum'. Schemes were planned, constructed and operated by Umgeni Water in consultation with community and tribal authorities, using internal staff as well as private-sector consultants and contractors, but with limited interaction with local government structures. Capital expenditure and net operating costs were financed by Umgeni Water. Assets were owned by Umgeni Water, and operating deficits (if any) were funded through cross-subsidisation from the bulk water sales revenue.

Since 1996, Umgeni Water has been involved as an implementing agent for over 40 rural water and sanitation projects on behalf of the Department of Water Affairs and Forestry (DWAF), and more recently on behalf of district municipalities in their capacity as Water Services Authorities (WSAs), using capital funding provided by external agencies such as DWAF and the Consolidated Municipal Infrastructure Programme (CMIP). No new RAWSP projects have been initiated by Umgeni Water since 1996. Table 17.1 highlights the differences between Umgeni Water's previously implemented RAWSP schemes and the externally funded RDP schemes which are now being developed and operated.

Umgeni Water's RAWSP schemes	Externally funded RDP schemes
Funded, owned and operated by Umgeni Water	Funded, owned and operated by others
Water sales revenue owned by Umgeni Water	Umgeni Water appointed as an implementing agent by DWAF or (more recently) by Water Services Authority
Operating deficits funded by Umgeni Water through tariff cross-subsidisation	Capital funding and operating deficits fully recoverable from funder or WSA
Traditional project management through Umgeni Water's (former) Corporate Services, New Works and Operations Divisions, with support from Finance and Administration and Scientific Services Divisions	Full project life-cycle project management by IA Services Business Unit (including planning, construction, commissioning and initial operation and maintenance stages) by using both internal Umgeni Water specialists and private-sector consultants and contractors
Capitalisation of assets	Direct project-related costs, programme management costs and IA fees charged to projects
Negative impact on tariffs if operating at a loss	No capitalisation of assets, and no impact on Umgeni Water's tariff
Long-term human and financial resource commitments by Umgeni Water	Opportunities for Umgeni Water staff development, and partnerships with both the public and the private sector
RAWSP schemes are no longer the *de jure* responsibility of Umgeni Water (to be transferred to the relevant Water Services Authorities)	Umgeni Water facilitates the transfer or hand-over of schemes to the relevant Water Services Authority on completion of the project

DWAF = Department of Water Affairs and Forestry; RAWSP = Rural Areas Water and Sanitation Plan; RDP = Reconstruction and Development Programme; WSA = Water Services Authority

TABLE 17.1 Comparison between RAWSP and RDP water schemes

17.2 The context of provision of water and sanitation services within South Africa

Much has been achieved within the water sector in South Africa since the Department of Water Affairs and Forestry published its first *White Paper on Water Supply and Sanitation* in November 1994. However, because of the significant institutional and legislative changes that have taken place, a new Strategic Framework for Water Services (DWAF 2003a) has been published in order to take into account the changing role of DWAF, municipalities and water boards, new national water policies (including an emphasis on sustainability) and a new financial framework. This document addresses the full spectrum of water and sanitation services (not only basic services) as well as the overarching policy issues pertaining to institutional, regulatory and financial frameworks, and integrated planning. It has been informed by a set of guiding principles that reflect international best practice, grouped under the following headings: (i) social; (ii) economic and financial; (iii) environmental and technological; and (iv) institutional and management.

These principles may be summarised as follows:

Social principles

- Everybody has a right to basic water supply and sanitation.

- A strong and active civil society has an important role to play in the water sector.

- Women should play a central role in the planning, provision and management of water services.

- Education is a vital component of water services in achieving and sustaining health and quality-of-life benefits.

Economic and financial principles

- Water services infrastructure to be publicly owned.

- Water services must be provided in accordance with sound business principles in order to ensure sustainability.

- Water tariffs and effective credit control are important components of any strategy to support sustainability.

- Demand management should be given as much attention as supply expansion in planning of water services and water resources planning.

- Water services should be provided and managed in such a way as to maximise their potential to support local economic development.

Environmental and technological principles

- Water services should take into account their impact on the natural environment and seek through remedial measures to minimise any negative impacts.

- Technology should be chosen rationally and appropriately.

Institutional and management principles

- Roles and responsibilities for government should be clearly defined.

- Regulatory and operational responsibilities should be separated.

- User and community participation is important.

- Ongoing capacity building is necessary.

- Information should support monitoring and evaluation.

- The public sector is the preferred provider of water services; nevertheless, the private sector has an important role to play.

The strategic framework clarifies the roles, responsibilities and interrelationships between the various players within the water sector, provides a financial framework within which to work, and includes sections on planning, delivery and sustainability, and a chapter on support, monitoring and regulation.

17.3 Umgeni Water's role as an implementing agent in reducing rural water and sanitation backlogs

Umgeni Water has been involved as an implementing agent in KwaZulu-Natal since 1996, and has provided rural water and sanitation infrastructure and management support to over 40 local communities in accordance with the guidelines issued by DWAF as part of the government's Community Water Supply and Sanitation Programme (CWSS). In terms of the new Strategic Framework for Water Services, the role of municipalities as Water Services Authorities will become more dominant, and DWAF will move away from being directly involved in the delivery of services to that of sector leader, supporter and regulator. It is fully the responsibility of local government, rather than national government, to ensure access to and provision of water and sanitation services. Government funding will increasingly shift towards two consolidated grant mechanisms directed at local government: the equitable share and the proposed municipal infrastructure grant (MIG), which is anticipated to be in place by 1 April 2005. WSAs may choose to implement their own projects or appoint water boards, non-governmental organisations (NGOs) or private-sector companies as implementing agents. Umgeni Water will therefore have to compete for this type of work in future.

Every municipality must seek to achieve the integrated, sustainable and equitable social and economic development of its area, for urban, peri-urban and rural areas alike. WSAs are required to prioritise projects and develop policies and regulations related to the water sector. Social, economic, financial, technical, institutional and environmental issues are to be included in the WSA's Water Services Development Plans (WSDPs). Two of DWAF's more far-reaching policies are the 'Free Basic Water' policy and the 'Free Basic Sanitation' policy which aim to support access to basic services by all; WSAs are required to determine the manner in which they are to be implemented within their areas of jurisdiction. Active community involvement at grass-roots level and by elected councillors remains critically important in the development of the more remote rural areas.

It is within this context that Umgeni Water will be required to function as an implementing agent, in partnership with the WSAs and funders. Current rural water and sanitation projects are located within the Ilembe (DC29), uMgungundlovu (DC22) and Sisonke (DC43) District Municipality areas (see Fig. 17.1). By way of illustration, one water project, which has been implemented by Umgeni Water, is described below.

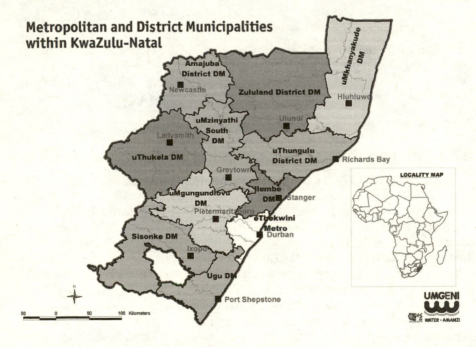

FIGURE 17.1 The region in which Umgeni Water operates

17.3.1 KwaSandanezwe Water Scheme: a brief case study

KwaSandanezwe is a relatively remote traditional rural community situated in the rolling hills of the KwaZulu-Natal midlands, situated on a plateau to the south of the uMkhomazi River, under the Vezokuhle Tribal Authority in the Sisonke District Municipality's area of jurisdiction. A project business plan for the water scheme was prepared by Umgeni Water and approved by DWAF in 1996. The construction stage started in 1997, and the scheme was commissioned in December 1999. Since then the scheme has been operational, supplying up to 25 litres/person/day of potable water to about 6,000 people within 200 metres of each household, in accordance with DWAF's guidelines.

The scheme is supplied by one main spring and two smaller supplementary springs, a bulk gravity supply system comprising three main pipeline routes (approx. 13.5 km long, 160–50 mm diameter), 16 pre-cast storage reservoirs (with storage capacity of more than 24 hours) and 22.5 km of reticulation pipelines (75–32 mm) supplying water to 50 standpipes. The current limiting scheme capacity is the sustainable yield of the water source, estimated to be 310 m³/day. Pipelines have been designed for an increase in both water consumption (up to 60 litres/person/day) and population growth (up to 10,500 people) over a 20-year period. The estimated final capital cost of the scheme is in the order of US$600,000, and has been fully funded by DWAF.

The scheme is currently being managed by a local water committee (LWC) consisting of 11 volunteer members and 3 employed staff members. The LWC fulfils an interim role as water services provider. Formal hand-over from DWAF as project funder to Sisonke District Municipality as WSA is due to take place during 2004 in order to comply with legislation related to local government, the Water Services Act and the Division of Revenue Act. Documentation will include asset registers, closure reports, record drawings, and operation and maintenance instruction manuals.

Throughout its involvement with the scheme, Umgeni Water as implementing agent has:

1. Liaised and worked closely with the community-elected project steering committee (PSC) and other development committees in the area, the tribal authority, local government departments and with DWAF

2. Appointed consulting engineers, project managers, institutional and social development practitioners, and awarded contracts to contractors in terms of Umgeni Water's targeted procurement policies and procedures which have been approved by the State Tender Board

3. Applied appropriate technologies and used local labour and labour-intensive methods wherever possible during the construction stage of the scheme

4. Generally carried out all the financial, contractual and project management functions related to the scheme on behalf of the WSA and DWAF.

A technical audit was carried out by DWAF in October 1999, and it was concluded that the scheme could be sustainable in both technical and financial aspects, as there were no buy-in costs for water, no pumping charges and limited purification costs. The tribal authority and the community was actively involved, but it was recommended that ongoing support be given by way of regular follow-up visits in order to ensure the smooth operation and maintenance of the scheme.

Umgeni Water has always placed great importance on the institutional and social development aspects of the scheme during the project life-cycle in order to ensure that the various needs of the community, tribal authority, local government authorities and the funder were taken into consideration and, wherever possible, met. As already mentioned above, this was being done in the context of a significantly changing legislative and institutional landscape. From the start of the project, the project steering committee (PSC), which included community members representing each area of the scheme, met on a regular basis and, through an interactive and consultative process, planned the scheme and went on to manage it, in order to meet the basic water needs of the people in the project area. Of necessity, physical, technical, environmental, social, institutional and financial aspects had to be considered.

Umgeni Water formed a multidisciplinary project management team (PMT) which met on a regular basis about a week before the PSC meetings were held on-site in order to ensure that the project was fully understood by all the institutional actors and that the message conveyed to the PSC and the community at large was not a confused one. Optimal results were achieved when there was a clear understanding of the roles and responsibilities of the various parties involved in the PMT, and where there was mutual trust, respect and co-operation within the team, and between the team members and the PSC. As far as possible, there was an attempt to avoid stereotyping the 'engineer' and the 'social facilitator/trainer', and opportunities for learning from each other and broadening experiences were provided.

During the construction stage, a technical management committee (TMC) was formed as a subcommittee of the PSC in order to assist the contractor with recruitment of labour, obtaining permission from householders for the contractor to lay pipelines or build structures on their properties, and assisting with labour disputes. Towards the end of the construction period, a local water committee (LWC) was elected to carry out the required tasks of operating, maintaining and administering the scheme once it had been commissioned and was operational. On commissioning of the scheme, both the PSC and the TMC were disbanded.

Capacity-building and training programmes were developed for each of four target groups: the community, the PSC, the TMC and the LWC, in accordance with the training needs assessment and training plan which was included in the project business plan. The objective was to create within the community the skills, ability, confidence and capacity to take ownership and responsibility for the implementation, management and sustainability of water schemes and secure an enabling environment for health. Water and sanitation-related health and hygiene issues and equity-related issues were regularly mentioned and discussed in meetings. Training sessions were held to develop management at local level through training and capacity-building initiatives that promoted financial, administrative, communication and good governance skills. PSC and community meetings were used to ensure that this was taking place and that participants had a fair understanding of their responsibilities and expected commitment to build strong structures to take on the management of the scheme. The PSC and LWC included representation by officials and politicians from local government and from the tribal authority. Youth and women were actively encouraged to become involved with all aspects of the scheme.

Efficient construction was made possible through site meetings and the involvement of the contractor, TMC, the engineer, works inspectors and local labour representatives. Local labourers were used to instil a sense of ownership among the community as well as to create jobs and develop skills for local people. During the construction stage, two people were identified and sent for training in plumbing skills to ensure that the local people would have the skills to deal with operation and maintenance duties. A scheme manager was also identified, someone who had been a member of the PSC since project inception, who had an intimate knowledge of the scheme, and who had been part of the capacity building and training exercises that the PSC and LWC went through. In order to encourage entrepreneurial development, local subcontractors were used to transport materials to site.

An assessment of the training effectiveness was carried out, both quantitatively and qualitatively. The expected attendance figures were seldom achieved, possibly because the social and cultural commitments of the community were not taken into account. These were found to be critical in ensuring the sustainability of the training programme and the project programme in general. The age of PSC members may also have been a problem: 80% of the PSC members were over the age of 55. This caused difficulty in understanding and assimilating what was taught. Ill-health and unfavourable weather conditions, which affected the condition of the roads, were also contributing factors to the poor attendance. Women's attendance at training sessions was generally good (above 50%), but this does not imply adequate levels of participation. Observations at PSC and community meetings indicated difficulty on the part of women to contribute at meetings.

Issues relating to cost recovery options and the location of the water office tested the PSC's decision-making and conflict resolution skills in a practical way. As part of their training, the PSC visited another water project, which helped them to understand how the coupon system worked, which was to be introduced in the scheme. Examples of success achieved through training included the following:

1. Sub-wards worked together and agreed on how the water scheme should be developed (historically, development projects were done in isolation).

2. The project opened the community's mind to seek funds for other development initiatives such as roads and electricity.

3. The PSC understand the need to pay for services (whether this has been fully understood by the whole community is yet to be seen).

4. The management structure (LWC) was representative of all the wards, youth, women and the tribal authority.

Challenges that require ongoing attention include vandalism, unauthorised connections and the improvement of cost recovery in order to achieve some measure of financial sustainability.[1]

17.4 Issues and concerns facing the water sector in addressing rural water and sanitation backlogs within targeted time-frames

It is the opinion of many South African water authorities that the targets set by the global community in Johannesburg to reduce backlogs in water and sanitation and attain sustainability of water services provision within the stated time-frames are ambitious and will not be achieved unless a concerted and co-ordinated effort is made, and appropriate and adequate resources are mobilised. Discussions at the Water Dome during the World Summit highlighted the common view that the water sector as an integrated whole has a vitally important role to play in achieving the overall global objectives of reducing poverty and increasing food security for all people (IWMI 2002). In the past, the programmes in South Africa have been too narrow in their scope to achieve that objective. It is hoped that this will change with the introduction of the consolidated municipal infrastructure grant (MIG) funding mechanism due to come into effect on 1 April 2005, and the increasing role that local government, in particular those municipalities designated as Water Services Authorities, will be required to play in service delivery.

A concern with much of the material presented at the Johannesburg meetings is that they seemed to ask questions and suggest areas of research rather than provide specific and implementable proposals. Indeed, there were some suggestions that funding was available from a variety of sources, and the difficulties lay in the lack of suitable projects and programmes to which it could be applied. One pamphlet, issued by the Africa Water Task Force (AWTF), complained 'So why is there a perception that funds are not available?' and answered by saying: 'Basically, the problem is the paucity of well-prepared projects that can be undertaken by technically and financially sound water companies or authorities in a regulatory environment based on transparent rules of the game' (AWTF 2002).

There are therefore many challenges and opportunities for organisations such as Umgeni Water, and certainly others within the water sector. In response, the nation of South Africa has set the following water sector targets (DWAF 2003b):

- Apply the 'free basic water service' policy to all people, with access to a basic service by 2004

---

1   Further details relating to each stage of a typical rural water project may be found in a paper prepared by the author entitled 'Appropriate Technology for Water Supply' (Stephen 2000). Other papers written on various aspects of the management of rural water schemes may be found on Umgeni Water's website (www.umgeni.co.za).

- Basic water services to all schools and clinics by 2005

- Education on hygiene and wise use of water at all schools by 2005

- Provision of at least basic water supply services to 8 million more people by 2008

- Provision of at least a basic sanitation service to an additional 18 million people (3 million households) by 2010

- Education to 3 million households receiving a basic sanitation service by 2010

There are many significant challenges and opportunities for municipalities, water boards, NGOs and the private sector to become involved with the attainment of the above-mentioned targets. The following critical success factors are suggested:

- 'Think globally, but act locally.' This will ensure that lessons learned from the 'home base' can be offered (possibly in an adapted form) to other geographical markets, and vice versa.

- Establish partnerships and strategic alliances with both public- and private-sector players, and explore ways of doing business in new and creative ways while maintaining the shared objectives of achieving cost-effective and sustainable solutions, and improving the quality of life of the benefiting communities or individuals.

- Recognise that the provision of infrastructure, however appropriate or cost-effective, is not sufficient to ensure ongoing provision of water services in a sustainable manner. Appropriate contractual arrangements and management-support systems must be developed and implemented.

- Identify areas where there is a need for capacity building and training at both community and local government levels, and provide appropriate training and skills-development programmes.

- Influence water-sector policies and procedures based on practical experience and lessons learned from the widest possible range of practitioners involved with rural development.

- Acknowledge, appreciate and respect the inherent capabilities and resources available from within the community, and make a commitment to use such resources. A major challenge centres on the way in which community management can be scaled up (IRC 2002).

- Deliver a consistently high-quality service which exceeds expectations, and maintain a passion, commitment and enthusiasm for serving the rural poor.

17.5 Conclusion

There is no doubt that South Africa has undergone major changes in a number of areas since its first democratic election in 1994. Water-sector reforms have been significant and far-reaching, the devolution of powers and functions between the various tiers of government is in the process of being finalised, and mechanisms for the funding of capital projects, institutional capacity-building grants and operational requirements for the delivery of services are being consolidated. Policies and legislation relating to both the water sector and local government are being aligned in order to bring about greater efficiencies and effectiveness, intended to benefit end-users and improve the quality of life of all, especially the poor. It is within this context, and as part of this process, that the future role of water boards is being keenly debated.

Whereas it is generally accepted that the South African water and municipal legislative and policy framework has been guided by international 'best practice', it is necessary to critically consider the manner in which the policies will be implemented in order to successfully achieve the desired national objectives and goals. For the water sector the challenges are to:

1. Increase the rate of infrastructural delivery in order to reduce the backlogs in water and sanitation

2. Provide ongoing water and sanitation services in a sustainable manner

3. Improve people's health and their quality of life

4. Reduce poverty

5. Improve food security

Umgeni Water has been involved with the provision of water and sanitation services to the rural areas of KwaZulu-Natal since 1989, and has as part of its strategic plan of 2002 indicated that it intends to continue with this work in partnership with both local government and private-sector players, within its chosen markets in South Africa, other countries in Africa and parts of Asia.

The global community has indicated that considerable sums of money will be made available to address water and sanitation backlogs. Access to, and the effective use of, funds for both capital development and operation and maintenance expenditure remain major challenges and provide new opportunities for Umgeni Water and others within the sector at this time.

References

AWTF (Africa Water Task Force) (2002) *Africa Water Facility: Towards the Development of a Facility to Finance the Water Sector in Africa* (pamphlet issued by AWTF at the World Summit on Sustainable Development, Johannesburg, August/September 2002).

DoF (South Africa Department of Finance) (1999) *Public Finance Management Act (No. 1 of 1999)* (Pretoria: Department of Finance).

DWAF (South Africa Department of Water Affairs and Forestry) (1997) *Water Services Act (No. 108 of 1997)* (Pretoria: DWAF, www.dwaf.gov.za).

—— (1998) *National Water Act (No. 36 of 1998)* (Pretoria: DWAF, www.dwaf.gov.za).

—— (2003a) *Strategic Framework for Water Services, September 2003* (Pretoria: DWAF, www.dwaf.gov.za).

—— (2003b) *Attaining the WSSD Vision 21 Goals: South Africa's Intervention Strategies* (pamphlet issued jointly by DWAF [www.dwaf.gov.za], Department of Health [www.doh.gov.za], Water Research Commission [www.wrc.org.za] and Umgeni Water [www.umgeni.co.za] at the 3rd World Water Forum, Kyoto, Japan, March 2003).

IRC (International Water and Sanitation Centre) (2002) *Community Water Supply Management* (Delft, Netherlands: IRC, www.irc.nl/manage/index.html).

IWMI (International Water Management Institute) (2002) *Water and Sustainable Development in Africa: An African Position Paper* (published on behalf of the Africa Water Task Force; Pretoria: IWMI, www.iwmi.org).

Stephen, D.A. (2000) 'Appropriate Technology for Water Supply', paper presented at the *3rd ESAR/IWA Conference*, Swaziland, October 2000, www.umgeni.co.za.

Umgeni Water (2002) *Annual Report, 2002* (Pietermaritzburg, South Africa: Umgeni Water, www.umgeni.co.za).

Part 5
Regionally focused case studies: urban environments

18

The demand-side versus the supply-side approach

THE CASE FOR SUSTAINABLE MANAGEMENT OF WATER SUPPLY IN DEVELOPING COUNTRIES

Lingappan Venkatachalam

Institute for Social and Economic Change, India

Provision of good-quality drinking water to households in developing countries generates considerable private and social benefits. Therefore water supply to such households is a priority in the social development of many developing countries. Supply of potable water is considered a direct and effective intervention in improving public health. However, owing to the problem of asymmetric information and the huge 'sunk cost' involved, the responsibility of implementing water supply schemes rests mainly with the government sector, though the private sector also plays a crucial role in this area in some developing countries (see Whittington *et al.* 1991).

In the public policy arena, one of the main questions often confronted by water supply authorities in developing countries is why a large number of water supply schemes fail to achieve the underlying objective of efficiency, equity and sustainability (see Rogers *et al.* 2002) in generating benefits to users. Some studies attribute this failure to the existence of a 'vicious circle' (see Griffin *et al.* 1995) or to a 'low-level equilibrium trap' (Singh *et al.* 1993) which is characterised by a poor quality of service, a low level of preference for services by households, a low level of household willingness to pay and a low level of revenue to the water supply authority, which in turn leads to a poor-quality service. As a remedial measure, it is suggested that an increase to the revenue component of the scheme by manipulating the pricing mechanism would be a suitable way to break free from this trap. However, real world experience suggests that even those water supply schemes that are adequately financed are usually not able to fulfil the stated objectives. An immediate question that arises is that if financial weaknesses cannot fully explain the failure of such schemes, what are the factors that can better explain the phenomenon? As Griffin *et al.* (1995) point out, the socioeconomic and institutional factors that are supposed to influence the preferences of the users are site-specific in nature; this implies that the sustainability of water supply schemes depends mainly on these same site-specific factors. But it should be noted that in many cases these factors are contradictory to the goals set by the water supply authorities at the local level, thereby undermining the real objectives of the scheme.

In this chapter I try to tease out these contradictions in a systematic way, on the basis of information obtained from a case study in a developing country. More precisely, I argue that there are contradictions between the preferences of the users or beneficiaries regarding various components of proposed water supply schemes (described as a demand-side approach) and the water supply authorities' specified objectives for the scheme (described as a supply-side approach). Analysis of these contradictions suggests that broader policy options such as the provision of an improved service and the manipulation of tariffs may provide useful aspects of water supply policy-making in developing countries.

This chapter is divided into three parts. Section 18.1 provides a general background of the study area and various components of the proposed water supply scheme, including the nature of the policy package proposed by the water supply authority. Section 18.2 highlights the contradictions between the supply-side approach and the demand-side approach in relation to the proposed water supply scheme under study. Finally, in Section 18.3 the various policy implications of the findings are discussed.

18.1 Background

The study area, Othakkalmandapam (hereafter referred to as Mandapam), is a suburban town of Coimbatore City, Tamil Nadu, India. Coimbatore City, the second largest city in the State of Tamil Nadu in terms of population, is one of the major industrial centres of Southern India. The total population of Coimbatore Urban Agglomeration (Coimbatore UA) increased from 10.91 million in 1991 to 14.46 million in 2001, with a decadal growth rate of 32.49% (Goverment of India 1991, 2001). The demand for water from the household and industrial activities in the Coimbatore UA increased rapidly, giving rise to water scarcity in and around the city.

The population of Mandapam town was 9,870 in 1991, rising to 11,198 in 2001. The decadal growth rate of population during this period stands at 13.45%. According to the 2001 census, 10.26% of the total population of this town belong to the scheduled caste (SC), which is a socially and economically deprived group in India. Nearly 30% of the households in this town are engaged in agricultural activities, approximately 39% are engaged in industrial activities and the remaining households are employed in the service sector, the government sector and other commercial activities. The average monthly income per capita of the town stands at Rs827 (1997 estimate).[1] Around 11% of the population in the town live below the poverty line.[2]

The water supply authority of Mandapam is a local government agency (called the town *panchayat*), which is also responsible for providing other local public

---

1   1 US$ = Rs46 as at the exchange rate prevailing in 1997.
2   According to the Government of India, the poverty line for urban area is Rs264 per person per
     month.

goods such as streetlights, public sanitation and so on. The town depends entirely on groundwater for public supply. Though there are a few ponds in the town and a small river flowing through the town, these sources for most of the year are dry, except during the very short rainy season. Under the existing water supply scheme public supply of water in the town is effected through 568 individual connections to houses, 80 public taps and 24 ground-level reservoirs. A flat rate of Rs20 per month is collected for the individual household connections, but the water from the public taps is supplied free of cost.

At present, two different methods are being followed to provide the water supply to households. Sub-surface water, pumped with use of electric motors, is stored in two overhead tanks and distributed to households, to a few industrial units and to commercial establishments. On average, water is supplied for 1–3 hours a day, depending on the amount of water stored in the tank and the availability of electricity.[3] Households store water for use during the rest of the day. Apart from individual connections and public taps, the water supply authority has installed 31 hand pumps in different parts of the town, 27 of them in working condition at the time of this study. Of the 27 hand pumps, only 2 are in frequent use by households, as these are the only hand pumps providing what is believed to be relatively good-quality drinking water. In the case of private sources, approximately 5% of households have installed their own bore-wells (i.e. tube wells) within the premises of their houses. A considerable number of households also collect water from the agricultural bore-wells located in the nearby villages of the town. As far as households are concerned, the present water supply situation has the following weaknesses:

- The level of service is of low quality.

- The distribution of water to different parts of the town is inequitable.

- The quality of the water is very poor.

Clearly, many households would like a new water supply scheme that overcomes these problems.

Based on the estimate made by the water supply authority in 1997, the availability of water per capita in Mandapam stood at 40 litres per capita per day (lpcd) whereas the government-required norm for semi-urban areas in the State of Tamil Nadu is 80 lpcd. Moreover, the water supplied to the industry and the commercial establishments under the existing scheme has been found to be completely inadequate. To bridge the gap between supply and demand, as well as to address the above-mentioned problems at the household level, the water supply authority, assisted by the World Bank, has inaugurated a water supply scheme—the Pillur Scheme—to be implemented in the Coimbatore region. The Pillur Scheme draws water from the Bhavani River flowing about 40 km north of the Coimbatore local planning area. The Tamil Nadu Water Supply and Drainage Board (TWAD), a public-sector agency responsible for providing water supply and drainage to urban and rural areas in the State, will undertake the overall implementation of the Pillur Scheme. Operations and maintenance (O&M) at the local level is to be the responsibility of the respective

3   Power shortage is one of the problems in Tamil Nadu and, in different parts of the state, power is generally rationed.

local government agency. The Pillur Scheme will benefit households and industrial and commercial establishments located in part of Coimbatore City as well as 21 suburban towns and 523 wayside villages, including Mandapam town.

Of the proposed quantity of 553 kilolitres per day (kld) to be delivered to the study area under this scheme, households will get 457 kld, commercial establishments will get 64 kld and the industrial sector will get 32 kld. The total cost to Mandapam Town for the Pillur Scheme is Rs12.5 million, of which Rs9.8 million constitutes the apportionment cost and Rs2.7 million the distribution cost. The town has to repay 25% of the total project cost, which comes to around Rs3.1 million, the remaining amount being considered as a grant. The present study was conducted prior to implementation of the scheme in order to understand the relationship between supply-side and demand-side approaches.

18.2 The supply-side approach versus the demand-side approach

The water supply authority in Mandapam Town has identified policy positions for different components of the proposed scheme. These include: the number of individual house connections to be provided to 'willing' households (approximately 500), the amount of one-time advance payment to be collected from these households (Rs4000 per connection), the monthly water tariff (Rs60) and the number of additional public taps to be installed (24 extra). It should be noted that the households are free to choose different options. They may elect to transfer from the existing scheme to the new scheme, to utilise both the existing and the new scheme, to obtain an individual house connection or to have access to public taps.

18.2.1 The survey

To understand the way in which the policy has been formulated by the officials, and to investigate the acceptability of different components of the policy package to the actual users, towards the end of 1997 my colleagues and I conducted a survey among 206 randomly selected households in the town. The households were selected from each of the 11 administrative wards of the town.

A stratified random sampling method was used to select the sample households. First, the property tax list was used to stratify the households into six income categories (based on the level of property tax paid); then, from each category, sample households were selected proportionately with use of a simple random method.

We used a contingent valuation (CV) survey (see Mitchell and Carson 1989) to elicit information from households. Before the main survey, rigorous pre-testing was carried out among 30 households in the study area, the CV scenario being framed on the basis of the results of this pre-testing. In-person interviews, as recommended by a panel of the National Oceanic and Atmospheric Administration (NOAA 1993), were carried out with an adult member (above 18 years of age) in each sample household. These interviews lasted from between 45 minutes to an hour.

The drinking water was the good under valuation, and an open-ended elicitation technique was used in the survey, since the open-ended technique was found to work well. During the interview, we also used two enumerators with a sociology and social work background so that water-related issues could be effectively discussed with the women respondents of the households.

In the scope test (investigating the provision of water in terms of quantity supplied) we split the sample into two sub-samples to look at the willingness to pay (WTP) for two levels of supply (each sample being assigned a single level of supply for investigation—that is, households were asked WTP questions based on only one level of supply). The results of this test suggested that the difference between the WTP values for the two different quantities of water was statistically significant. A test for detecting the strategic bias (by way of assessing the performance of various independent variables in the econometric model) revealed that the results were free from strategic bias. Therefore, it was concluded that the results obtained through the present CV study are valid (Venkatachalam 2000).

Table 18.1 summarises some of the major results of the study, and these will be discussed in the following sections.

During the survey, we found that the supply-side approach and the demand-side approach are in contrast to each other on many different aspects of the proposed water supply scheme. In Section 18.2.2 this 'mismatch' between the two approaches is elucidated.

18.2.2 The official announcement, uncertainty and the reduced propensity of the households to participate in the Pillur Scheme

Though household support for individual connections depends on endogenous factors such as income and education, in the study area we found that what is perceived to be a long delay in the implementation of the Pillur Scheme resulted in a reduction in the willingness of some of the households to participate. In large part, the approach adopted by the officials in communicating the implementation of the scheme was responsible for the uncertainty created among these households. As households remember it, the first announcements about implementation of the Pillur Scheme—through *tandora*[4] as well as through the press—was made by officials during 1996. Through these announcements the households were informed that the Pillur Scheme would be implemented 'soon' and that households willing to have individual connections under this scheme should submit their application to the officials of the town. These households were required to pay Rs200 towards the application fee immediately and Rs1,000 as a one-time advance payment once the household was selected for an individual connection. On the basis of this announcement, some of the households started applying for individual connections. Meanwhile, another announcement by the officials stated that there would be a delay in the implementation of the scheme because of some 'technical

---

4   *Tandora* is a method of signalling the announcement of official decisions of the local administration through use of drum beaten by a specially appointed person.

Quantity investigated	Result
Number of sample households willing to have an individual connection[a]	182
Mean WTP for advance (in rupees)	2,368.13
Mean WTP for monthly tariff (in rupees per month per 10,000 litres of water)	32.19
Percentage of households willing to have to individual connection for an advance payment of Rs4000	17.5
Percentage of individual connection holders willing to have individual connection under the Pillur Scheme	88[b]
Percentage of women respondents willing to connect to individual connections	92[c]
Percentage of sample households willing to pay for public taps	68.44[d]
Mean WTP for public taps (rupees per month per 10,000 litres of water)	8

[a]   Number of households in sample = 206
[b]   That is, 94 of 107 current holders of an individual connection
[c]   Number of women respondents = 48
[d]   That is, 141 of the 206 households

WTP = willingness to pay

TABLE 18.1 Summary of the major findings of the study regarding the Pillur Scheme

Source: author's survey

reasons'. The households were also told that there might be an 'upward revision' in the advance payment and monthly tariff to be paid under the Pillur Scheme. For these reasons the applications already submitted by some of the households became invalid, and they were asked to submit fresh applications (which would cost them an additional Rs200). As a result, some of the households previously supportive of the Pillur Scheme decided to withdraw.

Our survey results showed that 182 of the 206 sample households were willing to connect to individual connections and that the remaining 24 households were not. Of the 24 'non-interested' households, 10 cited 'uncertainty' over the commencement of the Pillur Scheme as the reason for their decision. According to these households, the repeated announcements, the frequent demand for an application fee, the subsequent revision in advance payment and the delay in the commencement of the Pillur Scheme were all part of the strategy of 'rent-seeking' by the officials. They pointed out that if the officials were interested only in 'rent-seeking', rather than taking steps to bring the scheme into operation, they would no longer wait for the scheme to commence. Rather, they decided to seek other solutions such as making their own investment, especially in terms of digging bore-wells or continuing to collect water from existing sources.

Clearly, the officials' approach encouraged some households to stay out of the scheme. thereby reducing the 'benefit that would have been achieved if these households had participated'.[5] The survey results indicate that around 5% of the total 'non-interested' households in the town would have been covered under the scheme if the water supply authority had communicated properly regarding the scheme. Though rent-seeking by officials is a regular phenomenon in the town, discussions with various officials revealed that there were indeed some technical problems in implementing this scheme and that this problem had to be dealt with by the TWAD engineers in pumping stations. All that the local officials did was to exploit the opportunity to maximise their own benefits by way of rent-seeking. This problem may be attributed to the existence of asymmetric information, not only among the officials and households but also among different government organisations dealing with water supply schemes. It may be inferred that greater transparency about the implementation of the scheme would facilitate smooth communication between the water supply authority and the households and would encourage more households to participate.

18.2.3 Fixing the advance payment

Fixing the level of advance payment for individual connections also resulted in a reduction in the benefit that would have occurred not only to the households but also to the exchequer of the town. During 1997, the TWAD officials, in consultation with the officials in the town, decided to fix the advance payment for each individual connection under the Pillur Scheme at Rs1, 000. A few months later, the officials decided to raise the advance payment to Rs4,000 per connection so that the revenue obtained from advance payment plus the monthly tariff would be sufficient to repay Rs3.1 million to the TWAD and to meet the likely expenditure on O&M. The figure of Rs4,000 had been arrived at by the officials on the assumption that only the 500 households belonging to the highest income group[6] in the town would be willing to pay for individual connections and that a higher level of advance and monthly tariff was needed to fulfil the objective of maximising revenue. The underlying implication of this assumption was that even if the advance payment were reduced to enable more households to participate the marginal number of households willing to connect would be small. This view was not supported by our survey, which found that the number of households willing to apply for individual connections would go up considerably if the amount of advance payment were reduced to Rs2,500. Of the 182 households willing to obtain an individual connection, only 32 households (17.5%) were willing to pay an advance payment of Rs4,000 and above, but an additional 150 (or 82.5%)

---

5 An implication of this statement is that the repeated announcements and the long delay in implementation also resulted in the discouragement of certain other households who would otherwise have made investments in private water supply.

6 According to the officials, these are households in which the annual income is Rs48,000 or above.

households be prepared to pay for individual connections if the advance payment were reduced to Rs2,500.

It may be concluded that, before any advance payment and monthly tariff for individual connections can be fixed, officials need to calculate a break-even point, which is the advance payment that will not only attract the maximum number of potential applicants for individual connections but also meet the revenue target. This should be based on a realistic assessment of the possible number of households that would be willing to pay for individual connections.

18.2.4 One-time payment versus payment in instalments

As we have seen in Section 18.2.3, a considerable number of households are willing to pay something for an individual connection, but less than the proposed advance payment of Rs4,000. In case this proved to be the minimum figure to fund the scheme, our survey investigated whether there was any alternative way in which these households could be encouraged to pay for the connection. Households were asked to consider whether they would pay Rs4,000 if it could be done on instalment basis. Around 70 (or 47%) of the 'willing' households were found to prefer paying on an instalment basis, preferably monthly. On an average, the realistic monthly payment would stand at Rs600 per month for these households.[7] Interestingly, one such instalment system already exists in the town. Many of the 650 textile mill workers in the town have reached an agreement with the mill management that management pays the advance for those workers willing to have new connections and recoups the money by deducting around Rs300 from the workers' monthly salary. This indicates that the introduction of instalment payments for the advance would attract more households to join the scheme, which would also increase the revenue to the exchequer. Three different options may be considered for poorer households:

- An instalment system could be introduced under which each household would be asked to pay a certain, small, amount on monthly basis.

- The officials could consider providing individual connections at a sub-sidised rate.

- The local banks and government credit agencies could extend credit facili-ties to these households to enable them to meet instalments on an advance payment.

18.2.5 Existing connections versus new connections

According to the water supply authority, the technical components of the Pillur Scheme, such as the overhead tanks, distribution lines, advance payment and water

---

7 However, it should be noted that some of the remaining households reported that they were not interested in an instalment system because the total advance to be paid remained the same and was unaffordable even if it was paid on an instalment basis.

tariff, would be kept entirely separate from similar components of the existing local public water supply scheme. This is necessary because all the revenue from the existing scheme is currently reinvested in that scheme, whereas the revenue from the Pillur Scheme has to be repaid to the TWAD. Hence all applicants for individual connections under the new scheme will be required to lay new pipelines, even if they already have a pipe link to the existing scheme. In consequence, the new connection will cost every applicant an additional lump sum of Rs2,000 towards engineering costs such as new pipes, installation charges and so on. Households with individual connections under the existing scheme complain that Rs2,000 towards the engineering cost would be an additional burden for them (bringing the initial payment to Rs6,000). However, because the water from existing sources is not of good quality, as noted in Section 18.1, these households remain willing to take up a Pillur Scheme connection as well.

One suggestion from these households was that Pillur water could be supplied through the existing connections so that they could at least save the engineering cost. Interestingly, 88% of the households with individual connections under the existing scheme were willing to have a new connection in addition to the existing connection. An immediate question that arises here is that if these households take up Pillur Scheme connections then why there is a need to retain the existing connection that provides poor-quality water? The reason is that these households are uncertain about the reliability of supply of Pillur Scheme water over the coming years and believe that if there is any discontinuity they can continue to get water from the existing connection.

The survey indicated that, if the arrangement of supplying Pillur Scheme water through existing pipelines was accepted by the officials, more of the households with individual connections at present would be willing to have a new connection. If it is not allowed then there would be either an additional financial burden to the households or there will be financial loss to the town if the households decide not to connect.

18.2.6 Willingness to pay for water tariff: individual connection

The water tariff for the individual connection under the Pillur Scheme has been fixed at a flat rate of Rs60 per month (up to 10,000 litres), three times the tariff rate of Rs20 under the existing scheme. As in the case of advance payment, the rate of the monthly tariff was fixed on the assumption that only a few households would opt for individual connections and so a monthly tariff of Rs60 would be necessary to meet the required amount for repayment of the loan. The survey indicated that although a large number of households felt that doubling the existing rate (i.e. to Rs40 per month) might be acceptable (though unaffordable for some) there was no justification for tripling it for the new individual connections. Households wanted to know the basis of fixing Rs60 per 10,000 litres of water: simply fixing a tariff without any concrete basis (such as quantity supplied, reliability and so on) did not make sense to them. In fact, most households were more concerned about the actual *quantity* of water to be supplied under the Pillur Scheme. According to the households, although the officials claimed that 10,000 litres of water per month would be supplied, the actual quantity will be much less because of unreliability as well as unequal distribution of water across the town.

In our survey we hypothesised two different levels of quantity of Pillur Scheme water to be supplied to the households on a reliable basis and asked respondents about their willingness to pay for one of those levels. The results showed that the average willingness to pay for water supplied through individual connections was Rs32.19 per 10,000 litres (Table 18.1). Since the monthly tariff has a major influence on household support for the scheme, the fixing of the monthly tariff by the water supply authority should have been a much more considered, transparent process.

A major requirement of the Pillur Scheme is the installation of meters and the determination of a tariff on the basis of the meter reading. The water supply authority decided to install meters for all individual connections so that excess consumption could be charged appropriately (at the rate or Rs2 for every additional 1,000 litres of water consumed). Even though this proposal was considered acceptable by some of households, many others opposed it. Two reasons were cited. The first was that the installation of meters and water charges on the basis of meter reading would encourage rent-seeking behaviour among the officials. It was thought that some of the politically powerful households might try to bribe the officials rather than pay the tariff for additional consumption of water. The second reason related to a perception that meters are not always reliable and might be triggered by air flow, leading to payment of a higher tariff for water not received. Moreover, the installation of meters was considered an additional financial burden. For reasons such as these the majority of the households felt that the present system of a flat rate per month was the preferred option but that other measures such as the regulation of the supply of water to different localities should be adopted to check over-consumption.

Around 63% of the households willing to opt for individual connections opposed the introduction of meters. However, if meters are considered necessary for curtailing excess consumption, it appears that people's apprehensions regarding their installation could be mitigated by the adoption of clearer methods of measurement and billing (see also Section 12.2.7 on attitudes to metering).

18.2.7 Quantity of water to be supplied

As mentioned in Section 18.1, the official estimates put the current availability of public supply at 40 lpcd. The water supply authority proposed to increase this to a total of 80 lpcd, with the additional 40 litres being drawn from the Pillur Scheme. However, we have observed two aspects: (a) our survey results showed that, at present, at the household level, the average per capita availability of water from all the sources was approximately 88 litres per day, not 40 litres as the officials claimed; and (b) the quantity of water to be supplied though the Pillur Scheme on a daily basis will actually raise the water availability to 128 lpcd (i.e. 88 litres at present plus 40 litres from the Pillur Scheme), and not 80 litres. The mismatch between the official estimate and actual water availability at present is the outcome of the method of quantification used by the officials. The official estimate takes into account only the public supply from individual connections and public taps, whereas the total supply of water at the household level includes some from other sources such as hand pumps, agricultural bore-wells and so on. It should be noted that, if the quantity to be delivered under the Pillur Scheme is determined on the basis of the official estimate, then it would actually result in excess supply at the household level. As we have already seen, at present almost all households get enough water. However the *quality* of water from the existing sources is often unsatisfactory[8] and many households therefore prefer the better water that can be obtained under the Pillur Scheme. On an average, the quantity of Pillur Scheme water required by households is approximately 25 lpcd. A few households suggested that water from current sources and the Pillur Scheme water could be supplied on alternate days so that good-quality Pillur Scheme water could be used for drinking and cooking and the local supply could be used for other purposes. They felt this would allow effective use of good-quality Pillur Scheme water without wastage.

It is important that the officials should aim to supply only the required amount of good water in view of the scarcity and opportunity cost of water. We conclude that there are three alternative options by which an optimum amount of water from the existing and Pillur Scheme could be supplied:

- Pillur Scheme water may be supplied for a restricted period each day so that the households can use this water for drinking and cooking, allowing water from other sources to be used for other purposes.

- Pillur Scheme water and local water may be supplied on alternate days or alternate time-periods.

- Meters should be installed in all the individual connections and extra charges (in addition to a minimum charge) imposed for water taken in excess of the prescribed limit.

18.2.8 Location of public taps

The water supply authority has proposed to install 25 public taps under the Pillur Scheme (in addition to 80 public taps under the existing scheme) distributed across the town so that each administrative ward would get at least two public taps under the Pillur Scheme. However, in wards 9 and 11, where the majority of upper-income households live, the households prefer *not* to collect water from public taps but to have individual house connections, as a symbol of their economic status. A total of 41 households, almost all of them located in the upper-income area, expressed their unwillingness to collect water from public taps. In contrast, in wards 1 and 2 most of the households belong to the lower-income category and prefer public taps since the households in these wards consider the advance payment and monthly tariff for the individual connection unaffordable.

One factor that influences a household's willingness to collect water from a particular service is the 'neighbourhood effect'. That is, a household's decision to opt for

8 The households, in general, assess the quality of the water in terms of three criteria: namely, its taste, its ability to boil food and its ability to preserve leftover food for the next day's use (i.e. the remaining rice cooked in the night is preserved with the water and is eaten the next morning).

an individual connection or to collect water from a public tap is influenced by the practice of neighbouring households. In order to maximise overall benefits, as well as promote equity, officials should install more public taps in low-income settlements and locations where the majority of households elect to use this source of water

18.2.9 Willingness to pay for water: public taps

The official policy is that the Pillur Scheme water supplied through public taps will be free. The strong assumption of the officials in the town is that the households will not be willing to pay for public taps because that has not been the practice in the past. This view is contradicted by the survey, which found that 141 (68.44%) sample households were willing to pay for public taps, provided the supply was reliable (Table 18.1). The average amount these households were willing to pay for water was around Rs8 per 10,000 litres. Indeed, a considerable number of low-income households felt that paying would encourage officials to ensure that public taps offered a reliable and continuous water supply.

Many of these households also expressed social concerns; they indicated that since the supply of water through public taps involved a cost to the government this cost should be borne by the user. However, a few households pointed out that the property tax collected by the officials at present included a component for public taps, so they were already paying for the service. Overall, however, it may be noted that 68.44% of all households were willing to pay for public taps, something the policy-makers should take note of.

18.3 Discussion and conclusions

The policy implications of the results of the present study are manifold. The results suggest that the government's water supply policies themselves negatively affect the sustainability objective of the Pillur Scheme because they are framed to serve a very narrowly defined objective: namely, the generation of revenue, rather than the overall goals of good water management and social welfare. It should be noted that if the supply-side approach incorporates various components of the demand-side factors then not only will revenue increase but also social welfare could be maximised on a sustainable basis. In other words, water supply policies that work *with* the preferences of the users will always lead to a 'non-zero-sum game' in which a 'win–win' situation can be achieved in the longer run.

The present study has found that a few basic changes to the existing policy at the local level, based on the preferences of the users, would lead to the achievement of the three major objectives: efficiency, equity and sustainability in the water supply scheme. For example, among other things, use of a discriminatory initial advance payment depending on the willingness to pay, an instalment system for payment in advance, differential water tariffs for different income groups, the allocation of more public taps in those areas where the lower-income households live and the fixing of a reasonable tariff for public taps will increase benefits to the users as well as to the government agency providing the water supply service. In addition, one of the implications of the study is that the private sector can play a part in providing water supply, particularly with regard to certain components such as maintenance and billing. However, more research is required in this area before any policy decision should be made.

An important consideration is that, although changes in the water supply policies at the local level may be desirable, the water supply authorities in general are constrained by many exogenous factors that prevent them from taking appropriate decisions, especially in a developing-country context. For instance, the water supply authority at the local level in India often does not have the political power to make even minor changes because the overall policy is formulated by the politicians and bureaucrats at the state level, who may have a vested interest in maintaining the current system and perhaps have less understanding of local conditions. The prevailing historical, cultural and institutional framework for the state as a whole is based on the general notion that provision of water is the responsibility of the government and therefore should be supplied either at highly subsidised rate or free of cost. The legal system in India also makes it difficult to implement appropriate changes in policy. For instance, placing a tariff on water from public taps becomes a legal issue in India. Therefore, even though communities and households are willing to accept change, it is even more important to work towards the modification of political and legal systems at the macro level. Only in this way will the achievement of the goals of water supply schemes at the local level be made possible.

References

Government of India (1991) *Census of India* (New Delhi: Government of India).
—— (2001) *Census of India* (New Delhi: Government of India).
Griffin, C.C., J. Briscoe, B. Singh, R. Ramasubban and R. Bhatia (1995) 'Contingent Valuation and Actual Behaviour: Predicting Connections to New Water Systems in the State of Kerala, India', *The World Bank Economic Review* 9.3: 373-95.
Mitchell, R.C., and R.T. Carson (1989) *Using Surveys to Value Public Goods: The Contingent Valuation Method* (Washington, DC: Resources for the Future).
Rogers, P., R. de Silva and R. Bhatia (2002) 'Water is an Economic Good: How to Use Prices to Promote Equity, Efficiency and Sustainability', *Water Policy* 4.1: 1-17.
Singh, B., R. Ramasubban, R. Bhatia, J. Briscoe, C.C. Griffin and C. Kim (1993) 'Rural Water Supply in Kerala, India: How to Emerge from a Low-Level Equilibrium Trap', *Water Resources Research* 29.7: 1,931-42.
US NOAA (National Oceanic and Atmospheric Administration) (1993) 'Report of the NOAA Panel on Contingent Valuation', *Federal Register* 58.10: 4,602-14.
Venkatachalam, L. (2000) *Economic Valuation of Water Used in the Household Sector: A Contingent Valuation Approach in a Developing Country Context* (unpublished PhD thesis in economics; Madras: University of Madras).
Whittington, D., D.T. Lauria and X. Mu (1991) 'A Study of Water Vending and Willingness to Pay for Water in Onitsha, Nigeria', *World Development* 19.2–3: 179-98.

19
Water supply in Singapore
CHALLENGES AND CHOICES

Kim Chuan Goh

National Institute of Education, Singapore

Arguments regarding water supply and consumption range from the liberal concept that access to wholesome water of sufficient quantity and quality is a basic human right and one of the most fundamental conditions for human development (Gleick 2000), to that of water as a resource that should be charged at a cost that reflects its true worth. In Singapore, while the need to make water inexpensive for everyone is important, it is equally important that water supply be judiciously managed to ensure effective use and minimal wastage. Here, available water is limited and dependence on foreign sources is becoming uncertain. Greater independence from foreign sources means that production of water domestically will have to be approached through unconventional methods and at higher costs, and therefore the application of market principles is no longer an option but a necessity. Thus the need to pay careful attention to this aspect of water as a socioeconomic good is nowhere greater than in this island republic.

This chapter examines the water supply situation in Singapore where the limited area of 640 km², a highly urbanised population of 4 million, and a vibrant economy have made the water issue of strategic importance and a national priority. The challenges facing this island-state in the past and, more importantly, in the future, and the choices it has to make to increase water supply, will be examined.

19.1 Sources of water supply

19.1.1 External sources

Thirty years after the foundation of Singapore in 1819 the population of Singapore had grown from 150 to 50,000 inhabitants, spurred by its role as the port of call for the peninsula. By 1920, when its population touched 400,000, supply from existing hill reservoirs on the island was stretched to the limits. Attempts were initiated to seek sources from Johor on the southern tip of the Malay Peninsula across the

Straits of Johor. The Gunung Pulai Scheme was selected and developed and water was supplied to the island through an agreement signed in 1924 between Singapore, a Straits settlement, and the Johor State, both under British colonial rule. In subsequent years new schemes were developed and the Tebrau River Scheme nearer Johor Bahru town was completed in 1953. Water was conveyed to the island via a 1,600 mm pipeline along the causeway from Johor Bahru. A decade later, the Skudai River Scheme and the Johor River Scheme were added; they became operational in 1964 and 1967, respectively, but they were preceded by agreements signed in 1961 and 1962. Some of these schemes were expanded in the 1980s while a new project on the Linggui River in the same state was developed and completed in 1993. In the same year a new agreement was signed between the sovereign republic of Singapore[1] and the Johor state. Johor currently accounts for half of Singapore's daily water needs of 1,299 million m³/day (286 mgd).

Given that a significant amount of water comes from outside its borders, and since water supply is a vital element of its national security, Singapore has been looking towards diversifying its external sources of supply. Indonesia was a logical choice, specifically from the larger islands closer to its borders. In the economic recovery following the mid-1980s recession, the Riau Province of Sumatra was identified not only as a potential economic growth area for Indonesia where Singapore could play a part but also as a potential supplier of water. Water could be conveyed from the Riau islands to Singapore via sub-marine pipelines. An agreement between the two countries, signed in 1991, provided for 4,545 million m³ (1,000 million gallons) of water per day from the Riau Province to Singapore. Sungei Kampar on Sumatra was identified as another potential supplementary source of water for the Riau islands, which could be developed with Singapore's participation. Moves were initiated to develop the water supply on Bintan for the neighbouring islands in Riau and for Singapore. In fact, two agreements were signed between the two countries on 29 January 1993: one was a memorandum of understanding to develop water resources in the Sungei Kampar Basin in Sumatra for sale to Singapore (which would also benefit the rest of Riau Province) and the other was an agreement to jointly develop an industrial estate in Bintan (*Straits Times* 1993). Unfortunately, the economic downturn of 1997/98 and the subsequent political uncertainty in Indonesia put paid to these well-intentioned plans, and Singapore's reliance on Malaysia for its water remains. But this reliance is undesirable in light of the recent deterioration in bilateral ties between the two countries.

19.1.2 Domestic sources

Impoundments and reservoirs

Singapore has several impounding reservoirs inland including Seletar, Peirce and MacRitchie, which occupy 12.3 square miles (about 30 km²) and 12 square miles of protected catchment and unprotected catchment areas, respectively, and which

---

1   Singapore's status changed from a Straits settlement to become a part of Malaysia in 1963 and an independent island republic in 1965.

belong to eight streams flowing into the partial pumpe[...] increase storage capacity, seven estuarine reservoirs ha[...] ming the river mouths. In the early 1970s Singapore re[...] national priority all available water resources on the i[...] through short-term and long-term schemes (Sung 1972)[...] island's area had been utilised for water collection, th[...] domestically available water was still significant. It was [...] to maximise collection of surface resources by extendin[...] miles (about 75 km²) of collection grounds to 156 square miles (or about 484 km²; 75% of the island's total area) was proposed. Given that geological conditions limited the availability of groundwater (Chou 1972), the plan focused instead on retrieval of stormwater and water recycling.

Stormwater run-off

Harnessing stormwater at minimum cost requires proper land-use planning and pollution control to ensure that stormwater run-off can be efficiently collected and that pollution levels are low. Pollution control policies and enforcement acts were drawn up and promulgated, and, by the 1980s, Singapore was seeing the benefits of these measures. Stormwater harvesting from urban land was consistent with the overall policy of land use in this land-scarce republic, in which land was seen as too valuable for its use to be restricted to a single purpose such as for housing. In the words of the Minister for National Development:

> If we designate more land for water catchment, there will be less land for
> housing and other developments. The reverse is also true. Optimising and
> maximising the use of land and water helped the country to overcome
> constraints to a certain extent (*Straits Times* 1996a).

Water supply schemes had to be planned to co-exist with other land users and innovative approaches to land use had to be thought out. Given this resolve, Singapore was the first country in South-East Asia to develop viable stormwater run-off schemes.

Among the various schemes, the Bedok and Lower Seletar Schemes are the largest. Surface water for these schemes comes mainly from the housing estates and new towns of Ang Mo Kio, Bedok, Tampines and Yishun and the area near Changi International Airport. Water is conveyed to the storage reservoirs of Bedok and Lower Seletar. One important feature of this scheme is the emphasis on close co-ordination between several agencies, such as the Housing Board Development (HDB), the Ministry of the Environment (ENV) and the Planning Department, in order to ensure that water collected from urban surfaces is low in pollutants. Such co-operation and co-ordination between agencies sharing land use in catchment areas ensured that pollution did not result from their development projects (Sung 1972). Thus industries and other potential polluters were excluded from the catchments, construction and erosion curbed, and the drainage system designed in such a way that it channels water through concrete channels to suitable collection ponds situated at topographic low points. An automatic monitoring system ensures that only discharges produced by heavy storms resulting in run-off above a certain

re collected. The 'first flush', which washes off all accumulated pollutants
the catchment, bypasses the stormwater collection facility and flows directly
the sea (*Public Utilities Board Digest* 1987).

Over the years a number of such schemes have been implemented, and rainwater
from as much as half of the island, including new towns, has been harnessed. One
example of the innovative approach to stormwater collection is making use of the
empty space under the interchange of the Seletar and Bukit Timah expressways for
a water collection pond. The space is the size of two football fields with a depth of
four Housing Development Board (HDB) storeys (*Straits Times* 1996b).

One obvious concern in collecting water in this way is its quality. Analysis of the
water collected showed that, for all parameters measured, the quality is comparable
to that produced from natural upland catchments, and Table 1, adapted from Lee
and Nazarudeen (1996), gives an indication of the high quality of stormwater
collected in reservoirs. The low-lying nature of the Bedok area accounts for the
higher conductivity values, and the coastal soils account for the higher sulphate
content. For all other parameters including heavy metals and bacteriological counts
the stormwater collected at the Bedok reservoir is of good quality.

Recycling and water reclamation

Recycling of water used in homes and industries is an attempt to augment water
supplies locally, treating and using it as a resource rather than letting it flow as
waste to the sea. Recycling efforts in Singapore started in 1966 when the Jurong
Industrial Water Treatment Plant was commissioned to supply industrial water to
the Jurong Industrial Estate. This water comes from treated sewerage effluent and
is meant for industrial use in the Jurong area as well as by several oil refineries. In
general, the Singapore government encourages industry and private enterprises to
recycle water, and liberal tax rebates have been provided for factories that install
water-saving plants under the Economic Expansion Incentives Act.

An example of a successful programme is that implemented by the semiconduc-
tor company, STMicroelectronics, which has invested S$3.9 million[2] since 1995 into
three water recycling systems in its wafer fabrication plant and to date has saved
almost S$11 million. This translates into a recycling rate of 44% of its water usage,
or 4.1 million m[3] of water saved in the past 3 years (*Straits Times* 2003c).

Under pressure to reduce dependence on supplies from Malaysia, Singapore has
aggressively embarked on increasing treatment of waste-water effluent, allowing
development of a new product, 'Newater', to standards higher than industrial
water. A four-stage process brings waste-water to a quality that is better than that
produced by the Public Utilities Board,[3] and exceeds the United States Environmental Protection Agency (US EPA) and World Health Organisation (WHO) standards on
all parameters. Treatment begins with the conventional waste-water treatment
process, followed by microfiltration to remove suspended solids, colloidal particles,
bacteria, some viruses and protozoan cysts, through reverse osmosis to filter all bac-

2   US$1 = S$1.76.
3   www.pub.gov.sg/NEWater_files/newater_quality/chart.html

Parameters	Bedok Reservoir (stormwater)		Upland Reservoir (natural forested run-off)	
PHYSICAL				
Turbidity (NTU)	1.0–5.9	2.4	1.4–5.6	2.9
Conductivity (mmhos/cm)	263–529	340	16–37	25
pH value	6.7–7.9	7.4	5.7–7.3	6.3
CHEMICAL (mg/l)				
Total organic carbon	1.0–4.1	2.9	2.0–4.0	3.1
Ammoniacal nitrogen	<0.02–0.03	<0.02	<0.02–0.55	0.02
Nitrate nitrogen	<0.10–0.32	0.16	<0.10–0.17	<0.10
Total solids	162–246	205	16–32	25
Suspended solids	2–8	4	7–10	8
Phosphate	<0.03–0.04	<0.03	<0.03–0.04	<0.03
Sulphate	22–34	27	2–4	3
METALS (mg/l)				
Iron	0.01–0.15	0.04	0.40–0.71	0.52
Manganese	0.001–0.016	0.005	0.001–0.015	0.005
Arsenic	<0.005	<0.005	<0.005	<0.005
Cadmium	<0.0005	<0.0005	<0.0005	<0.0005
Chromium	<0.005	<0.005	<0.001–0.002	<0.001
Lead	<0.001–0.002	<0.001	<0.001–0.002	<0.001
Copper	<0.002–0.011	0.006	<0.002–0.045	0.023
BACTERIOLOGICAL				
Coliform (counts/100 ml, 37°C, 24 h)	2–120	18	2–56	14

NTU = Nephelometric Turbidity Units

TABLE 19.1 Raw water quality comparison for some parameters, 1994

Source: Lee and Nazarudeen 1996: 37

teria, viruses, heavy metals and other harmful substances, and finally to ultraviolet disinfection to guarantee complete purity of water, free of any organisms.[4]

This water meets the requirements of industries such as the wafer fabrication plants and some commercial buildings, but the intention is to mix with reservoir water to supplement domestic supply. A pilot plant built in 2000 was able to demonstrate the feasibility of reclaiming high-grade water from treated used water using the processes described above. As of 21 February 2003, 2 million gallons

4 *Ibid.*

(about 9,000 m³) a day, or 1% of consumption, will be blended with raw water in the Bedok, Kranji and Upper Seletar reservoirs (*Straits Times* 2003a). This amount will increase to some 10 million gallons (about 45,000 m³) a day in 2011, or 2.5% of consumption.

19.1.3 Desalination of sea water

Desalination to augment water for use in Singapore has been considered for some time but it was not adopted as a matter of policy until recent years. Cost was one compelling reason for this reluctance; also, in the early 1990s there was optimism that sources of water from outside Singapore could be diversified through the signing of agreements to develop water schemes in Bintan and the Riau Province. To date nothing has come from these agreements and the need for desalination has become urgent. In February 2000, the Public Utilities Board (PUB) was given permission to source desalinated water from private companies developing desalination plants under the single wholesale buyer market structure. This is expected to produce some 91,000 m³/day (20 mgd) with the supply to come on stream in 2005.

Although desalination as a viable option to augment water is a new venture for Singapore, for many years it has been the main means of supplying water for the Shell oil refinery complex on Pulau Bukom. Here 90% of the water supply need of the complex is obtained from desalination and only 10% from the PUB source, mainly to meet the drinking needs of the workers.

Although desalination costs under current improved technology are still higher than traditional means of treatment, Singapore has decided to go ahead in the belief that new technologies will reduce the costs further. It is envisaged that this source of supply will ultimately produce some 12% of Singapore's daily water needs.

19.2 Reduction of water loss in the system

Water supplied from metered sources must be accounted for; the lower this unaccounted-for loss, the more efficient the water supply system. Losses during conveyance can be due to several factors: leakage, pipe breakages, delayed response and repair work, and water theft. In many developing countries unaccounted-for water (UFW) may be as high as 30–60% of metered water supply. While technical problems can be solved by replacing old pipes and attending to repairs promptly when reported, water theft must be tackled through legal means. High wastage is a drain on the system: huge revenues are lost and the UFW could easily meet the needs of a significant proportion of the population that has no access to clean water. Singapore is determined to tackle the problem of wastage due to loss within conveyance although by the standards of many countries, including developed ones, its UFW was low, only 11% in the early 1980s.

The PUB has intensified efforts to reduce this loss by implementing various programmes and water conservation measures including leakage control, full and accurate metering policy, proper accounting of water use and strict legislation on water thefts. Better-quality and corrosion-resistant pipes were used to replace old ones made of galvanised iron, which had been chemically attacked by the acid sulphate soils, and there is stricter supervision of pipe-laying work to ensure that newly laid pipelines are watertight. An island-wide survey was conducted of all unlined galvanised iron connecting pipes and unlined cast-iron pipes in the water distribution system. Arising from this a comprehensive programme to replace these pipes was undertaken beginning in 1983 in the western part of the island and ending in 1993 in the central part. Another measure taken in conjunction with this comprehensive effort to cut unaccounted-for loss is a nationwide leak detection programme carried out throughout the year. The objective of the programme is to check the soundness of the entire network at least once a year (PUB undated). Tied to the above is the quick response to public reports of leaks and rectification of faults. Where meters are at fault in causing unaccounted-for loss, the older meters are replaced by more accurate electromagnetic flowmeters which are highly accurate. Any illegal draw-off is dealt with by legal means and stringent enforcement. With all these measures in place, PUB has been able to conduct a proper accounting of water supplied and used with the result that, in the first four years, unaccounted-for losses declined from 10.6% in 1989 to below 7% in 1992 (PUB undated). Since then a value of 6% UFW has been maintained.

19.3 Demand management

Singapore's industrial water demand is still less than that of domestic consumption, accounting for less than 50% of total consumption. The types of industry that consumed large amounts of water (average consumption above 100,000 m³/month) in 1984 and 1995 are shown in Table 19.2. From the table it is evident that the main water-consuming industries have changed from the 1980s to 1990s. In the 1990s manufacturing of electronic products and components was the main industrial activity; wafer prefabrication is highly intensive in the use of water. Also, more governmental and educational establishments consume more than 100,000 m³/month now than in the 1980s.

Domestic demand is still predominant. In 1995 three components of domestic use made up some 80% of the total: showers (45%), toilet flushing (18%) and laundry (14%). The rest was accounted for by dish washing, food preparation and other house-cleaning activities. Consumption of water per household per day increased from 648 litres in 1987 to 736 in 1994. Per capita consumption based on resident population shows an increasing trend from 164.8 litres per day in 1987 to 204.6 in 1997. Although by the standards of many cities the per capita water consumption in Singapore is relatively low, greater savings of water could still be achieved by targeting the three main water-consuming activities.

In 1981 a Water Conservation Unit was created in the Public Utilities Board. Since then, a comprehensive public education programme has been put in place to create awareness among Singaporeans and to encourage conservation and reduce wastage. The PUB website provides tips to consumers on how to conserve water and many other items including teachers' kits that could be used to support the teach-

Type of account	Number of accounts	Average consumption (m³/month)
1984		
Petroleum refineries	5	553,601
Hotels	43	433,831
Manufacturing of electronic products and components	23	249,305
Port facilities	10	185,092
Manufacturing of transport equipment	14	158,058
Manufacturing of textile except apparel	9	126,339
Temporary supplies for building construction	24	117,075
Manufacturing of products of petroleum and coal	1	110,852
1995		
Manufacturing of electronic products and components	43	1,330,785
Hotels	42	697,110
Petroleum refineries	6	639,420
Defence establishment	20	362,581
Landlord supplies for office buildings	24	253,563
Medical, hospitals, etc.	9	223,463
Prisons and places of detention	9	218,313
Manufacturing of transport equipment	9	211,901
Education establishments	4	197,329
Manufacturing of chemical products	9	163,806
Manufacturing of products of petroleum and coal	1	160,986
Beverage companies	5	133,494
Landlord supplies for office buildings and flats		117,828
Manufacturing of fabricated metal products	10	114,269
Manufacturing of textile except apparel	8	112,281

TABLE 19.2 Water consumption beyond 100,000 m³ per year by industry, 1984 and 1995

Source: PUB (personal communication, 13 November 1995)

ing of the importance of water to primary school pupils. Another public education drive was the Save Water Campaign in 1995, making use of the mass media. The Civil Defence Force also organises water-rationing exercises to simulate emergency situations in which supplies are shut down for a few hours and residents in HDB estates obtain their water from collection points on the ground floors of apartments. In 1992, the PUB jointly with HDB introduced the low-capacity flushing cistern (LCFC) for toilets, which uses 3.5–4.5 litres per flush, approximately half that of older designs, in all new public housing estates. This became mandatory from 1997 for all new developments and building renovations involving the replacement of toilet cisterns (*Straits Times* 1997).

In the most recent effort to encourage effective use of water by residents and to create awareness of the strategic importance of water to Singapore in the light of the bilateral problems with Malaysia over water, a programme for 'Water Efficient Homes' was launched on 23 February 2003. Data for 1999 shows that private houses consume the most water, averaging 35 m^3 per month while condominiums, private flats, HDB five-room and bigger flats, and HDB four-room flats consume an average of 20 m^3 per month.[5] It was felt that a 5–8% reduction in household consumption of water could be achieved by using simple water-saving devices such as thimbles and bags for toilet cisterns. This programme will eventually involve some 80% of homes in Singapore (*Straits Times* 2003b).

The pricing mechanism is an important instrument for improving efficiency of water use. Singapore has long had universal metering and the rates charged have been revised a number of times in the last decade. The rates differentiate between users, but for domestic users, two block rates are charged for consumption of less than 40 m^3 per month and more than 40 m^3 per month. To ensure that the lower-income households are not unduly burdened by increases in water rates, HDB provides utilities rebates based on the size of the HDB flats as a surrogate for household income. Families in smaller flats obtained higher rebates than those living in larger flats. The tariffs also include a water conservation tax for all types of user, and the tax is higher for the larger domestic consumers. This targeting of domestic consumers is understandable given that domestic consumption still is higher than industrial and commercial consumption put together.

The management of the water supply system in Singapore has been under the Public Utilities Board, which operates as a private-sector entity. While mindful of the need to ensure that low-income families have access to potable water, it has to balance this objective with the need to price water as a scarce commodity to ensure efficiency in water usage. The PUB has evolved a water supply management system that is efficient and profitable. In further enhancing efficiency, in 2000 PUB awarded a contract to Intergraph South East Asia to provide the next-generation Geospatial Resource Management System which 'will facilitate enterprise-wide data exchange and integration for enhanced decision support among PUB's broad user base'.[6]

5   Statistics Singapore, www.singstat.gov.sg/papers/snippets/water.html, 2003.
6   www.intergraph.com/utilities/mainpages/util082400.htm

19.4 Challenges, choices and costs

Singapore has long recognised that, given the limited water available internally, it must seek to increase its supply from outside sources, but over-dependence on foreign sources, whether from Malaysia or Indonesia, is undesirable in the long run. The complexity of the treaty arrangements with Malaysia has never been more obvious than in recent years when issues of pricing and extension of supply after the expiry of the treaties have been debated, sometimes acrimoniously.

Singapore currently draws water from Johor under two agreements. The 1961 contract gives Singapore rights to extract 86 million gallons (400,000 m³) of water per day from the Pontian and Gunung Pulai Reservoirs and the Tebrau and Skudai Rivers, while under the 1962 agreement Singapore can draw up to 250 mgd (1.15 million m³) from the Johor River. Although the latter agreement runs until 2061, the former expires in 2011 and, given the short period remaining, Singapore is anxious to secure water supplies beyond that deadline. The agreement that expires in 2011 is the focus of disputes; demands have been made by Malaysia and rebuttals have been provided by Singapore. Malaysia perceived that the 1961 and 1962 agreements, under which Singapore pays Malaysia for raw water at 3 Malaysian cents per 1,000 gallons, were 'lopsided and exploitative at a ridiculous rate' (quoted in *Sunday Times* 1998).

The maximum yield from these sources is 138 million gallons per day (627,000 m³/day). Singapore supplies Johor with up to 12% of the water it receives, or not less than 4 million gallons (18,000 m³) per day. Johor can request more treated water up to a maximum not exceeding the yield from the Pulai catchment. Singapore has to pay rental for the land reserved for its waterworks at a rate of s$5 per acre (0.4 ha). Provision is made for water rates review 25 years from the day of signing. The 1962 agreement was similar to the first with a few additions: Singapore has the right to draw up to a maximum of 250 million gallons (1.15 million m³) a day from the Johor River, at the same rate as before; the agreement is valid for 99 years and will expire in 2061, and the water rates are to be reviewed. Singapore rebutted the accusation of exploitation by pointing out that it costs MYR$2.40[7] to treat 1,000 gallons of water while Johor buys the treated water from Singapore for only MYR$0.50, the price agreed by the two parties. Johor then sells the treated water at an average price of MYR$3.95, which means that Singapore is subsidising water supplied to Johor consumers.

19.5 Conclusions

Given the strategic importance of water to Singapore's survival and development, and the risks of over-dependence on external sources, measures to make the island-state more self-sufficient must be pursued. Available water must be 'stretched' in its use by reducing consumption, wastage and unaccounted-for losses. Further,

7   US$1 = MYR$3.90

reclamation of waste-water for re-use through the application of technology and desalination are necessary options. Singapore has approached the challenge holistically, with some measure of success. Because water is so important to Singapore, it is willing to invest resources to make this objective possible. New developments in technology have also helped to reduce the costs of recycling and desalination such that the gap between the cost of raw water production and the cost of water supplied through recycling and desalination has narrowed considerably.

Singapore is dealing with the limitations of water supply through an efficient water supply system characterised by the following:

- There is comprehensive long-term planning.

- Desalination and recycling are features of water production activity.

- Costs are not a factor in ensuring additional supply.

- Losses in the system are kept to a minimum.

- The population is constantly reminded of the importance of conserving water.

References

Chou, T.C. (1972) 'Groundwater Investigations in Singapore', in *Proceedings of the Regional Workshop on Water Resources, Environment and National Development*, Singapore, 13–17 March (Science Council of Singapore and the National Academy of Sciences of USA): 3-16.

Gleick, P.H. (2000) 'The Changing Water Paradigm: A Look at Twenty-first Century Water Resources Development', *Water International* 25.1: 127-38.

Lee, M.F., and H. Nazarudeen (1996) 'Collection of Urban Stormwater for Potable Water Supply in Singapore', *Water Quality International*, June 1996: 36-40.

PUB (Public Utilities Board) (undated) *Unaccounted-for Water: Singapore's Experience* (Singapore: PUB).

Public Utilities Board Digest (1987) Stormwater Collection in Sungei Seletar/Bedok Water Scheme', *Public Utilities Board Digest* 7 (June 1987): 24-28.

Straits Times (1993) 'Two New Pacts to Boost Ties', *The Straits Times*, 30 January 1993.

—— (1996a) 'Innovative Way to Solve Limited Land, Water Supply', *The Straits Times*, 6 August 1996.

—— (1996b) 'Pond Under Flyover to Collect Storm Water', *The Straits Times*, 6 August 1996.

—— (1997) 'A Must for New Buildings: Cisterns that Use Only Half the Water of Existing Ones', *The Straits Times*, 23 March 1997.

—— (2003a) 'Newater Flows into Reservoirs', *The Straits Times*, 21 February 2003.

—— (2003b) 'Big Savings in Little Ways', *The Straits Times*, 24 February 2003.

—— (2003c) 'They Spend Millions but Saved More', *The Straits Times*, 24 February 2003.

Sunday Times (1998) 'Singapore Sells Subsidized Water to Johor', *The Sunday Times*, 6 September 1998.

Sung, T.T. (1972) 'Water Resources Planning and Development, Singapore', in *Proceedings of the Regional Workshop on Water Resources, Environment and National Development*, Singapore 13–17 March (Science Council of Singapore and the National Academy of Sciences USA): 17-25.

Biographies

Fenda Akiwumi worked as a hydrogeologist for 14 years on the UNDP/FAO Land Resources Survey Project (subsequently Land and Water Development Division, Ministry of Agriculture and Forestry) in Sierra Leone and as an environmental consultant in the mining industry. She teaches geography and geology at Hill College, Texas, USA, and continues to write on water resources development in Sierra Leone from an interdisciplinary perspective. She holds a master's degree in hydrogeology from University College London, London University, UK. She is currently enrolled in a PhD programme in Environmental Geography at Texas State University, San Marcos, TX, specialising in water policy and management.
fa1010@txstate.edu

Juliet Bird is a graduate of the Universities of London and Melbourne. For much of her career she was at the Melbourne College of Education, where she lectured in Geography and Environmental Science. Later she transferred to the Department of Geography at the University of Melbourne, where she lectured in water resources management. She was a member of the Cooperative Research Centre for Catchment Management and a consultant on river and water management. She is now a Fellow of the Department of Geography, and chairs the Landscape Committee of the National Trust of Australia (Victoria).
julietfb@unimelb.edu.au

Davide Bixio, with an MSc in environmental engineering (Genoa University, 1996), specialised in water resources engineering and did a postgraduate in corporate management (2001). He worked as a staff co-operator at Genoa University. He joined AQUAFIN—the largest Belgian waste-water treatment utility—in 1997, where he has held various positions, including that of risk analyst. His main activity focuses on the optimisation of investment projects and of the operation of waste-water treatment infrastructure. Currently his work is oriented mainly towards water recycling and re-use and international consulting.
davide.bixio@aquafin.be

Jennifer Bremer is an adjunct professor of public policy and business at the University of North Carolina at Chapel Hill and directs the Washington branch of the Kenan Institute of Private Enterprise, where her work focuses on removing constraints to expanded infrastructure investment in developing countries, corporate community engagement and the role of business in international development.
Jbremer@kenan.org

Jonathan L. Chenoweth is a lecturer in the Centre for Environmental Strategy, University of Surrey, UK. He graduated from the University of Melbourne in 2000 with a PhD that examined institutional structures for the management of the Murray-Darling and Mekong River Basins. He has conducted research in Australia, South-East Asia, the Middle East and Europe in the areas of environmental policy and water resources management.
j.chenoweth@surrey.ac.uk

Greet De Gueldre has a PhD in science (biology) from Antwerp University in 1988 and has been working with AQUAFIN since 1992. During her career she has executed and managed several research and design projects related to the treatment of urban waste-water. She is currently head of the research and product development department of the company.

Professor **Diane Dupont** holds a PhD in economics. Her research involves a number of areas including those related to fisheries regulations, environmental valuation, and water pricing and demand. Her work has been published in *The Journal of Environmental Economics and Management*, *American Journal of Agricultural Economics* and *Environmental and Resource Economics*.

diane.dupont@brocku.ca

Dimitriou Elias is a geologist and environmental scientist with a degree in geology from the University of Athens, an MSc in Environmental and Ecological Sciences from Lancaster University, UK, and is a PhD candidate in Water Resources Management at University of Athens Department of Geology. He has professional expertise in hydrology, geology and water resources management and significant experience in project management and wetland hydrology. He has been a research assistant at the Hellenic Centre for Marine Research, Athens, since 2000. During this period he has supported several applications of environmental modelling, GIS techniques and use of remote sensing data in environmental analysis.

elias@ncmr.gr

Luis Fernando Gallardo Cabrera, a biologist, was formerly manager of IMPLAN (Municipal Institute of Planning) at Aguascalientes at the time of writing the chapter in this volume. He is now General Director of MAPLE Environmental Consulting, Aguascalientes.

l_gallardo4@hotmail.com

Carl Ulrich Gminder has been working part-time as a research assistant at the Institute for Economy and the Environment since 2001. He is also a freelance consultant for strategic, organisational and sustainability management. His PhD thesis explores the systemic method of organisational constellation for translating sustainability strategies into action.

Ulrich.Gminder@unisg.ch   www.gminder.de

K.C. Goh is professor of geography, National Institute of Education, Nanyang Technological University. He has taught undergraduate courses on water management issues as well as supervised doctoral research in hydrology. His research has been mainly in hydrology and water management in the South-East Asian region. He has taught in Malaysia, Brunei and, over the past 12 years, in Singapore.

kcgoh@nie.edu.sg

C.T. 'Kip' Howlett is Secretariat of the World Chlorine Council, Vice President of the American Chemistry Council, and executive director of the Chlorine Chemistry Council (CCC). Formed in 1993, the CCC is involved in science, research, product stewardship, government relations and public information regarding chlorine and chlorine chemistry. The CCC represents companies that produce chlorine or use chlorine chemistry to make products, ranging from medicines to high-performance plastics, that meet the most essential needs of modern society. Mr Howlett has a BA from the Johns Hopkins University and a law degree from Willamette (OR) University.

kip_howlett@americanchemistry.com

Eric Johnson has been involved in the fields of small-scale rural water supply, sanitation, health, community conflict and altenative energy use for the past 15 years. He has been extensively invloved in the training of professionals, technicians and community leaders throughout Latin America. During the last four years he has served as a representative of the Environmental Health Project in the Dominican Republic, aiding in the implementation of USAID-funded institutional assistance to the national rural water supply agency there. He has also recently served as an advisor providing guidance on economically rational use of renewable energy under funding granted by the US Department of Energy.

ericjohnson@igc.org

Areti Kontogianni holds a degree in Agricultural Economics and a PhD in Environmental Economics and Policy from the University of Aegean. She has been working as a Research Fellow for the University of Thessaly in several research projects for the National Marine Park of Northern Sporades and as a scientific collaborator for the Greek Ministry of External Affairs Committee on European Environmental Policy and International Environmental Relations. She is currently a Senior Research Associate at the Laboratory of Applied Environmental Economics (EREOPE) and a CSERGE Associate Fellow. Her current research interests include the ecological/economic approach to the non-market valuation of ecological functions, integrated watershed and coastal zone management, stakeholder analysis, and participatory management.

akonto@env.aegean.gr

Liz Mann joined Oxfam Australia, known as Oxfam Community Aid Abroad within Australia, in 1997 as the Project Officer for the Horn of Africa. After spending two years in that post she took up a position as the Mozambique Field Representative and spent three years based in the capital, Maputo, managing rural development, HIV/AIDS and advocacy programmes before returning to Melbourne for two years as the Southern Africa Regional Co-ordinator. In January 2004 she left Oxfam Australia and is now based in the UK working with the International HIV/AIDS Alliance as Senior Programme Officer: East and Southern Africa.

lizmann@iprimus.com.au

Steven Nebiker is a specialist in water resource management and water and waste-water treatment. He is a project manager for HydroLogics Inc., a management consulting firm specialising in simulation of water resource systems and conflict resolution using mathematical software. Steven has masters' degrees in environmental engineering and business administration from the University of North Carolina at Chapel Hill.

snebiker@hydrologics.net

Thomas Nowak is a PhD student and assistant lecturer at the University of Düsseldorf. His main research focus is sustainable development and networks. As part of his PhD thesis he is working with the Gerling Sustainable Development Project GmbH in a project on Milos aimed at creating a desalination plant powered by geothermal energy. This project relies heavily on a functioning network of actors from different fields.

thomas@nowaks.net

David Lloyd Owen runs Envisager, a consultancy advising companies, institutions and governments about economic, competitive and regulatory drivers in water and waste management markets. He heads the advisory board of the Pictet Water Fund and is a member of Glas Cymru Cyf. His books include the *Masons Water Yearbook* (Masons Solicitors, London, six editions, 1999–2004) and *European Water: Market Drivers and Responses* (CWC, 2002).

david@envisager.co.uk

Leslie Morris is a planner with an interest in social and environmental issues within a development perspective, particularly in urban environments. She is currently working as a consultant in water and sanitation issues.

leslieamorris@yahoo.co.uk

Professor **Steven Renzetti**'s research is concerned with the economics of water resources. He is the author of *The Economics of Water Demands* (Kluwer, 2002). In addition to teaching and research, Dr Renzetti has acted as a consultant for a number of government agencies including Environment Canada and the World Bank.

steven.renzetti@brocku.ca

Arno Rosemarin is Communications Director and Senior Researcher at the Stockholm Environment Institute. He has authored over 40 papers dealing with water pollution, including eutrophication of freshwater and marine systems, and is currently managing the Sida-sponsored EcoSanRes ecological sanitation programme (www.ecosanres.org).

arno.rosemarin@sei.se

Dieter Rothenberger works as a senior researcher at the Centre for Innovation Research in the Utility Sector (CIRUS) at the Swiss Federal Institute for Environmental Science and Technology. He also looks back on many years of experience in his earlier work with a major German utility in developing and implementing private-sector participation projects.

dieter.rothenberger@gmx.de

Konstantinos D. Sarantakos holds a degree in Agricultural Sciences from the Agricultural University of Athens and an MSc degree in Environmental Management and Policy from the University of the Aegean. He is a PhD candidate in Non-market Valuation of Environmental Resources, University of the Aegean. He has been a research associate at the Hellenic Centre for Marine Research since 2002. During that time, he has worked in several research projects, concerning the sustainable management of water/coastal resources. His recent research interests include: non-market valuation of environmental resources, integrated management of inland water resources and coastal zone, and GIS and remote sensing applications in water and coastal zone management.

ksarant@ncmr.gr

Mayling Simpson-Hebert is a medical–environmental anthropologist. She has authored numerous papers on sanitation, hygiene education and community participation in water and sanitation and is a co-author of the books *Ecological Sanitation* (SIDA, 1998; Stockholm Environment Institute, 2004), *Sanitation Promotion* (World Health Organisation, 1998) and *A Paper's Life: Serbia's Roma in the Underworld of Waste Scavenging and Recycling* (WEDC, Loughborough University, 2005). She is currently Regional Health Advisor for Catholic Relief Servicxes in East Africa (Nairobi) and resides in Ethiopia.

maylingsh@yahoo.com

Professor **Michalis S. Skourtos** obtained his PhD in Economics from the University of Frankfurt. He has been Professor of Environmental Economics and Policy at the University of Aegean since 1987. He is also an honorary research associate of the Centre for Social and Economic Research on the Global Environment (CSERGE) and he has served in a number of Greek and international advisory and scientific bodies including the Environmental Committee of the Greek Ministry for External Affairs (chairman), the Governing Board of Joint Research Centre, the Environmental Economics Committee of DG XII (ENVECO), and the Greek MAB (UNESCO) Committee. He has co-authored and edited five books and some 20 chapters on environmental economics policy. His recent research interests include: non-market valuation of environmental goods, economic instruments in pollution abatement, integrated management of water and coastal resources and socioeconomic scenarios of environmental change.

mskour@env.aegean.gr

David Stephen is a professional civil engineer, has a Master of Business Administration (MBA) degree, and has had 20 years' experience in the water sector in South Africa. He has worked for the national Department of Water Affairs and Forestry, a large private-sector consulting engineering firm and has been with Umgeni Water since 1997. He is a member of the South African Institution of Civil Engineers (SAICE) and a fellow of the Water Institute of Southern Africa (WISA). David has presented papers at a number of national and international conferences, seminars and workshops on topics relating to the management of rural water schemes. At Umgeni Water, he has programme-managed the externally funded rural water and sanitation programme on behalf of local government and communities within KwaZulu-Natal.

david.stephen@umgeni.co.za

Dr **Daniel Terrill** is a senior consultant in the Australian economic consultancy firm ACIL Tasman. He specialises in the application of economics to the management of infrastructure issues, particularly in the fields of water, environment and regional development. He is also an experienced economic modeller, especially spatial modelling involving the application of geographical information systems (GIS) to a range of economic policy and planning issues. In addition to his role with ACIL Tasman, he is also a research fellow with Department of Economics at the University of Melbourne.

d.terrill@aciltasman.com.au

Chris Thoeye, with an MSc in bioengineering (University of Ghent, 1980), specialised in wastewater treatment and aquaculture, and has worked as a researcher and staff co-operator at various universities. Having joined AQUAFIN in 1993, since 1996 Chris has been a research co-ordinator, managing all research projects in AQUAFIN, of which several are international projects.

Bernhard Truffer works as a senior researcher at the Centre for Innovation Research in the Utility Sector (CIRUS) at the Swiss Federal Institute for Environmental Science and Technology. For the past ten years he has been conducting research on the sustainable transformation of infrastructure sectors.

truffer@eawag.ch

Dr **Lingappan Venkatchalam** is an Assistant Professor in the Economics Unit of the Institute for Social and Economic Change (ISEC), Bangalore, India. He obtained his PhD in economics from the University of Madras, India (through the Madras Institute of Development Studies) in 2002. Before joining ISEC, he served as a consultant–environmental economist at the Ministry of Environment and Forests, Government of India, and the Water Resources Orgainsation, Government of Tamil Nadu, from 1998 to 2002. His teaching and research interests are in environmental economics, new institutional economics and behavioural economics.

venkat@isec.ac.in

Uno Winblad is a consultant architect–planner specialising in the relation between the physical environment and human health. From 1993 to 2002 he was in charge of SanRes, an international research and development programme funded by Sida, with projects in China, Vietnam, South Africa, Uganda, Bolivia, El Salvador and Mexico. He is a co-author of the book *Ecological Sanitation* (SIDA, 1998; Stockholm Environment Institute, 2004) and *Sanitation without Water* (Macmillan, 1985) as well as of a large number of papers and reports on environment and health.

uno440@netscape.net

Abbreviations

AIDS	acquired immuno-deficiency syndrome
ARC	American Red Cross
AWTF	Africa Water Task Force
BOD	biological oxygen demand
BOO	build–own–operate
BOOT	build–own–operate–transfer
BOT	build–operate–transfer
BSC	balanced scorecard
BSS	bottom support system
BWC	Berlin Water Company
CAASA	Concessionária de Agua y Alcantarillado de Aguascalientes Socieda Anonima
CAP	Common Agricultural Policy (EU)
CAPAMA	Comisión de Agua Potable y Alcantarillado del Municipio de Aguascalientes (Aguascalientes Water and Sanitation Commission)
CCC	Chlorine Chemistry Council
CEO	chief executive officer
CMIP	Consolidated Municipal Infrastructure Programme (South Africa)
CNA	National Water Commission (Mexico)
COD	chemical oxygen demand
CV	contingent valuation
CWSS	Community Water Supply and Sanitation Programme (South Africa)
DBP	disinfection by-product
DEA	data envelopment analysis
DSM	demand-side management
DWAF	Department of Water Affairs and Forestry (South Africa)
ECDP	Environmental and Community Development Programme
ecosan	ecological sanitation
EMAS	Eco-Management and Audit Scheme (EU)
ENV	Ministry of the Environment (Singapore)
EPA	Environmental Protection Agency (USA)
EPC	engineering, procurement and construction
ESAC	Espaccio de Salud AC (Mexico)
ETOSS	Ente Tripartito de Obras y Servicios Sanitarios (Brazil)
ETTAC	Environmental Technologies Trade Advisory Committee (USA)
EU	European Union
FAO	Food and Agriculture Organisation (UN)
FYROM	former Yugoslavian Republic of Macedonia
GNP	gross national product

GOLR	general organisation for land reclamation
GSDP	Gerling Sustainable Development Project GmbH,
HDB	Housing Board Development (Singapore)
HIV	human immunodeficiency virus
IADB	Inter-American Development Bank
IAWQ	International Association on Water Quality
IBT	increasing block tariff
IFC	International Finance Corporation
ILO	International Labour Organisation
IMF	International Monetary Fund
INEGI	Institute Nacional de Estadistica Geografia e Informatica (Mexico)
IPCS	International Programme on Chemical Safety
IPO	Initial Public Offerings
IRC	International Water and Sanitation Centre
ISO	International Organisation for Standardisation
JUMI	joint use municipal–industrial
kld	kilolitres per day
KPI	key performance indicator
LCFC	low-capacity flushing cistern
LOLR	local organisation for land reclamation
lpcd	litres per capita per day
LWC	local water committee
MDG	Millennium Development Goal
MIG	municipal infrastructure grant
MIGA	Multilateral Investment Guarantee Agency
MMRG	management, maintenance and repair group
NAFTA	North American Free Trade Agreement
NGO	non-governmental organisation
NIE	new institutional economics
NOAA	National Oceanic and Atmospheric Administration (USA)
NOAEL	no-observed-adverse-effect level
O&M	operations and maintenance
ODA	overseas development assistance
OFWAT	Office of Water (England)
OPIC	Overseas Private Investment Corporation
ORC	organic ranking cycle
PA	principal–agent
PC	public choice
PDI	potential daily intake
PEC	predicted environmental concentration
PKN	phosphorus, potassium and nitrogen
PMT	project management team
PNEC	predicted no-effect concentration
PR	property rights
PSC	project steering committee
PSP	private-sector participation
PUB	Public Utilities Board (Singapore)

PVC	polyvinyl chloride
QRA	quantitative risk assessment
RAWSP	Rural Areas Water and Sanitation Plan (Umgeni Water)
RDP	Reconstruction and Development Programme
RPI	retail price index
RWE	Rheinisch-Westfälische Elektrizitätswerke
SABESP	Companhia de Saneamento Basico do Estado de São Paulo
SADM	Servicio de Agua y Drenaje de Monterrey
SAUR	Société d'Aménagement Urbain et Rural
SBSC	sustainability balanced scorecard
SC	scheduled caste
SKAT	Swiss Centre for Appropriate Technology
STP	sewage treatment plant
TECO	Tampa Electric Company
TMC	technical management committee
TWAD	Tamil Nadu Water Supply and Drainage Board
UA	Urban Agglomeration
UAW	unaccounted-for water
UN	United Nations
UNAC	União Nacional de Camponeses
UNEP	United Nations Environment Programme
UNICEF	United Nations Children's Fund
USAID	US Agency for International Development
USDC	US Department of Commerce
UV	ultraviolet
VBU	Vorstandsabteilung Beauftrage und Umweltschutz (Shared Service Department for Operations Officers and Environmental Affairs, BWC)
VIP	ventilated improved pit
VLOM	village-level operation and maintenance design
WATSAN	water and sanitation
WBCSD	World Business Council for Sustainable Development
WFD	Water Framework Directive (EU)
WHO	World Health Organisation
WRN	Water Relief Network
WSA	Water Services Authority (South Africa)
WSDP	Water Services Development Plan (WSA)
WSSCC	Water Supply and Sanitation Collaborative Council (Netherlands)
WSSD	World Summit on Sustainable Development
WTP	willingness to pay

Index